HAUNTED
HOUSES

BARBARA VILLIERS, DUCHESS OF CLEVELAND.

From the mezzotint after Wissing

HAUNTED HOUSES

CHARLES G. HARPER

SENATE

Haunted Houses

First published in 1907 by Cecil Palmer Ltd, London

Copyright © Charles G. Harper 1907

This edition first published in 1994 by Senate,
an imprint of Random House UK Ltd,
Random House, 20 Vauxhall Bridge Road,
London SW1V 2SA

Reprinted 1996

ISBN 1 85958 068 8

Printed and bound in Guernsey by
The Guernsey Press Co Ltd

PREFACE

"*Do you believe in ghosts?*" *asked a gentleman of Madame du Deffand.*

"*No,*" *replied that witty lady,* "*but I am afraid of them.*"

There are very many people who, without the least danger of being accused of wit, do not believe in ghosts, and yet are afraid; it is, in fact, the attitude of the world toward the supernatural. Most people whose mental digestion of the marvellous, as exemplified by the pretensions of patent medicines and company promoters, is quite robust will refuse to believe in ghosts, and yet there must be few whose hair has not been stirred and whose hearts have not beat an unusual tattoo at the sound of a Something inexplicable in the watches of the night: a Something that is not rats, nor burglars, nor the wind, nor anything readily associated with things of earth. We declare there are no such things as spirits, and disbelieving—tremble; without, like Madame du Deffand, striving after epigram.

In the registers of the church of Edwinstowe, Nottingham-shire, there is said to be an entry of a man who died of fright on seeing the Rufford ghost; the "little old lady in black" who is supposed to haunt Lord Savile's magnificent seat, Rufford Abbey, hard by. He probably did not believe in ghosts, but the appearance of something out of the common scared the life out of him, all the same.

While apparitions have not yet been scientifically "placed" and accounted for, and while no alleged spirit has been made to stand and thoroughly explain itself, to the satisfaction of cold inquirers, few will have the hardi-hood to declare, in discussing the return of disembodied spirits and the haunting of houses, that there is "nothing in it." The many more or less authentic ghost-stories told for many centuries, and very widely believed, forbid any such attitude on the part of thinking people.

v

PREFACE

A belief in ghosts has always been as widely distributed among all the peoples of the earth as the Religious Idea itself. Even in the remotest islands of distant seas, and among the most unlettered savages, religion has been ever found, and as invariably the belief in ghosts. If this were a work upon the philosophy of religion and of the supernatural (instead of being merely an attempt to interest and amuse) it could be conclusively shown, I have no doubt, that a belief in religion necessitates that of the existence of ghosts : and vice versa. But we must leave that to the professors.

CHARLES G. HARPER.

PETERSHAM, SURREY.

PREFACE TO THIRD EDITION

A few slight alterations and corrections have been made in the new edition now called for. Among them (not conveniently to be made in the body of the book) is one referring to the Bishop of Winchester's ghost-story (pp. 86–88). The Vicar of Stone near Aylesbury, writes me : " I remember referring to this story when the late Francis Paget, then Bishop of Oxford, was present. Bishop Paget said to me, when I had finished : ' Ah ! but have you ever heard the sequel of that ? ' and went on to say that when Bishop Wilberforce told it to intimate friends, he added, ' I know that story is true, because I made it up, out of my own head.' " Again I emphasise that one cannot always place a premium upon the word of a Bishop ; and indeed, if Wilberforce's phrasing is correctly given, can one follow the reasoning.

C. G. H.

SEPTEMBER, 1927.

CONTENTS

vii

LIST OF ILLUSTRATIONS

HAUNTED HOUSES

INTRODUCTORY

Unhinged, the iron gates half-open hung,
  Jarred by the gusty gales of many winters,
That from its crumbled pedestal had flung
  One marble globe in splinters.

The wood-louse dropped, and rolled into a ball,
  Touched by some impulse, occult or mechanic ;
And nameless beetles ran along the wall
  In universal panic.

The subtle spider, that from overhead
  Hung like a spy on human guilt and error
Suddenly turn'd, and up its slender thread
  Ran with a nimble terror.

O'er all there hung the shadow of a fear ;
  A sense of mystery the spirit daunted ;
And said, as plain as whisper in the ear,
  The place is haunted !
                The Haunted House, TOM HOOD.

THE ancient sense of human life beset on all sides by
heavenly watchers and diabolic enemies is not extinct.
It lies dormant and forgotten, but ready at call when
occasion comes ; and so, too, the deep-seated belief in
the spirit-world is proof against any boast of disbelief.

13

It is a heritage from immemorial ancestors which one must needs accept.

But, nevertheless, the era of the " haunted house " has long been on the wane. There is too much intellectual priggishness prevalent nowadays for the fine old crusted tales of the Moated Grange and its spectral inhabitants to attract more than an amused tolerance, as things only fitting for children. To an age which knows so much more than was known fifty years ago, and therefore presumes that it has arrived at a complete knowledge of all there is to know in heaven and earth, talk of spirits is—what a more august subject was, in the words of St. Paul, to the Greeks—" foolishness."

In times such as these, when the traditional robin on his snow-clad spray of holly has been banished from the Christmas card, and such un-Christmassy things as roses and tropical flowers are pictured instead, the time-honoured tales of Christmas parties are outworn and disregarded, and hair-raising stories of ghosts, told by the flickering fire before the lights are lit, no longer form a delightfully appetising prelude to the Christmas dinner ; nor, later, send the guests to bed with raw nerves that jump at every shadow. That kind of thing was worn threadbare in Christmas numbers many years ago, but the time is already circling round to the old convention again. Only, it is a little unfortunate that much of the appropriate setting of ghost-stories has been destroyed. There are many blood-curdling legends, but their native homes have largely been demolished, and in some cases rebuilt ; and ghosts do not very appropriately haunt houses less than a hundred years old. Ghosts and newly completed—even newly furnished —houses are antipathic things. You require, for a moderately complete installation, a manor-house, with wine-cellars, a butler, old family portraits (not necessarily those of your own family), and if you can manage old oak panelling and tapestry hangings (let them, if possible be " arras ") so much the better. Such is a moderate specification of requirements ; but the ideal appointments, now that in these days the typical country house is warmed with hot-water pipes and lighted by electricity, and has telephones, and is in every way up to date, are difficult to find. In the ideal haunted house, or Christmas scene of ghost-stories, the guest, primed with ancestral horrors, went to bed with apprehension, leaving the warm dining-room for some vast woebegone chamber, with a bed like a catafalque and hangings of a bygone age ; with mysterious cupboards in which a dozen family skeletons might reside, and with a floor whose every board had a separate and distinctive squeak. It would nowadays be difficult to secure a house-party on such terms.

Manor-houses we have still with us, but their number, as compared with the myriads of newly built " villas " in the suburbs, is woefully small. You cannot hope to find a White Lady on the staircase of a £30 house down Wandsworth way, or a Radiant Boy domiciled in a Brompton flat ; and an ancestral drummer who parades the premises, prophetically drumming disaster, is not to be expected within hail of Finsbury Park. This is very sad, for a family ghost is a possession that in these times, when antiquities are prized, would be greatly welcomed by many estimable folk. The Uncanny and the Inexplicable, seated invisible (but yet making their presence felt) by the hearthstone, would themselves give a *cachet* of respectability, or, at least, of long descent, to a domestic circle ; and so long as they did not play their ghostly parts so earnestly as to send the servants into hysterics and render the house uninhabitable, would thus be prized possessions. There would be nothing, for example, to fear from the gentle spook or spooks who, on the impeccable authority of Henry Kingsley, used to share residence of Barnack Rectory, Northampton- shire, with the Kingsley family, and only make its or their presence known by stertorous breathings, rustlings, and scratchings, and by stroking the heads of the children, who at last grew quite familiar with, and unafraid of, it and used to call it pet names ! Ghosts of this kind are the low comedians of the spirit world.

It is much better to read of " the breath of the bogy in your hair," as Robert Louis Stevenson phrases it, than to *feel* that chilling breath in some mouldy corridor.

Cold and gruesome gusts that may indicate open casements or a broken window-pane, but stir the hair of the nervous and make it bristle as though the phantasmal hands of some White Lady had been run through their locks, are not liked when personally experienced ; and up-to-date visitors nurse an odd prejudice against the dark staircase of the goblin hall, hung with the sombre portraits of ancestors who, afflicted with a Family Curse, step out of their frames at the sound of the midnight bell.

Ghost-stories, tales of haunted houses, and weird family legends lend themselves to varied treatment. The Psychical Research Society has inquired very learnedly into these subjects, and has published a number of very highly interesting volumes, about the size of small haystacks ; but, very generally, the names of places and people are withheld, and so, to the general reader, the accounts are not particularly interesting. Other tales of haunted houses range from the grisly to the merely flippant ; nor is there often any firm foothold of ascertained fact to help the inquirer in this, one of the most interesting and pregnant of studies. Phantasmal appearances and other unaccountable manifestations have been dismissed by the matter-of-fact as trickery, hysteria, credulity, or—more grossly still— as the results of indigestion ; or have been ascribed to mists, draughts, owls, rats, and what Tennyson finely calls " the shrieking rush of the wainscot mouse." They have, no doubt, often been all these things ; but, quirk and quibble them how you will, there is yet " more in heaven and earth than is dreamt of in our philosophy " ; and since we believe in, though we cannot comprehend, the Hereafter, the necessary corollary would seem to be a belief in the existence, and the occasional appearance, of spirits.

We have at least one striking instance in the Bible to support a belief in the existence of the spirits of the dead, and even in the possibility of summoning them. This is to be found in the famous incident of Saul and the Witch of Endor, in which " the woman that hath a familiar spirit " raised the ghost of Samuel. The

" witch " was, of course, nothing more or less than what we should now style a " medium."

A book that should give an account of all the alleged Haunted Houses and Family Curses would of necessity be a work in many volumes. In these pages will be found a representative selection ; the houses that are no longer in existence, such as Hinton Ampner manor-house, being ' generally omitted. The stories range through every emotion, from tragedy, through comedy, to farce ; and from the well authenticated to the absolutely denied. But the especial attention of the sceptical is invited, in the Family Curses, to the extraordinary fulfilments of prophecies, certainly known to have been made centuries before the disasters foretold—for prophecies are generally predictions of woe—came to pass. There is, it may be added, an opening for a prophet who will foretell prosperity and joy. Such a one is keenly desired ; but it may sadly be suspected that he will not soon be found.

I am a haunted man. Haunted by ghosts of days dead and gone ; haunted with regrets and by the faces and voices of those who were dear to me : the well-remembered friends of old, who have passed into the Beyond, where, let us hope, there is peace and joy. I beliieve there is, beyond these fleeting scenes, that place where the good and excellent friends whom one misses so greatly have gone, and that they are not wholly unconscious of what passes here. Dear friends ; perhaps they know us even better now than then ; and it may be they rejoice in our joys. They cannot sorrow overmuch at our sorrows ; because, if they know anything at all, they must know how small a space of time it all is.

This consoles me a very great deal for the turmoil of these days, when life, as I see it, is very like some over-populated ant-heap kicked over by a wanton foot : the unhappy inhabitants of it hurrying hither and thither without sense of direction. But I am by no means an unhappy man ; indeed no. Life is the greatest of all practical jokes, if you can but have the wit to see it. And I, beg to say that my regrets, whatever they be, are certainly not for a misspent youth. They are the

regrets which must come to all, whether saint or sinner.
I love to be haunted in the manner I have described, by
the thoughts of those dear ones. Thank God for one's
friends. Without them, and the memory of them when
they are gone, what would this be but some pitiful
pilgrimage ?

And, as for those who were not friendly ; for the
scornful, the spiteful, the malicious ; well, I suppose
they have gone to their own place. Let us say to the
bosom of Ahrimanes. This may be unchristian ; but
it is eminently human.

I have never seen a ghost ; never have had, so to
speak, the ghost of a chance. Although I have sought,
the quest has been in vain. But I have had my uncanny experiences ; which, if you please, I will keep to
myself. Some things are sacred. And I have been to
spiritualist séances, and have found them so extremely
unsatisfactory that I do not propose to attend any more.
All bunkum, my dear sirs. That way madness lies. I
knew once a man who made a habit of those affairs.
His brother had been a musician of some eminence, and
he claimed that the brother's spirit possessed him when
he sat at the piano and played. He proceeded to play
to me ; and he honestly believed his performance to be
equal to, let us say, Liszt, or some other great master.
But never in my life had I heard such horrible discords,
so abominable maunderings, as I listened to then.
" Isn't it wonderful ? " he asked. It was indeed ; nay,
more—incredible. The man was mad. His glance
sufficiently proclaimed the fact.

But since the foregoing remarks were written, I have
heard much modern so-called " music " broadcast by
the B.B.C., and perhaps, after all, the man of whom I have
written was not insane. He must have been possessed
by the spirit of an early deceased, one of those modern
composers who despise melody because they can't
produce it.

Well, then, here be truths. But haunted houses ? I
have slept in such : in " haunted " rooms, but no visitant
from the unseen world has ever troubled me there.
That is either because I am a commonplace person (a

theory I don't like to entertain), or else because those all-wise spirits knew that if they appeared I should make what journalists call " copy " out of them. They declined to put in an appearance, to be interviewed ; and I know of no sort of subpœna by which a spook could be summoned to attend. " I can call spirits from the vasty deep," says the braggart Glendower. " But will they come when you do call ? " sardonically asks Hotspur. Precisely : they will come—if at all—when they choose.

This is a book for the winter evenings.

> Hark to the sighing of wind in the trees,
> List to the flying of icy-cold breeze.
> An eerie night, when elf and sprite
> May fitly work their deeds of spite.

Let us draw up our chairs to the cheerful glow of the fire. The curtains are drawn, to shut out the wintry cloud-wrack in the sky, through whose flying scud the moon peeps with pallid face. The wind booms in the chimney ; it is good to be at home.

This is the time for ghost stories. Switch off that electric light, that modern miracle which has disestablished the olden reputation of many a " haunted house." We will sit in the fitful blaze of the coals ; or better still, in that of the wood-logs, for much illumination is fatal to such talk as we are to have. It is a talk of ghosts, of family curses and of the inexplicable in general.

CHAPTER I

HAUNTED PALACES

The Tower of London—St. James's Palace—Hampton Court—
Richmond Palace.

> His house . . .
> Was haunted with a jolly ghost, that shook
> The curtains, whined in lobbies, tapt at doors,
> And rummaged like a rat : no servant stay'd.
> TENNYSON.

ROYAL palaces should, by all the canons of the supernatural, be haunted. If convulsions of nature happen,
according to old belief, when the great die, and if—as
was certainly the case—the death of Oliver Cromwell at
Hampton Court Palace and the coincidence of an exceptional storm were thought to have some mysterious
affinity, it should be the merest commonplace to see
ghosts in ancient palaces. Some such legend has taken
root at Kensington Palace. It was there that George the
Second died, October 25th, 1760. He had long been
kept within doors by ill-health, and—hasty, choleric
personage that he was—bore it ill. The winds, too, were
in the wrong quarter, and kept back the ships carrying
anxiously awaited and long overdue dispatches from his
beloved Hanover.

Thus it was that, during his last hours, the King was
continually gazing from the windows, up at the curious
weather-vane, bearing the conjoined ciphers of William
and Mary, that to this day twirls upon the cupola of
the quaint tower forming the principal entrance to the
Palace. He died before the wind changed; and still,
they say, at night a ghostly face peers from the old
windows at that weather-sign, and a voice asks irritably,
in broken English, " Vhy tondt dey come ? "

If one spot more than any other should be haunted,

that place is assuredly the Tower of London. Many
are the brave and the true ; many, too, the brave and
yet the false, who have suffered at the hands of the
executioner on Tower Hill, or the equally fateful Tower
Green, outside the church of Saint Peter-ad-Vincula,
whose grim name—Saint Peter-in-the-Fetters—is so
thoroughly in keeping with the history and the spirit
of the place.

But the historic personages whose lives were cut
short by the headsman's axe, or who dragged out a long
and hopeless captivity within the massive walls of the
grim fortress, sleep untroubled the long sleep of centuries.
No stories are told of Anne Boleyn, of Lady Jane Grey,
of Lord Guildford Dudley, of Raleigh, revisiting the scene
of their last hours on earth ; and the tales of ghostly
shapes that haunt the precincts of the Tower on the eve
of the Sovereign's death are—well, romantic.

But the very remarkable story told in 1860 by
Edward Lenthal Swifte, sometime Keeper of the Crown
Jewels, has elements of the fantastic and the horrible
which leave the ordinary ghost-story far behind. Mr.
Swifte never ceased to believe in the supernatural
character of the inexplicable occurrence he narrates.

" I have often purposed," he says, " to leave behind
me a faithful record of all I personally know of this
strange story. Forty-three years have passed, and its
impression is as vividly before me as on the moment of
its occurrence.

" In 1814 I was appointed Keeper of the Crown Jewels
in the Tower, where I resided with my family till my
retirement in 1852. One Saturday night in October,
1817, about the ' witching hour,' I was at supper with
my wife, her sister, and our little boy, in the sitting-
room of the Jewel House,* which—then comparatively
modernised—is said to have been the ' doleful prison '
of Anne Boleyn, and of the ten bishops whom Oliver
Cromwell piously accommodated therein. For an
accurate picture of the *locus in quo* my scene is laid, I
refer to George Cruikshank's woodcut in p. 384 of
Ainsworth's ' Tower of London.' The room was—as it

* In the Martin Tower.

KENSINGTON PALACE : THE CLOCK TOWER

still is—irregularly shaped, having three doors and two windows, which last are cut nearly nine feet deep into the outer wall ; between these there is a chimney-piece projecting far into the room, and (then) surmounted with a large oil picture. On the night in question, the doors were all closed, heavy and dark cloth curtains were let down over the windows, and the only light in the room was that of two candles on the table. I sate at the foot of the table, my son on my right hand, his mother fronting the chimney-piece, and her sister on the opposite side. I had offered a glass of wine and water to my wife, when, on putting it to her lips, she paused, and exclaimed, ' Good God ! what is that ? ' I looked up and saw a cylindrical figure, like a glass tube, seemingly about the thickness of my arm, and hovering between the ceiling and the table ; its contents appeared to be a dense fluid, white and pale azure, like the gathering of a summer cloud, and incessantly mingling within the cylinder. This lasted about two minutes, when it began slowly to move before my sister-in-law ; then, following the oblong shape of the table, *before* my son and myself ; passing *behind* my wife, it paused for a moment over her right shoulder (observe, there was no mirror opposite to her in which she could there behold it). Instantly she crouched down, and with both hands covering her shoulder, she shrieked out, ' O Christ ! it has seized me ! ' Even now, while writing, I feel the fresh horror of that moment. I caught up my chair, struck at the wainscot behind her, rushed upstairs to the children's room, and told the terrified nurse what I had seen. Meanwhile, the other domestics had hurried into the parlour, where their mistress recounted to them the scene, even as I was detailing it above stairs."

The comparative insensibility to, or receptiveness of, phenomena of this kind, which divides human beings into " matter-of-fact " people and into the class from which spiritualistic " mediums " emerge, is illustrated here by Mr. Swifte's statement that, although he and his wife distinctly saw this uncanny shape, neither his sister-in-law nor his son beheld it.

Scepticism met Mr. Swifte at every turn when he

told his story next morning, and the chaplain put it to him, " if one person might not have his natural senses deceived ? And if one, why might not two ? " A very dangerous argument for a minister of religion, dealing professionally with the supernatural (which is the basis of religion) to indulge in ; and Mr. Swifte very pertinently answered, " If two, why not two thousand ? "— an argument which would reduce history, secular or sacred, to a fable.

" Our chaplain," he continued, " suggested the possibilities of some foolery having been intromitted at my windows, and proposed the visit of a scientific friend, who minutely inspected the parlour, and made the closest investigation, but could not in any way solve the mystery." He suggested that if he were allowed to bring his scientific apparatus and place it upon the table, or if he could plant it on the walls near the window, and have the curtains raised, he could produce a similar illusion ; but he did not undertake to reproduce it under the conditions which accompanied its original appearance, nor did he go so far as to explain how an illusion could produce the physical sensation of seizing one by the shoulder.

It was true, as Mr. Swifte candidly remarks, that, a few days before, some young ladies residing in the Tower had been producing apparitions, but no one ever explained how it could be possible for them to introduce anything of the kind into the room where this extraordinary occurrence took place ; and the mystery remained a mystery.

Mr. Swifte further recounts the story of a singular incident that took place a few days after his own terrible experience. " One of the night sentries at the Jewel Office, a man who was in perfect health and spirits, and was singing and whistling up to the moment of the occurrence, was alarmed by a figure like a huge bear issuing from under the Jewel Room door. He thrust at it with his bayonet, which stuck in the door, even as my chair had dinted the wainscot ; he dropped in a fit, and was carried senseless to the guard-room.

" When on the morrow I saw the unfortunate soldier

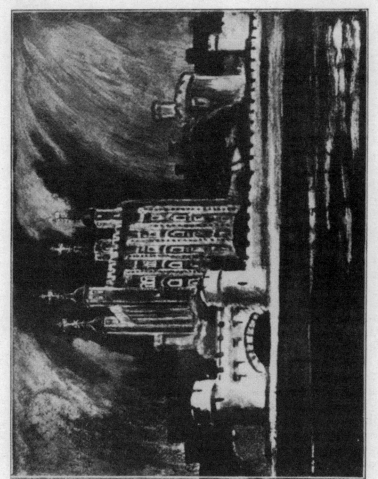

THE TOWER OF LONDON

ST. JAMES'S PALACE

in the main guard-room, his fellow-sentinel was also there, and testified to having seen him at his post just before the alarm, awake and alert, and had even spoken to him. I saw the unfortunate man again on the following day, but changed beyond my recognition ; in another day or two, the brave and steady soldier, who would have mounted a breach, or led a forlorn hope with unshaken nerves, *died*—at the presence of a shadow.

The soldier was buried some days later, with due military honours, in the long-since-abolished churchyard of St. Katharine's-by-the-Tower.

Whether or not the soldier died from the effects of seeing a genuine apparition, or was merely the victim of a practical joke, was never known ; but the guards were doubled immediately after this affair, and no more apparitions appeared. It is remarkable, however, to read in the memoirs of Sir John Reresby, a hundred years earlier, how a somewhat similar apparition was observed at York Castle, where a piece of paper, fluttering along the ground, was seen to change into a monkey, and then into a bear, and then to accomplish the amazing feat of squeezing between the door and the doorstep, through a space that would hardly have done more than admit the passage of a coin.

Only one story is associated with St. James's Palace, and that is some two hundred years old. It seems that in the times of Charles the Second and his brother and successor, James, there resided at the Palace, in handsome suites of apartments, two Frenchwomen of considerable notoriety in their age : the Duchess of Mazarin and Madame De Beauclair. They had formerly been housed in that famous Royal seraglio, the Palace of Whitehall ; but, upon its almost complete destruction by fire, were given house-room here, and then completely forgotten by their kingly and ducal protectors, in favour of fresher faces. In the cold shade of obscurity, the women, who had been in some sense rivals, became close companions, and their conversation often dwelt upon the future life, and the possibility of the spirits of the dead communicating with surviving friends. This resulted in their entering into a compact that, whoever of the two should first die should, if possible, communicate with her friend and inform her of her condition in the other world.

At last the Duchess of Mazarin died. In her last illness, she was reminded by Madame De Beauclair of their compact, which in those last solemn moments was duly ratified ; and there, for some years, the story halted. No message came to Madame De Beauclair from the other side ; and she grew a thorough sceptic in all things supernatural, becoming highly indignant with those who differed from her in these matters.

Some months after a heated argument with a lady on this subject, a servant from Madame De Beauclair called hurriedly upon the lady in question and stated that his mistress entreated her to come at once, adding that if she desired ever to see Madame again in this world she must not delay.

The lady, suffering from a severe cold, and hearing from the servant that Madame De Beauclair appeared to be in good health, hesitated to comply ; but presently received a still more urgent message, accompanied by such convincing evidence of the seriousness of affairs as the gift of a jewel-case containing all Madame De Beauclair's jewellery.

The lady hurried to St. James's Palace forthwith, accompanied by a gentleman, who afterwards narrated the story.

Madame De Beauclair, after a very few introductory words, told them that, although apparently in the best of health, she would in a very few hours have passed from this life into that other existence whose reality she had once doubted. She had seen the spectre of her departed friend, the Duchess of Mazarin.

" I perceived not how she entered ; but, turning my eyes towards yonder corner of the room, I saw her standing in the same form and habit as in life. Fain would I have spoken, but had not the power of utterance. She took a little circuit round the chamber, seeming rather to swim than walk ; then stopped beside that Indian chest, and, looking at me with her usual sweetness, ' Beauclair,' said she, ' between the hours of twelve and one to-night you will be with me.' "

At the time when Madame De Beauclair told her story it was close upon twelve o'clock. Those present tried to assure her that there was nothing of any significance in her vision, but they had scarce begun to speak when the clock struck twelve. She exclaimed, " Oh! I am sick at heart," and, although she did not appear to be suffering from any known ailment, grew rapidly worse. Mrs. Ward, her attendant, applied some drops, but without effect, and in about half an hour she died, exactly as the apparition had foretold. It was stated, in conclusion, that " Madame De Beauclair was neither vapourish nor superstitious."

But Hampton Court Palace is richest of all the old Royal palaces in ghost stories, and the continuity of them and the constant succession of people who have " seen a somethink " must strike even the most sceptical as singularities worth investigating. Starting with the concession of a belief in ghosts, there is every reason why Hampton Court should be haunted. Wolsey, the proud Cardinal who originally built it, and was impelled by the instinct of self-preservation to make a present of his great palace to Henry the Eighth, in the hope of regaining the estranged affections of his master, should certainly haunt this, among the last scenes of his broken ambition ; and the spirits of certain unhappy Queens, wives in succession of the " professional widower," should with equal certainty trouble the midnight galleries. If we may give credence to oft-repeated tales, they do. No one has ever claimed to have seen the form of the Cardinal, and not even that most unhappy Anne Boleyn has been observed ; but the ghosts of Jane Seymour and of Katharine Howard are reported to be frequent visitors. Jane Seymour, who by crafty intrigue supplanted her Queen and former mistress in the dangerous affections of Henry, and died ultimately, a year later, is said, clothed in white, to walk forth from the Queen's apartments, carrying a lighted taper, and to perambulate the stairs and the Silver Stick Gallery. And this, although no expense was spared at her funeral ; one thousand two hundred masses being paid for to ensure the repose of her soul. Possibly the number was not sufficient to expiate the treachery of the ex Maid-of-Honour.

The spirit of Queen Katharine Howard was said to be more unseemly, and has, they say, been known to wake the echoes of the galleries with her shrieks ; even as she did in that last sad scene of her life there. Historians tell how Katharine, the fifth wife of Henry the Eighth, was suddenly placed under arrest in the Palace, but escaped from her guards and ran along the gallery to the Chapel, in which the King was then hearing Mass. She had reached the Chapel door when the yeomen of the guard interposed, and, seizing her, hurried her back, screaming, to her arrest ; while the King, although the sound of her lamentation was clearly heard in the Chapel, made no sign.

Most of the victims of Henry's political and connubial quarrels ended with a noble dignity ; but this unfortunate girl—she was only in her twentieth year when she was beheaded on Tower Hill in 1542—could not give up the beautiful world around her and contemplate death by the headsman's axe with that proud philosophy ; and strove and fluttered pitifully in her gilded cage.

The Haunted Gallery, as it has often been styled of late years, was for a long period used as a lumber-room, where moth-eaten tapestries, pictures out of repair, and veteran articles of furniture, hopelessly worm-eaten, were stored ; but the Office of Works at last cleared out the lumber, disestablished the immemorial cobwebs, stopped the holes of rats and mice, and, after thoroughly renovating the Gallery, opened it to the public on April 1st, 1918 : a significant date, those will say who do not believe in ghosts.

Nothing has been heard or seen of the unquiet spirit of Queen Katharine Howard since that spring-cleaning. The proper *milieu*, the traditional setting of mystery and decay, has been destroyed, and it is certainly too much to expect a sixteenth century ghost of delicate suscepti-bilities to pervade apartments reeking of newly applied paint, putty and varnish.

It should be said that Mr. Ernest Law, who years ago made a special study of Hampton Court, believes neither

in ghosts in general nor in the especial habitués of this
ancient Palace. Interviewed, as the person above all
others likely to speak with authority on the subject, he
was disappointingly matter-of-fact. He said :

" I am often accused of having originated the ghosts.
Certainly, when I first began, scarcely anyone knew of
their existence, and they were not recognised with the
unanimity they deserve—as they now are. I have met
only one man who has ever actually seen any of the
Palace spectres ; he was a sentry, who was frightened
out of his wits by a woman in a flowing robe of white,
who took a mean advantage by vanishing when he
challenged her. Unfortunately he did not recognise her.
As to the recent revival of these tales in the Press, I fancy
it is probably due to a new resident of journalistic tastes,
who, learning of them for the first time, thought them
new. It has proved a great bother to other residents, as
many of them have had difficulty in retaining their
servants, owing to the ghost-stories. In fact, I have been
asked to ' lay the spectres '—in the Press ; and it is only
on the understanding that you will mention that I do not
believe in the tales that I can relate them to you. I
don't believe in any ghosts whatever." With that
preamble, Mr. Law proceeded to make a midnight
assignation with the interviewer, to explore the historic
pile, in quest of experiences.

" That evening — a glorious moonlight night "—
writes that journalist, " we met in the sombre precincts
of the old Tudor Palace. As soon as the lights were
turned out Mr. Law set forth on a voyage of exploration
for ghosts.

" ' I have been searching for these spectres for
upwards of thirty-five years,' said he, ' and have never
met one yet, much to my disappointment ; but I live
in hope. As to the spirit of Anne Boleyn being rampant
here, as stated in some newspapers, I never before
heard of the story, and I rather suspect that someone
must have seen Jane Seymour and not recognised her.
I wish a snapshootist would bring his kodak down here
and get a photo of her—it is much needed by historians.'

" By this time we were in the deserted dusky

THE HAUNTED GALLERY, HAMPTON COURT

cloisters. Our footsteps clanked loudly on the stones, and awoke a thousand hollow echoes in the midnight stillness. Dark rain-clouds had veiled the moon, and began to pour down a steady drizzle, which pattered drearily on the ground. A slight fitful breeze moaned weirdly down the long corridors. Our surroundings were certainly such as to inspire one with gruesome feelings. Tall and gaunt, the massive towers and gables stood out against the chequered sky and threw gloomy uncertain shadows about us. Not another soul did we meet. The exaggerated noise of a scrap of paper caught by a sudden gust and hurtling along the stone flags startled us both. Presently we stopped at a door ; the drip, drip, of the rain and the sighing of the wind only intensified the oppressive silence, which Mr. Law suddenly broke.

" ' This leads to the " Haunted Gallery," where Katharine Howard is supposed to prowl about, shrieking, on nights such as this,' he said. His key grated in the lock, the heavy door groaned on its hinges, and then shut behind us with a mighty bang that went echoing and re-echoing down the interminable dusky galleries and sent a shiver through one's marrow. It was dark—inky dark, until the eyes got accustomed to a faint glimmer struggling through peep-holes in the shutters. Following my guide as best I could up broad staircases, through vast cold rooms, down long passages, all still and weird and dark, we came at length to an enormous apartment. ' Here we are,' said Mr. Law, and his words went ringing round the giant chamber in unending echoes, though his voice sounded thin and small in the empty vastness. Groping in the gloom, his intimate knowledge of the place enabled him to find an old-world cane-bottomed bench, which he dragged with a harsh grating sound to where I stood. Then cautiously he undid the noisy shutter of one window, and the great iron bar swung back with a loud clang, and admitted a faint streak of light. The scene outside was dismal and weird—a narrow rain-soaked court, clothed in deep shadows and surrounded by high walls with huge black glittering eyes of windows. Above were dusky streaks of clouds hurrying over the sky and hiding ever and anon the moon. We sat down and waited. Mr. Law began to tell his ghost-stories. Drip, drip, went the rain ; sw-ough, s-s-sweigh, moaned the wind. Strange Dutch faces stared out of the gloom and fixed us with their eyes from their sombre backgrounds and old-fashioned frames on the opposite wall. All else was lost in darkness.

" Mr. Law's voice, drowned in its own echoes, continued the narration of the spectre legends. Suddenly, above the sound of the rain and wind, there came to our ears a long low moan, which rose and fell. Mr. Law stopped abruptly. We started to our feet. The moan was succeeded by another—louder, more prolonged, more agonising. It grew in intensity, rose to a hideous shriek, then gradually died away again to a low wailing groan. Shriek followed shriek, shrill and loud—human, horribly human, as of a woman in torture, yet unearthly and gruesome. My blood ran cold. The sounds grew nearer and more awful. Then distinctly we heard footsteps, slow, uncertain, and shuffling. They approached. The shrieks sounded close at hand. A clanking, jingling sound, like rattling chains, jarred on our ears at each footfall. We heard the door at the far end of the gallery grate back upon its hinges, and a strange glow of light in the doorway revealed a bowed figure, as a shriek more piercing than the rest made us both start. Mr. Law walked bravely forward. The figure stood motionless. Then I heard my companion at the far end of the corridor address it.

" ' Why, hallo ! good evening, Blundle ! '

" ' Good evenin', Mr. Law. Nasty damp night. I wonders you isn't afeerd o' the rhumatis. *I* wouldn't be a-settin' 'ere if I could be abed, I know.'

" ' I'm looking for ghosts with a friend. We thought you were one. But what was all that shrieking just now ? '

" ' It was on'y them infarnal cats.'

" I had come forward now, and joined in a hearty laugh at our own expense as the old night watchman shuffled off with his jangling keys and his glimmering lantern.

" ' Well, that accounts for Katharine Howard, at any rate ! Let's get back to my house, it's wretchedly cold here.' And we returned to Mr. Law's apartments, where, in the warm dining-room, he concluded his tales."

But these queenly wraiths are mere rumours compared with the remarkable tales told of the ghost of Mistress Sibell Penn, foster-mother to Jane Seymour's son, Prince Edward (afterwards Edward the Sixth). She was appointed nurse to the Prince in October, 1538, a year after the death of his mother. Mrs. Penn was so devoted a foster-mother that she was in high favour with the King, his father ; and when the Prince grew up, and in turn became King, she was one of the personages held in foremost consideration at Court. He died of consumption, in 1553, in his sixteenth year, and Mrs. Penn was left as bereaved almost as if she were his mother. Apartments were afterwards allotted to her at Hampton Court, and there she died, from an attack of smallpox, November 6th, 1562. She was buried in the old church of Hampton-on-Thames, and an imposing monument in the taste of that age was erected to her. In 1829 the old church was ruthlessly demolished, and the present structure, a monument to the debased architectural practice of the time, was reared in its stead. In the wholesale irreverent overturning of everything, during this rebuilding, the grave of Mrs. Penn was rifled and her memorial removed, being placed eventually in the entrance lobby of the present building. The accompanying illustration will show, more clearly than words can explain, what the monument is like ; but it is impossible to show on so small a scale the long metrical epitaph which, in the quaintly eloquent Elizabethan style of mortuary verse, narrates her many virtues :

Pen here is brought to home, the place of long a bode
Where vertu guided hathe her shippe into the quyet rode.
A myrror of her tyme, for vertues of the mynde
A matrone suche as in her dayes the like was herd to find.
No plant of servile stocke, a Hampden by discent
Vnto whose race 300 yeres, hathe frendly fortune lent.

MRS. PENN'S TOMB

THE GATEHOUSE, RICHMOND PALACE

To Courte she called was, to foster vp a Kinge
Whose helping hand, long lingring svtes to spedie end did bring.
Twoo quenes that scepter bare, gave credytt to this dame
Full manye yeres in Court she dwelt, without disgrace or blame.
No house ne worldly wealthe, on earthe she did regerde
Before eche joye, yea and her life, her Prince's health prefard ;
Whose long and loyall love, with skilful care to serve,
Was svch as did throvgh heavenly help, her Prince's thankes
　　deserve.
Woolde God the grovnd were grafte, with trees of svche delight,
That idell braines of frvctfvll plantes, might find jvst cavs to
　　writ,
As I have plyed my pen, to praise this Pen with all,
Who lyeth entombed in this grave, vntill the trompe her call.
This restinge place beholde, no svbject place to bale,
To which, perforce, ye lokers-on, yovr fietinge bodyes shale.

The ghost of Mrs. Penn, it was said, began to haunt
her old rooms at the Palace very soon after her grave at
Hampton Church had been disturbed. Odd sounds, as
of one working a spinning-wheel, were heard, with the
sound as of a person muttering to herself, through the
wall of a large room in the south-west wing of the Palace ;
and, on search being made, following a report of these
remarkable noises, an entirely forgotten room was discovered, in which was found an ancient spinning-wheel,
together with other odds and ends. The oak flooring,
it was said, was worn away where the treadle of the
spinning-wheel touched the boards.

Many people have, at one time or another, believed
they saw the ghost of Mrs. Penn ; and tales are told of new
residents at the Palace, who could not have been familiar
with the monument in Hampton Church, describing the
form they saw dressed in a long straight robe and with
close-fitting head-dress, exactly as the effigy of Mrs. Penn
is represented on her tomb.

Late in the sixties of the last century, a lady who
occupied a suite of apartments in the Palace—the " finest
almshouse in the world," as it has been called—assured
her friends that she was frequently troubled by the
rappings made by two invisible beings, who in this way
exercised upon the panelling of her rooms. She complained to the Lord Chamberlain, and the Lord Chamberlain passed on the complaint to the Office of Works, with

the result that in due course, after the matter had circulated through the requisite number of departments, she was informed that the jurisdiction of the First Commissioner did not extend into the spirit world. The sequel is singular. In 1871, when workmen were excavating in the cloister or covered way of Fountain Court, nearly opposite the entrance to this lady's rooms, two human skeletons were uncovered, at a depth of about two feet beneath the pavement. It was supposed that they were the remains of two soldiers of the time of William the Third, but it does not appear what was the evidence that led to this supposition. The remains were removed to Hampton churchyard, but whether the rappings ceased forthwith is not stated.

As recently as February, 1907, the ghostly reputation of the Palace came again before the public mind, in the reported adventure of a constable of the Metropolitan Police. A policeman, one thinks, should not readliy be convinced of ghostly manifestations. His duties render him, of all men, matter-of-fact and sceptical. There is, indeed, a latent cynicism in the police ; as a body, and individually. For the most thoroughgoing of materialists, you think, not unreasonably, to seek most hopefully in their unromantic ranks. Years of night-duty, of patrolling the midnight streets, of trying front-doors and area-gates, of persuading drunken men to go home quietly, and of flashing an exploratory bull's-eye into darkling basements, have acquainted the Force with nothing more supernatural than burglars. In all that while the constable's ears have been assailed by nothing more awful than the yells of nocturnal cats, eloquent with love and jealousy, whose demon cries are sufficient to disgust the most dreadful ghost of romance with his own poor efforts.

Yet it was a police-constable who flushed a whole covey of ghosts at Hampton Court Palace on a night of February, 1907 ; and not a young policeman, either. 265 T (for that appears to have been his style and title) had over twenty years' experience of tramping the midnight beat, at the regulation three-miles-an-hour gait, and if there be any class of man who, more than another,

knows what's what, it should be a police-constable with
twenty years' service at the back of him. Yet 265 T saw
" ghosts " ; and more, probably, than any living man
has seen assembled together on any one occasion. Briefly,
he stated that, while stationed in the precincts of the
Palace, about midnight, he saw a group of figures coming
towards him along one of the walks, and that when they
had advanced to within nine yards of where he was
standing, the whole party vanished.

" On this particular night," he said, " I went on duty
at the east front of the Palace at ten o'clock, and had to
remain there until six o'clock next morning. I was quite
alone, and was standing close to the main gates, looking
towards the Home Park, when suddenly I became conscious of a group of figures moving towards me along what
is known as the Ditton Walk. It is a most unusual thing
to see anyone in the gardens at that time of night, but I
thought it probable that some of the residents in the
Palace had been to a party at Ditton and were returning
on foot. The party consisted of two gentlemen in evening dress and seven or nine ladies. There were no
sounds except what resembled the rustling of dresses.
When they reached a point about a dozen yards from
me I turned round and opened the gates to let them in.
The party, however, altered their course, and headed in
the direction of the Flower Pot Gates, to the north of the
gardens. At the same time there was a sudden movement amongst the group ; they fell into processional
order, two deep, with the gentlemen at the head. Then,
to my utter amazement, the whole crowd of them vanished ; melted, as it seemed to me, into the air. All this
happened within nine yards of where I was standing, in
the centre of the broad gravel walk in front of the Palace.
I rushed to the spot, looked up and down, but could see
nothing or hear nothing to explain the mystery."

Most police-constables, in these sceptical times,
would exercise a wise discretion, and say nothing of such
a sight ; but, if the facts are as stated, 265 T, very
greatly risking the dangers of reporting such an unusual
incident, narrated what he had seen, and became at once
a public character. There are very many visitors daily

to Hampton Court in these times, and the very next day the baiting, or the martyrdom, of 265 T began. Spiritualists, disbelievers in ghosts, and idle people of all kinds, wanted to know all day, and for many days, the rights of the matter ; but the constable bearing that divisional letter and number professed entire ignorance of it. To the question, " Were you not the constable who saw the ghosts ? " he returned an unfailing and emphatic " No," and to all inquiries as to their number and their dress he invariably answered, " I don't know, and, what's more, I don't care."

Here we pause, to ask, with Pilate, " What is truth ? " Probably visions, and the seers of them, are discouraged at Hampton Police Station.

Tales of Queen Elizabeth, who, living and dead, has ever been the subject of scandal, were once frequently told (and believed) in connection with Richmond Palace. Queen Elizabeth died in the old Palace of Richmond at three o'clock in the morning of March 24th, 1603. For days she had lain there, at the point of death, in a stupor : and so ended that glorious reign. A curious tale was told at the time, and has been duly handed down, that a ghostly shape of the great queen was seen pacing the rooms of the Palace while she yet lay there alive but unconscious. It is a strange story, and worthy the attention of those interested in psychic phenomena. Stories told in after years of the old Gatehouse and other few remnants of the Palace being haunted have now finally become discredited.

CHAPTER II

Ripley Castle—Baddesley Clinton—Littlecote, and the story of
Wild Darell—Bisham Abbey and Lady Hoby—Woodcroft
Manor—Eastbury Park—The " Haunted House " at Egham
—Dalham Hall.

To tell of all the reputedly haunted houses would be
the work of a lifetime, and would grow wearisome to
the reader ; for, in general, a house has but to look
dark and forbidding, or to lack a while a tenant and
the attentions of the builder and decorator, for a ghostly
tenant to be speedily found for it in popular imagination.
In other instances, romantic old houses with impressive
picture-galleries will fire the imaginations of the servants and others, with amazing results. A choice
example of this type of " haunted house " is Ripley
Castle, Yorkshire, in which, at the head of the stairs, is
the portrait of a nun who is said to descend from her
picture at night and tap at the bedroom doors ; when,
if anyone says " Come in," in she comes. It is a rather
scandalous tale to tell about a nun, if you come to think
of it, but ghost stories are superior to the proprieties.

The moated house of Baddesley Clinton, in Warwick-
shire, has a thrilful reputation. It rejoices in secret
passages and hiding-holes, and has, or had, a peculiarly
devilish contrivance in the shape of a passage that led
directly, without warning, into the deep waters of the
silent moat. In the days when Baddesley Clinton was
new, it was only with the utmost discretion that one
visited such country houses, and never at all if one's
host had anything to gain by one's disappearance.

" What was that ? " a guest might ask, when that
undesirable *other* guest had been artfully induced to
stray into the moat, instead of walking into the banquet-
ing-hall, and with a splash had gone to a particularly
noisome death in the sewage-charged waters. (For we

BADDESLEY CLINTON

must recollect that in the " good " old days manor-
houses, granges, and noble castles and mansions of every
kind drained directly into the moats that surrounded
them.)

" Only a fish," the host would reply ; but the strayed
guest nevermore appeared ; and we may shrewdly suppose that the other who heard that splash made haste
to quit so chancy a lodging.

It would appear that Baddesley Clinton was built
by one of the Catesbys, and that it was purchased from
the representative of that family by one John Brome,
a successful lawyer who flourished in the reign of Henry
the Sixth. Brome was killed in London, in a dispute
with one Herthill over some property which Brome had
taken under a mortgage ; but it did not end so, for his
son Nicholas, three years later, waylaid Herthill and
so mauled him that he presently died. Holy Church
required that Brome should do penance for this, which
he accordingly performed ; but his troubles did not
end here, for, coming home unexpectedly one day, he
discovered his domestic chaplain " choking his wife
under the chin," as Dugdale quaintly phrases it. He
was not really choking the lady, as the antiquary's queer
spelling would lead some people to believe, but was
indulging in the playful, or amatory, performance of
" chucking."

Being a man of hasty temper, Brome slew the priest
on the spot, an act for which he duly got into serious
trouble again with the Church ; which was not content,
this time, with less than a parish church being especially
built at Baddesley Clinton, by way of expiation, and a
new steeple being erected to that of Packwood. Nicholas
Brome died in 1517, but whether it is he or the priest—
or perhaps both—who haunt the old manor-house is not
narrated. The church of Baddesley Clinton, built by
Nicholas Brome by way of expiating his hasty deed, is
still an object of curiosity.

One of the most fearsome tales told of ancient manor-
houses is the dark and gory legend of Littlecote, the grey
and rambling pile built in the closing years of the fifteenth
century by the Darell family in the pleasant and fertile

BADDESLEY CLINTON CHURCH

meadowlands beside the river Kennet, and sheltered
beneath the Wiltshire downs, midway between Hunger-
ford and Ramsbury. Leland styles the demense of
Littlecote " a right faire and large parke hangynge upon
the clyffe of a highe hille welle woddyd over Kenet "—
quaint spelling that should please admirers of the archaic.

The property came to the Darells, who were originally
from Yorkshire, by the marriage of the heiress of the
Costons, the old owners, to William Darell. The " Wild
Will Darell " of the famous story of Littlecote was a
descendant of this William.

No one will ever succeed in satisfactorily settling the
historic doubts as to the character and career of the
Wicked Will, who flourished in the extremity of wicked-
ness in the reign of Good Queen Bess. There are two
schools of thought in this matter. The one is content
to see Darell painted in the blackest of hues, while the
other would have us believe him a much injured man,
a paragon of virtue and patience under undeserved misfortune. The ancient legends of the country-side have
always agreed to regard him as a monster of iniquity :
which certainly is not conclusive evidence, for there
is no one so ready as your simple rustic to endow his
superiors with attributes that would not ill become the
devil himself.

The story of Will Darell is that of a wild young man,
master of Littlecote, but by no means master of his own
evil passions. It is a tale of a midwife, a Mrs. Barnes of
Great Shefford, being suddenly summoned one dark night
on a pretence of attending Lady Knyvett, of Charlton,
near by, and then being blindfolded and led on horse-
back to a quite different house. In a stately room of
this mysterious mansion was an equally mysterious
masked lady, for whom her services were required. The
legend then goes on to declare that a tall, slender gentleman, with lowering and ferocious aspect, " havinge uppon
hym a goune of blacke velvett," entered the room with
some others, and, taking the newly-born child from her
arms, without a word threw it upon a blazing fire in an
ante-room and crushed it with his boot-heel into the
flaming logs, so that it was entirely consumed.

LITTLECOTE

THE HAUNTED CHAMBER, LITTLECOTE

It is impossible to altogether discredit this story, because the depositions made by Mrs. Barnes of Shefford, taken down from her when she was upon the point of death, in after years, have been discovered. The statement was committed to writing by Mr. Bridges, of Great Shefford, a magistrate, and, as a cousin of Darell, not likely to wantonly spread baseless slanders to the injury of a family with which he was connected. The document certainly does not identify Darell or Littlecote, nor does it even hint at the identity of any place or person. But the discovery, about 1879, at Longleat, of an original letter from Sir H. Knyvett, of Charlton, to Sir John Thynne, of Longleat, dated January 2, 157⅝ (about the time of Mrs. Barnes's confession), brings us to the original rumours pointing to Darell and Littlecote. A Mr. Bonham was then residing at Longleat. His sister was well known to be living with Darell as his mistress, and the letter from Sir H. Knyvett was to rouse this Mr. Bonham to " inquire of his sister touching her usage at Will. Darell's, the birth of her children, how many there were, and what became of them : for that the report of the murder of one of them was increasing foully, and would touch Will. Darell to the quick."

Whatever the rumour and the gossip, the result of this letter is unknown. Aubrey, the historian of the county of Wilts, writing a hundred years later, tells us that Darell was brought to trial, and says, " Sir John Popham gave sentence according to law, but, being a great person and a favourite, he pronounced a *noli prosequi*." Aubrey's facts are all at sea here, for Popham did not become a judge until 1592, when Darell had been dead nearly three years. He was, however, Attorney-General at the time of Darell's supposed crime. But Darell certainly made over the reversion of Littlecote to Popham in 1586, and upon Darell's decease in 1589 he took possession. Aubrey's story is that this transaction was a bribe to procure Popham's services.

Mrs. Barnes is said to have brought about the identification of the mysterious house with Littlecote by the ingenious devices of counting the stairs and cutting a piece out of the bed-curtains. By fitting the piece of

curtain she had carried away into a corresponding hole
in the hangings of a bed at Littlecote, and by finding
the number of the stairs to agree, Darell's guilt is said
to have been brought home to him.

The death of this ferocious Will is said to have been
caused by his being haunted along the roads by the
apparition of a Burning Babe, which startled his horse
so that Darell was flung to the ground and his neck
broken. He is now, in old country lore, an apparition
himself, and haunts indifferently " Darell's Stile " and
the bedroom.

"Haunts," I have written; but who talks now
of Darell ? Long ago General Leyborne-Popham, who
died in 1843, burnt the historic bed-curtains, being so
much pestered by people who were interested in the
story. Later, at the great Littlecote sale, the bedstead
itself was disposed of and was removed to Parnham, in
Dorset, whence it was sold in July, 1910.

But it was about 1861 that the " haunted " nature
of Littlecote again was noted, in a curious circumstance.
A child in the Leyborne-Popham succession lay ill in
the house, in a room overlooking the entrance, which
is guarded by tall iron gates. The nurse, finding the
child to be desperately ill, sent an express for the parents,
and the next night she heard the gates flung open, and
a coach driven to the door ; and then the peal of the
bell. When the expected parents did not come to the
room, the nurse rose and opened the casement ; but all
was still, in the bright moonlight. Next day, when the
parents arrived, the child was dead. No one at the
time remembered to have heard of the legend, but many
years later, the child's father, Mr. Francis Popham,
found in an old chest a manuscript which referred to a
story that when the heir to Littlecote is about to die,
Wild Darell is supposed to drive up to the door in his
chariot.

In recent years Littlecote has had a sordid romance
by no means associated with the supernatural. It was
occupied by Gerard Lee Bevan, managing director of
the City Equitable Assurance. There he assembled
priceless collections of objects of art and lived in

magnificence. It all ended in a conviction for fraud in 1922, and a sentence of seven years' penal servitude.

Bisham Abbey, that lovely old residence on the banks of the Thames, in Berkshire, has long been reputed a haunted house. If historic associations of the most romantic kind make a predisposition to haunting, Bisham Abbey has every circumstance in favour of ghosts ; for it has been at different times a Preceptory of Knights Templar and a stately Abbey in whose noble church numbers of the great in history were buried. Greatest of them all was the imposing Nevill, the famous " Warwick the Kingmaker," who fell at the Battle of Barnet, in 1471, in the hour of defeat. Surely, if ever ghost walked, his should have haunted the shades of Bisham. But no such great figures have disturbed those sylvan lawns. They sleep well, gentle and simple, famous or obscure, who were buried here, and their very tombs have gone, together with the stones of the Abbey that sheltered them, in the complete destruction of the monastic buildings. The mansion now styled the " Abbey " is, in fact, only a portion of the domestic buildings, and has itself been refaced.

Boating parties on that most beautiful reach of the Thames are familiar with the ancient church of Bisham, standing close upon the banks of the river, and glimpse the old mansion near by, embosomed amid trees, its corbie-stepped gables peaking picturesquely into the sky. It is a beautiful old house, and essentially the same as when Henry the Eighth gave it (among others) to his discarded Queen, Anne of Cleves. It has long been the property of the Vansittart-Neale family, to whom, it is understood, the reputation of " haunted house " is by no means welcome.

From Anne of Cleves the property passed by exchange to the Hoby family, one of whom, Sir Thomas Hoby, was charged in the reign of Queen Mary with the custody of the Princess Elizabeth.

Sir Thomas does not appear to have had much leisure to enjoy his riverside retreat after the accession of Queen Elizabeth. He must have been a courtly and a gentle custodian, for the Queen who had, as Princess,

been his prisoner looked with favour upon him, and
employed him as Ambassador to France, where he died,
a very youthful Ambassador, at the age of thirty-six.

It is the unquiet spirit of his wife, Lady Elizabeth
Hoby, that has long been reputed to haunt the old
mansion. She was one of the four accomplished daughters
of Sir Anthony Cooke, of Gidea Hall, Essex, and married

LADY HOBY
From the crayon drawing by Holbein

Sir Thomas Hoby in 1553. Hoby died in 1566, in Paris,
as his epitaph states, and his widow brought home the
body to Bisham. She married again, in 1574, John,
Lord Russell, who died in 1584, and herself died in 1609,
aged 81, being buried beside her first husband.

Lady Hoby was a person of remarkable linguistic
and other scholarly attainments. She wrote Greek and
Latin verse, and composed religious treatises. So much

is certainly known ; and the story of the alleged haunting of Bisham Abbey, handed down from one generation to another, shows her, singularly enough, in complete accord with this character. It can readily be understood that a highly accomplished, and perhaps priggish, person such as Lady Hoby would not be likely to make sufficient allowance for the mistakes of a dull child, or the wilfulness of an idle one ; and the story goes that she was a cruel mother to her little boy William, who was slow at learning and untidy with his copy-books ; whose pages were not what neat copy-books should be, but slovenly, and disfigured with blots. Lady Hoby is said to have been in the habit of severely chastising the boy, and one day, when the copy-books had been more than usually blotted, she thrashed him so unmercifully that he died.

This story has long been current, and would seem to have been handed down by gossip from a remote period. Oral traditions have achieved even more remarkable vitality than this. The legend of the haunting seems to be almost equally old. It tells how the ghost of Lady Hoby is to be seen gliding from a bedroom, like Lady Macbeth, in the act of washing bloodstains from her hands in a basin of water carried before her like a vagrant, without visible means of support. Her identity may be established by comparing the spook with one among the old family portraits in the dining-room, in which Lady Hoby is represented with very white face and hands, and dressed in the coif, weeds, and wimple of a knight's widow. But those who are said to have seen the ghost have always declared that she appears (speaking after the manner of photographers) in the negative way, with *black* face and hands and white dress. A drawing by Holbein, among the collection at Windsor Castle, picturing the Court of Henry the Eighth, shows a portrait head of Lady Hoby, with hard features and a cat-like smile, not at all prepossessing.

A curious discovery was made at Bisham Abbey many years ago, supporting the old story of the blotted copy-books. During some alterations a sixteenth-century window-shutter was removed, when " a packet of antique copy-books was discovered, pushed into the wall between

BISHAM ABBEY

the joists and the skirting, and several of these books,
on which young Hoby's name was written, were covered
with blots."

But the rather daunting fact becomes presently
apparent that no " William Hoby " is to be discovered.

In Bisham church may be seen the magnificent
monument erected by Lady Hoby to her husband, Sir
Thomas, and to his half-brother, Sir Philip. Life-sized
effigies of the two knights lie side by side, and in front
is the lengthy epitaph :

> Syr Thomas Hobye married with Dame Elizabeth,
> daughter to Syr Anthonye Cooke, Knighte,
> by whome he had issewe fower children,
> Edward, Elizabeth, Anne, and Thomas Posthumus,
> and being Embassador for Quene Elizabetha in Fraunce
> died at Paris the . 13 . of July 1566 of the age of 36.

> Two worthye knightes, and Hobies bothe by name
> Enclosed within this marble stone do rest.
> Philip the fyrst, in Caesars court hathe fame :
> Such as tofore, fewe legates like possest.
> A diepe discoursing head, a noble brest :
> A courtier passing, and a curteis knight :
> Zelous to God whos gospel he profest :
> When gretest stormes gan dym the sacred light.
> A happie man, whom death hath nowe redeemd
> From care to ioye that can not be esteemd.
> Thomas in Fraunce possest the legates place.
> And with such wisdome grew to guide the same,
> As had increst great honour to his race,
> If sodein fate had not envied his fame.
> Firme in God's truth, gentle, a faithful frend :
> Wel lernd and languaged, nature besyde
> Gave comely shape, which made ruful his end :
> Sins in his floure in Paris towne he died :
> Leaving with child behind his woful wief ;
> In forein land opprest with heapes of grief.
> From part of which when she discharged was,
> By fall of teares that faithful wiefes do shead :
> The corps with honour brought she to this place
> Perfourming here all due unto the dead.
> That doon, this noble tombe she causd to make,
> And both thes brethern closed within the same :
> A memory left here for vertues sake,
> In spite of Death to honour them with fame.
> Thus live they dead, and we lerne wel therby,
> That ye, and we, and all the world must dye.

A woman, the contemplative stranger thinks, who could so barbarously torture the laws of rhyme and of spelling as to write " his woful wief " to rhyme with " grief," as above, would have been capable of anything ; but, apart from such criticism, the sentiments of that epitaph do not display anything but an affectionate nature : quite foreign to that of a woman who could so cruelly treat a child, and it should also be remarked that the received story of the child " William " Hoby does not agree with the facts narrated in the epitaph, in which no " William " appears. Lady Hoby's children were, in fact, as stated, four : two sons, Edward and Thomas Posthumus, both of whom grew up to manhood and became knighted ; and two daughters, Elizabeth and Anne, who died within a few days of each other, in 1570. By her marriage with Lord Russell, however, she had a son, Francis, who is recorded to have died in infancy.

Bisham remained in the Hoby family until 1766, when their descendant in the female line, Sir John Mill, held the estate. His widow sold it to the Vansittarts, who, in the person of Sir H. J. Vansittart-Neale, are there yet.

A very prominent recent monument in the church confronts you on entering. It is the figure in marble of a boy, kneeling in prayer at a desk, and dressed in a Norfolk-jacket suit. It represents George Vansittart-Neale, who died of peritonitis, in 1904.

Woodcroft Manor, or Woodcroft Castle, as it is sometimes styled, in the neighbourhood of Peterborough, is another reputed haunted house, and its gloomy exterior is in keeping with its reputation and with the tragic story that belongs to it.

Though the house was once a castle, the round tower seen to the left of the picture is almost the only relic of the early Edwardian times when the house was first built.

The stirring story of the place belongs to that disastrous period, the time of the Civil War between King Charles and his Parliament. It was a time when the old order of fighting Churchmen was not yet quite extinct ; and among these militant clerics loyal to the

King was Dr. Michael Hudson, one of His Majesty's chaplains.

With a view to holding in check the many bands of Parliamentary marauders who were pillaging Huntingdonshire, Dr. Hudson collected a body of yeomen for the purpose of waging a guerilla warfare against the enemy, but, after some initial successes, he was obliged to fall back upon Woodcroft Manor.

Here he was presently besieged, and defended the house stubbornly from morn till eve, and from room to room. At last, driven to the roof of the tower, and himself the sole survivor of the little band of defenders, he was engaged in combat with half a dozen of the Roundheads, who refused to accept his offer of surrender, and forced him over the parapet. There he clung desperately until the officer in charge of the party hacked off his fingers, when he fell into the moat which then surrounded the house.

The sorely wounded man, however, managed to struggle to the muddy bank, but was murdered there by his enemies, who hurried down from the tower and despatched him with their pikes.

That is why Woodcroft Manor has the reputation of being haunted. Lovers of the marvellous declare that the scene is again enacted in ghostly fashion, and that the clash of steel and cries of " Quarter ! " and " Mercy ! " are heard.

There is a finely ruinous old estate of fallen fortune and peculiar history in the neighbourhood of Blandford. Eastbury Park is the name of this haunted domain. Built out of the proceeds of vast and long-continued peculations from the Admiralty by George Dodington, in the middle of the eighteenth century, and afterwards allowed to fall into ruin by Earl Temple, a later owner, who could not afford to maintain so huge a place, and actually offered (in vain) £200 a year and free residence to anyone who would take the great mansion and keep it in repair ; it has long since been demolished, except or one wing only.

It is the ghost of Doggett, the fraudulent steward of that Earl Temple, which haunts the road and the long

WOODCROFT MANOR

EASTBURY

drive up from the park gates to the house. The neighbourhood knows Doggett very well indeed, and can tell you how, emulating the vaster frauds of him who built the place, he robbed his employer and oppressed the tenantry, and at last shot himself. Generally at the stroke of midnight, a coach with headless coachman and headless horses drives out and picks up Doggett down the road.

If you see an old-world figure at such a time, stepping into that horrid conveyance, you will recognise him as Doggett by his knee-breeches, tied with yellow silk ribbon. The headless coachman asks (out of his neck ?), " Where to, sir ? " and the ghost says, " Home " ; whereupon the horses are whipped up, and they drive back to the house. The shade of Doggett, entering, proceeds to the panelled room where he shot himself a century and a half ago—and shoots himself again !

Doggett was buried in the neighbouring church of Tarrant Gunville. That building was demolished and rebuilt in 1845, when the workmen, exhuming his body, found the legs to have been tied together with yellow silk ribbon. The material was as fresh and bright as the day it had been tied, and the body was not decayed. The credulous country folk averred that he was a vampire.

The whimsical story of a suburban villa at Egham that was said to be haunted, and would appear *not* to be haunted, was the subject of actions-at-law in 1904, 1906, and again in 1907. The owner of the house, Mr. Charles Arthur Barrett, brought actions to recover damages against Mr. Stephen Phillips, dramatist, certain daily newspapers, and the weekly paper *Light*, for circulating statements as to supernatural happenings on his property, and was duly awarded pecuniary consolation for the aspersions cast upon the house. The offence was technically, in legal phraseology, " slander of title."

A mediæval castle or an Elizabethan manor-house may, it appears, be haunted with advantage, but a modern suburban villa must be above suspicion of spooks. In the one case, the " haunted " character is thought to give a certain romantic charm ; in the other, it simply reduces the rental value, or even renders the house absolutely impossible, from the house-agent's point of view.

The house that was the subject of these actions in the King's Bench Division is the modern villa at Egham called "Hillside." In 1890 it was sold by one Mr. John Ashby to the plaintiff, who let it subsequently to a succession of tenants at £70 per annum. None of these tenants, it was stated, made any complaints. Then in 1903 it was rented by Mr. Stephen Phillips, who, it was alleged, heard inexplicable noises, and soon left, forfeiting the rent he had paid, and being obliged to take refuge in a local hotel from gruesome noises that suggested the strangulation of a child.

The *Daily Express*, hearing of the affair, in 1904 published an account of it ; the result being an action brought against the paper and Mr. Phillips. This was settled out of court for £200.

In March, 1906, when the libelled house was getting back its character once more, the *Daily Mail* published the following extract from *Light*, the organ of the occult :

" THE POET'S EXPERIENCE.

" About a year ago the poet-dramatist, Mr. Stephen Phillips, moved into the house at Egham. It was not long before he was disturbed by strange knockings and rappings, accompanied by footfalls, soft and loud, hasty and stealthy. As he sat quietly writing in his study, the door would open. He found the obvious explanation of a draught to be absurd. ' Draughts do not turn door-handles—and, on my life, the handle would turn as the door opened, and no hand was visible.'

" His little daughter told him that she had seen a small, old man creeping about the house, but there was no such person to be found. There was, however, a common reputation and local tradition that an old farmer had strangled a child fifty years ago in the vicinity of the house. The servants having incontinently fled, the poet was constrained to throw up his lease and do likewise. There is no report that the disturbances pursued him."

As a result of this, it was complained, the house remained empty, the best offers received being £500 for the purchase, and a five years' tenancy, with one year rent-free in which to " lay " the ghost.

It appeared that the house was built upon the site of an old cottage in which anything or nothing tragical might have happened ; but no one knew anything about a child having been strangled there, except some vague tradition that a farmer had committed such a crime in the vicinity about fifty years earlier.

According to a report of the case, " Mr. Finn, auctioneer and estate agent at Egham, said he had not been able to let the property. Mr. Phillips had complained to him that the doors in the house had opened without physical agency, and he was employing an expert to investigate the matter. The expert had slept in the house, and had attributed the noises complained of to the visitations of a child which had been strangled in the neighbourhood.

" Mr. Lowe : Did he say anything about a little old man ?—Nothing at all.

" Mr. Lush (cross-examining) : You know there are other things besides ghosts which stop houses being let. Are there not a very large number of motor-cars that pass the house ?—I should not say a very large number.

" It is in the main road from Virginia Water to London ?—Yes.

" Mr. Philip S. Head, auctioneer and agent, said the house in question had been on his books for over three years, but he had been unable to let it, though there was nothing in its external appearance which would debar people looking at it. He did not go out of his way to tell people who thought of taking the house the story about its being haunted.

" Mr. Lush, Q.C. (for the defendants) : I suppose you agree that the development of the motor-car traffic is a nuisance to houses on the main arteries out of London ? —I believe it is in some cases, but I don't think it affects Egham.

" You think the dust is rather enjoyable in some cases ? (Laughter.)—In some cases it would not be as serious as in others.

" His Lordship : Do you think the owner of a house like that can let it if he will only let it on a term of years ?

" Witness did not quite follow his lordship's meaning.

" ' Well, I have had some experience of houses,' said his lordship. ' Don't you think if he has got a house like that with a bad name, the only way to let it is to get some person to take it for a year without rent ? '

" The Witness : I think that would be a feasible plan.

" Mr. Charles Barrett, the plaintiff, said that if he had got a good tenant he would have been pleased to let the house on almost any terms."

The result was that the jury returned a verdict for the plaintiff for £90 damages against the *Daily Mail. Light,* whence the report was derived, had paid a sum into Court on account of damages more than the £10 awarded against the proprietors of that journal.

But the affair did not end here, for the defendant *Daily Mail* appealed successfully against the decision ; and at this point, for the present, matters rest.

The house, in no way, so far as appearance goes, different from the general run of modern villas, faces the Exeter Road, the great highway out of London into the West of England, and is situated half-way up the hill, beyond Egham, near the Holloway College. A policeman now inhabits " Hillside " as caretaker, and is prosaically of opinion that the " ghosts " of the house are rats ! According to local information, this was not the only house Mr. Phillips found impossible. It appears he took " The Quadrant," two doors off, for a term of three years, and left in a twelvemonth, paying the rent for the remaining two years without occupying the place.

At the Wandsworth County Court on October 23rd, 1911, Mr. Thomas Henry Wrensted, of Queen Victoria Street, sued Mr. William Atkinson, of Borough Road, S.E., for £10 13s. 4d., rent due in respect of house in Cathles Road, Balham.

Mr. Hanne, solicitor for the plaintiff, said the defendant objected to pay rent for the premises because, he alleged, the house was haunted by an old, grey-headed man.   He left the house and declined to pay after taking the premises for twelve months.

Mr. Hanne read a letter from Mrs. Atkinson to the plaintiff, in which she said : " Some noises we have heard give us no rest.   We have tried all the rooms to sleep in, but they are all alive.   Big bangs come at the head of the bedstead and wake us up.   One of my daughters had her face slapped.   One night some brass rails were flung across the room.   There are terrible bangs at the head of the bed and pattering up and down stairs.   Our dog whines and it is very restless.   Last week he was let loose, and the back door opened and the dog was admitted to the house, by whom we do not know. . . ."

In another letter Mrs. Atkinson said : " We left on Monday morning, so have had two good nights' rest and we all feel much better for it. . . ."

The Judge :   " Has the landlord investigated all these apparitions ? "

Mr. Hanne :   " He says he has never heard about these mysterious noises and appearances before."

The judge said that a plea of ghosts could not be

THE " HAUNTED HOUSE," CATHLES ROAD, BALHAM

"HILLSIDE," EGHAM

COMBE BANK

a successful reason for not paying the rent, and gave a verdict against the defendant.

We all know the " unlucky house." Every neighbourhood has such a one, which has brought—or has seemed to bring—ill-fortune to all who have resided therein. I know a noble seventeenth-century mansion that is in most respects (in the conventional phrase of auctioneers and estate-agents) a " desirable family residence." In every respect, that is to say, save one. Disaster has dogged the footsteps of those who have taken it—and has in the end overtaken them. Three persons who have lived there, at intervals extending over twenty-five years, have laid violent hands upon themselves and ended lives that had, for one reason or another, become too irksome to be faced any longer. One occupier shot himself in the house ; a gardener hanged himself behind the coach-house doors ; and a later occupant shot himself by the river-bank. The superstitious consider that if we knew the whole history of the mansion, we should have a longer tale of mischances to those sheltered by its ill-omened roof. But, strange to say, it does not long lack a new tenant.

One wonders, in the case of a reputedly " unlucky house," if the incoming tenant has been informed of its reputation, or if he enters upon his tenancy with his eyes open, and, like the furniture-removing people, " taking all risks." If he dares so much, he has my respectful admiration, and becomes at once an object of interest to myself in particular and to the neighbourhood in general. He earns an admiring or expectant interest, just as we look upon some intrepid explorer on dangerous ground, or some nimble trapezist : sincerely hoping he will come to no harm, but anticipating that he will. After all, we need not be thoroughly superstitious in refusing to reside in an " unlucky house." To be the centre of local interest under the circumstances attending such a tenancy must be distinctly unnerving in the end to various members of the household, and demoralising to the servants ; and desirable residences are not so scarce that one need be reduced to the straits of taking such an inimical house, or none.

DALHAM HALL

Dalham Hall, near Newmarket, built in 1704 by
Dr. Patrick, Bishop of Ely, long ago, rightly or wrongly,
earned the name, locally, of " unlucky Dalham."
Calamities, financial and otherwise, pursued—and overtook—a long line of its owners. Among these were the
Affleck family, who at last sold it to the late Mr. Cecil
Rhodes. The purchase was still a new thing when that
great man died, untimely, in 1902, in his forty-ninth
year.

Cause and effect ? Well, no : no one dare contend
so much in these days ; but the facts were duly noted at
the time by many newspapers ; and newspapers, it
should be observed, in freely paragraphing curious
coincidences of the kind, together with every provincial
" haunted house " or " ghost " story, keep alive very
effectually the dread beliefs and fearful imaginings
fondly thought by many people to be obsolescent.

Cecil Rhodes had thoughts of retiring, at the close of
a public life, to Dalham ; but, as we have seen, he died
unexpectedly, shortly after he had purchased the estate.
He left it to his brother, the popular Colonel Frank
Rhodes, to whom, the more thorough-going among the
marvel-mongers declared, the bequest proved fatal. At
any rate, he did not long survive the possession of it,
dying in 1905. Needless to say, the present writer does
not share that article of belief ; and, as evidence of good
faith, hereby declares his willingness to accept the
reversion, should there be those sufficiently faint-hearted
to renounce it. But a third, and even more startling,
event took place on April 4th, 1907, when the third
brother, Captain Ernest Frederick Rhodes, to whom the
estate had fallen, died at Dalham Hall, in his fifty-fifth
year. Dalham is now the property of Mr. F. W. Rhodes.

CHAPTER III

Spedlin's Tower—Cranford Park—Ham House and the Duchess
of Lauderdale.

THE following example takes us across the Border, into
the neighbourhood of Lockerbie, Dumfriesshire.

Spedlin's Tower was, in the reign of Charles the
Second, the residence, or at least the property, of Sir
Alexander Jardine, of Applegarth : a bold bad Baronet,
who had imprisoned in the dungeons of this old tower
overlooking the Annan a certain miller, one Porteous,
charged (with what degree of truth does not appear)
with being the incendiary of his own mill. It was while
this prisoner was languishing in the underground hold of
Spedlin's Tower that Sir Alexander Jardine was summoned to Edinburgh on urgent business, which so
engrossed his mind that, carrying with him the keys of
his Little Ease, he clean forgot the existence of the
unfortunate Porteous, until some days later. Suddenly
the horrible conviction dawned upon him that he had
left the miller in his lonely cell, without any possibility of
his making himself heard. Hurriedly the Baronet
entrusted the keys to a messenger, whom he bade hasten
to Spedlin's Tower ; but by the time that envoy had
arrived, the hapless Porteous was dead : starved to
death.

It was quite in order that the ghost of this miserable
prisoner should haunt the scene, and the neighbourhood
of Spedlin's Tower accordingly was very soon reported
to be unquiet with a shrieking spirit whose howls made
the blood of such cottars who lived within earshot run
cold.

The horror-stricken Baronet did what was possible.
He procured the services of a number of ministers of
religion, who undertook to " lay " the ghost, in the
Red Sea, or other appropriate resting-place ; or, at the

very least of it, to confine him within the dungeon wherein his mortal part had ended. The Red Sea, however, appears to have been a little beyond their powers, and Sir Alexander had to be content with the dungeon ; from which muffled cries of " Let me oot ! let me oot ! I'm deein' o' hunger ! " were long heard, accompanied by bird-like flutterings. When children thrust twigs through the keyhole, the hungry ghost would invariably tear off the bark and consume it !

When at last, about 1770, the Jardine family migrated across the Annan to their fine new mansion, the ancient Bible by whose aid the spirit had thus been kept within bounds was left behind. At last, in an age which did not comprehend the essential importance of the Bible being kept on the spot, it was taken away to Edinburgh, to be re-bound. That was the spirit's opportunity, which he took full advantage of by crossing the stream and invading the mansion, where he was credited with hauling the Baronet and his wife out of bed, and in general produced such terror that no time was lost in intercepting the Bible on its way and restoring it—and incidentally the ghostly but forceful Porteous—to the old tower.

But even ghosts seem to feel the ravages of time. Long, long ago, the old Bible was taken to Jardine Hall, and not within the memory of man has Porteous made any sign. Jardine Hall was sold by the family in 1884, but they still preserve the old black-letter Bible, printed in 1634, and now carefully enclosed within a strong brass-clamped box made from the ancient beams of the long-since roofless walls of Spedlin's Tower.

The mansion of Combe Bank (or Comb Bank) at Sundridge, in Kent, lately the property of Mr. William Spottiswoode, who died in 1883, has, with its beautiful park, been for some years past in the market, to be let or sold. It is associated with a singular chain of events, having been in 1756 the property of Colonel John Campbell, who in 1761 succeeded to the Dukedom of Argyll, as fourth Duke, and was afterwards given the additional title of Baron Sundridge, in acknowledgment—not of any remarkable public services—but of the less meritorious

SPEDLIN'S TOWER

than fortunate circumstance of being the owner of much
property in the parish.

To his third son, Lord Frederick Campbell, he presented Combe Bank ; and there Lord Frederick resided
with his wife, who had been wife, and subsequently the
widow, of the fourth Earl Ferrers, who was hanged at
Tyburn in 1760 for the murder of his steward. The
murder arose partly out of a petition for separation
brought by Lady Ferrers. In the judicial proceedings
evidence was given against the Earl by his steward,
John Johnson, whom that ill-balanced nobleman afterwards shot, in revenge. Even so far back as 1760,
when the privileged classes were allowed wide latitude, it
was not permitted to shoot stewards like rabbits, and so
Lord Ferrers was arraigned on the capital charge, and
greatly to his surprise, convicted and sentenced to be
suspended—where many another malefactor had swung
—at Tyburn.

It was very like a gala day in London when my Lord
Ferrers went forth from the Tower to be hanged. It
was done in style—if that were any satisfaction to the
central figure in the proceedings. He had dressed
himself in his wedding clothes, and set out upon that
four-miles journey seated in a landau with six horses.
In advance went a company of grenadiers, and a sheriff in
a carriage and six, plentifully decked with ribbons ; and
the rear was brought up by a troop of horse, the chariot
of the other sheriff, and—decently in the wake of this
brilliant procession—a mourning coach and a hearse.

A huge crowd watched the passing of this singular
assemblage, and an even larger crowd was waiting at
Tyburn. " I suppose," remarked Lord Ferrers sardonically, as they bowled along and noticed this concourse of
people, " I suppose they never saw a lord hanged, and
will never see another." He had hoped to be executed
on Tower Hill, where his ancestor, Queen Elizabeth's
Earl of Essex, had suffered, and had petitioned the King
that he should not be hanged at Tyburn. " I think it
hard," he exclaimed, on learning that his request had
been refused, " that I must die at the place appointed
for the execution of common felons " : but it would have

been harder if the place where so many of the brave and the true had suffered had been made the scene where one who had lowered himself to the condition of a felon was to die. They hanged him with a silken rope, as some concession to his rank, and he ended with all the air of a martyr, presuming even to prophesy. Lady Ferrers, it would appear, had given evidence that largely helped to convict him, and he cursed her, saying her death would prove even more painful than his. Strange to say, forty-seven years later, in 1807, Lady Frederick Campbell, as she was then, was burnt to death in one of the towers of Combe Bank. It was thought that she had fallen asleep beside the fire in her dressing-room, and so fallen into the fire-place. The accident was not discovered until the room was furiously blazing, and the only fragment of her ever discovered was a portion of one thumb, which is stated to have been duly interred in Sundridge church. Her ghost was long declared to walk the park at night, looking for that lost thumb; but has not been seen of late.

The house is a striking architectural composition, built of stone, and designed in imitation of the Villa Doria, at Rome.

The old mansion in Cranford Park, Middlesex, the seat of the Fitzhardinge Berkeleys for many a long year, and now that of Lord Fitzhardinge, is the home of ghostly servants, who, fortunately, do not appear to breathe down your neck at dinner or obtrude themselves upon " the quality." But " the quality," penetrating occasionally to the kitchen, have seen things not of this earth. The mansion is for the most part a heavy, scowling pile, rambling darkly, a mass of deep-toned red brick, over much ground in the picturesque park; and a more or less " modern " portion, with a double-bayed front, furnished with veranda-roofs on the first floor, looking weirdly like heavy, half-closed eyelids, has a not much more cheerful appearance. To the distant view, the house and church, framed as it were by the sullen waters of the river Crane and dark masses of trees, look sufficiently eerie.

It was the Hon. Grantley Berkeley who, in his

Recollections, first made public the " haunted " character
of the house. He, of all men—a typical robust English
sportsman, of the old roast-beef-and-bitter-beer type—
was the least likely ghost-seer, but he declares he—and
his brother with him—saw one. They had returned
home late, and went down into the kitchen, in search of
supper, all the rest of the household having retired long
before. In the kitchen they distinctly saw the tall
figure of an elderly woman walk across the room. Thinking it was one of the maids, they spoke to her, but the
figure vanished into thin air, and a search discovered
nothing at all. Grantley Berkeley's father, however,
used to describe how he saw a man in the stable-yard,
and, under the impression that he was some unauthorised
visitor to the servants' hall, asked him what he was
doing there. The man " vanished " without a reply.
Perhaps, after all, he was a real flesh-and-blood man, to
whom the sight of the horsewhip the Earl was carrying
would be a sufficient motive force.

Not, perhaps, very terrible ghosts, these of Cranford :
but it is just a trifle disconcerting, it will be conceded,
after old servitors have been decently interred in the
churchyard, with their services handsomely acknowledged
on good honest tombstones, to find them coming back
and haunting the kitchen, the pantry, and the housekeeper's room. The only advantages of ghostly butlers
or housekeepers are that they want no wages and claim
no perquisites. Whether, by the laws and ordinances
of the other world, they can have " followers " is doubt-
ful ; but one very obvious disadvantage is that other
servants will not work with them.

Ham House, situated in a fine damp position, amid
the meadows beside the Thames, midway between
Richmond and Kingston, is prominent among those
stately mansions whose very appearance presupposes
the supernatural. It is densely overshadowed by trees,
and the chief entrances to it, by the ancient wrought-
iron gates back and front, are, and long have been,
closed, the usual approach being by the stable-yard
on the west side. This singular disuse of the entrances
originally planned has itself given rise to many fantastic

CRANFORD PARK

and entirely fictitious legends ; but every circumstance,
historic and scenic, connected with Ham House is
provocative of tales of the marvellous. To begin with,
it was built originally by Sir Thomas Vavasor in 1610,
and intended as a residence for Prince Henry, the Prince
of Wales, eldest son of James the First. He was a
promising youth, and was to have resided with some
splendour at Ham House : hence the several fine mansions
at Petersham, near by, built at the same time, and
intended to have been occupied by the Court which he,
as Heir Apparent, would have maintained. But this
Prince died with tragical suddenness, not without hints
of poison, in 1612. He really died of typhoid fever,
at that time very prevalent ; but it is difficult (or was
in those days) for a prince to die a natural death.

No one, however, has presumed to take away the
character of Prince Henry. He sleeps sound enough,
and does not trouble the avenues of Ham. It is the
old Duchess of Lauderdale who, according to the stories.
revisits this—among others—of the scenes of her triumphs
and infamies in the period of the Commonwealth and
the reign of Charles the Second. The old dame's boudoir
remains as it was when she left it, and her silver-mounted
ebony walking-stick lies across the table ; and they *do*
say that the stick may be heard " rap, rap, rapping "
at the most untimeous hours, when no Christian is about,
nor, under the circumstances, would be doing aught
but putting his head under the bedclothes, for fear of
the uncanny.

The reason for the infamous old Duchess haunting
the place is to be sought in the story told by Mr. Hare :

" There is a ghost at Ham. The old butler there
had a little girl, and the Ladies Tollemache kindly
asked her to come on a visit : she was then six years
old. In the small hours of the morning, when dawn
was making things clear, the child, waking up, saw a
little old woman scratching with her fingers against
the wall, close to the fire-place. She was not at all
frightened at first, but sat up to look at her. The noise
she made in doing this caused the old woman to look
round, and she came to the foot of the bed, and, grasping

HAM HOUSE

the rail with her hands, stared at the child long and
fixedly. So horrible was her stare that the child was
terrified, and screamed and hid her face under the
clothes. People who were in the passage ran in, and
the child told what she had seen.   The wall was examined
where she had seen the figure scratching, and concealed
in it were found papers which proved that in that room
Elizabeth, Countess of Dysart, had murdered her husband
to marry the Duke of Lauderdale."

The foregoing is quoted as one of Mr. Hare's picturesque
ghost-stories ; which, however, have not the proper merit
of being accurate and historic. Elizabeth, Countess of
Dysart's first husband, Sir Lionel Tollemache, died in
Paris in January, 1669, Lady Dysart being then in London.
The Duke of Lauderdale's wife did not die until 1671.

CHAPTER IV

In discussing such subjects as these, it is always desirable to have the testimony of those whose good faith is not likely to be called in question. Thus, the ghost-story told by the Rev. Dr. Jessop, the well-known Norfolk cleric, is especially welcome. It was originally narrated by him in the *Athenæum*. In the pages of that journal he told how, on October 10th, 1879, he visited Lord Orford at Mannington Hall, for the purpose of consulting some out-of-the-way books in the library there. Arriving at four o'clock in the afternoon, he dined with his host and a company of four others. There was not, during the whole of the evening, any reference made to occult subjects, and at half-past ten the company separated. By eleven o'clock the only person downstairs was Dr. Jessop himself, engaged in the library, making literary references. The family, and the servants alike, had retired to bed.

Dr. Jessop was busily engaged, and had soon accumulated a pile of volumes beside him. He sat at a table near the fire, and, with occasional intervals for raking the fire together and warming his feet, was thus engrossed in writing and reading by the light of four candles in silver candlesticks, until close upon one o'clock in the morning. Then, thinking with some satisfaction that he would be able to conclude his labours in another hour, he rested awhile, and, winding his watch, opened a bottle of seltzer water. Presently he resumed work again, and came at last to the concluding volume.

" I had been engaged upon it about half an hour,"

says Dr. Jessop, " and was just beginning to think
that my work was drawing to a close, when, as I was
actually writing, I saw a large white hand within a foot
of my elbow. Turning my head, there sat a figure of
a somewhat large man, with his back to the fire, bending
slightly over the table, and apparently examining the
pile of books that I had been at work upon. The man's
face was turned away from me, but I saw his closely-
cut reddish-brown hair, his ear and shaved cheek, the
eyebrow, the corner of the right eye, the side of the
forehead, and the large high cheek-bone. He was
dressed in what I can only describe as a kind of ecclesiastical habit of thick corded silk, or some such material,
close up to the throat, and a narrow rim or edging, of
about an inch broad, of satin or velvet, serving as a
stand-up collar, and fitting close to the chin. The right
hand, which had first attracted my attention, was
clasping, without any great pressure, the left hand ;
both hands were in perfect repose, and the large blue
veins of the left hand were conspicuous. I remember
thinking that the hand was like the hand of Velasquez's
magnificent ' Dead Knight,' in the National Gallery.
I looked at my visitor for some seconds, and was perfectly
sure that he was not a reality. A thousand thoughts
came crowding upon me, but not the least feeling of
alarm, or even uneasiness ; curiosity, and a strong
interest, were uppermost. For an instant I felt eager
to make a sketch of my friend, and I looked at a tray
on my right for a pencil ; then I thought, ' Upstairs,
I have a sketch book ; shall I fetch it ? ' There he sat,
and I was fascinated : afraid, not of his staying, but
lest he should go.

" Stopping in my writing, I lifted my left hand
from the paper, stretched it out to the pile of books,
and moved the top one. I cannot explain why I did
this—my arm passed in front of the figure, and it vanished.
I was simply disappointed, and nothing more. I went
on with my writing as if nothing had happened, perhaps
for another five minutes, and had actually got to the
last few words of what I had determined to extract,
when the figure appeared again, exactly in the same

MANNINGTON HALL

place and attitude as before. I saw the hands close to my own ; I turned my head again to examine him more closely, and I was framing a sentence to address him when I discovered that I did not dare to speak. I was afraid of the sound of my own voice. There he sat, and there sat I. I turned my head again to my work, and finished writing the two or three words I still had to write. The paper and my notes are at this moment before me, and exhibit not the slightest tremor or nervousness. I could point out the words I was writing when the phantom came, and when he disappeared. Having finished my task, I shut the book, and threw it on the table : it made a slight noise as it fell—the figure vanished.

" Throwing myself back in my chair, I sat for some seconds looking at the fire with a curious mixture of feeling, and I remember wondering whether my friend would come again, and if he did whether he would hide the fire from me. Then first there stole upon me a dread and a suspicion that I was beginning to lose my nerve. I remember yawning ; then I rose, lit my bedroom candle, took my books into the inner library, mounted the chair as before, and replaced five of the volumes ; the sixth I brought back and laid upon the table where I had been writing when the phantom did me the honour to appear to me. By this time I had lost all sense of uneasiness. I blew out the four candles and marched off to bed, where I slept the sleep of the just, or the guilty—I know not which—but I slept very soundly."

As a pendant to this narrative may be mentioned the story quoted by Mr. Augustus Hare, of a clergyman brother of Sir Philip Egerton who had been given a living in Devonshire, and had not long been installed at the rectory when, coming one day into his study, he found an old lady seated there in an arm-chair by the fire. Knowing no old lady could be really there, and thinking the appearance must be the result of indigestion, he summoned all his courage and boldly sat down upon the old lady, who disappeared. The next day he met the old lady in the passage, rushed

FELBRIGG HALL

up against her, and she vanished. But he met her a third time, and then, feeling that it could not always be indigestion, he wrote to his sister in Cheshire, begging her to call upon the Misses Athelstan, sisters of the clergyman who had held the living before him, and say what he had seen.

When they heard of it, the Misses Athelstan looked inexpressibly distressed, and said, " That was our mother : we hoped it was only to us she would appear. When we were there she appeared constantly, but when we left we hoped she would be at rest."

A comparison of dates, and a reference to Crockford's *Clerical Directory*, indicates that the clergyman who was courageous enough to sit down upon a ghost was the Reverend Brooke de Malpas Egerton, and his rectory that of Uplyme, Devonshire, to which he was presented in 1873.

Some ten miles only from the scene of Dr. Jessop's adventure at Mannington Hall is Felbrigg, with its noble old hall, long the home of the Windhams, and built by one of them three hundred years ago on the site of the older residence of the Felbrigge family. William Windham, the patriotic statesman who died in 1810, was the last of the real Windhams, the nephew who succeeded him and adopted his name being a Lukin. With the notorious " mad Windham " who died in 1866, even the Lukin-Windhams ended, and Felbrigg Hall was purchased by a grocer of Norwich, John Kitton, who had made a huge fortune. He purchased everything as it stood, including even the family portraits and heirlooms of many Windham generations and the states-man's library, and, changing his name to Ketton, lived until 1872 at Felbrigg, as a country squire. When Augustus Hare visited Felbrigg in 1885 and saw the Miss " Cattons " (as by a whimsical error he misnames them), he found they had adopted the Windhams and all their heirlooms and traditions as though the vanished race were their very won. Said Miss Ketton: " Mr. Windham comes every night to look after his favourite books in the library. He goes straight to the shelves where they are : we hear him moving the tables and chairs about. We never disturb him, though, for we intend to be ghosts ourselves some day, and to come about the place just as he does."

But what many readers will probably think the most horrible ghost-story they have ever read is the following narrative told by Captain Fisher to Mr. Augustus Hare, and printed in the *Story of My Life*.

" Fisher," said the Captain, " may sound a very plebeian name, but this family is of very ancient lineage, and for many hundreds of years they have possessed a very curious old place in Cumberland, which bears the weird name of Croglin Grange. The great characteristic of the house is that never at any period of its very long existence has it been more than one story high, but it has a terrace from which large grounds sweep away towards the church in the hollow, and a fine distant view.

" When, in lapse of years, the Fishers outgrew Croglin Grange in family and fortune, they were wise enough not to destroy the long-standing characteristic of the place by adding another story to the house, but they went away to the south, to reside at Thorncombe near Guildford, and they let Croglin Grange.

" They were extremely fortunate in their tenants, two brothers and a sister. They heard their praises from all quarters. To their poorer neighbours they were all that is most kind and beneficent, and their neighbours of a higher class spoke of them as a most welcome addition to the little society of the neighbourhood. On their part the tenants were greatly delighted with their new residence. The arrangement of the house, which would have been a trial to many, was not so to them. In every respect Croglin Grange was exactly suited to them.

" The winter was spent most happily by the new inmates of Croglin Grange, who shared in all the little social pleasures of the district, and made themselves very popular. In the following summer there was one day which was dreadfully, annihilatingly hot. The brothers lay under the trees with their books, for it was too hot for any active occupation. The sister sat in the veranda and worked, or tried to work, for in the intense sultriness of that summer day, work was next to impossible. They dined early, and after dinner they still sat out in the veranda, enjoying the cool air which came with evening, and they watched the sun set, and the moon rise over the belt of trees which separated the grounds from the churchyard, seeing it mount the heavens till the whole lawn was bathed in silver light, across which the long shadows from the shrubbery fell as if embossed, so vivid and distinct were they.

"When they separated for the night, all retiring to their rooms on the ground-floor (for, as I said, there was no upstairs in that house), the sister felt that the heat was still so great that she could not sleep, and having fastened her window, she did not close the shutters—in that very quiet place it was not necessary—and, propped against the pillows, she still watched the wonderful, the marvellous beauty of that summer night. Gradually she became aware of two lights, two lights which flickered in and out in the belt of trees which separated the lawn from the churchyard, and, as her gaze became fixed upon them, she saw them emerge, fixed in a dark substance, a definite ghastly *something*, which seemed every moment to become nearer, increasing in size and substance as it approached. Every now and then it was lost for a moment in the long shadows which stretched across the lawn from the trees, and then it emerged larger than ever, and still coming on—on. As she watched it, the most uncontrollable horror seized her. She longed to get away, but the door was close to the window and the door was locked on the inside, and while she was unlocking it she must be for an instant nearer to *it*. She longed to scream, but her voice seemed paralysed, her tongue glued to the roof of her mouth.

"Suddenly—she could never explain why afterwards—the terrible object seemed to turn to one side, seemed to be going round the house, not to be coming to her at all, and immediately she jumped out of bed and rushed to the door, but as she was unlocking it she heard scratch, scratch, scratch, upon the window, and saw a hideous brown face with flaming eyes glaring in at her. She rushed back to the bed, but the creature continued to scratch, scratch, scratch upon the window. She felt a sort of mental comfort in the knowledge that the window was securely fastened on the inside. Suddenly the scratching sound ceased, and a kind of pecking sound took its place. Then, in her agony, she became aware that the creature was unpicking the lead! The noise continued, and a diamond pane of glass fell into the room. Then a long bony finger of the creature came in and turned the handle of the window, and the window opened, and the creature came in ; and it came across the room, and her terror was so great that she could not scream, and it came up to the bed, and it twisted its long, bony fingers into her hair, and it dragged her head over the side of the bed, and—it bit her violently in the throat.

" As it bit her, her voice was released, and she screamed with all her might and main. Her brothers rushed out of their rooms, but the door was locked on the inside. A moment was lost while they got a poker and broke it open. Then the creature had already escaped through the window, and the sister, bleeding violently from a wound in the throat, was lying unconscious over the side of the bed. One brother pursued the creature, which fled before him through the moonlight with gigantic strides, and eventually seemed to disappear over the wall into the churchyard. Then he rejoined his brother by the sister's bedside. She was dreadfully hurt, and her wound was a very definite one, but she was of strong disposition, not either given to romance or superstition, and when she came to herself she said, ' What has happened is most extraordinary and I am very much hurt. It seems inexplicable, but of course there *is* an explanation, and we must wait for it. It will turn out that a lunatic has escaped from some asylum and found his way here.' The wound healed, and she appeared to get well, but the doctor who was sent for to her would not believe that she could bear so terrible a shock so easily, and insisted that she must have change, mental and physical ; so her brothers took her to Switzerland.

" Being a sensible girl, when she went abroad she threw herself at once into the interests of the country she was in. She dried plants, she made sketches, she went up mountains, and, as autumn came on, she was the person who urged that they should return to Croglin Grange. ' We have taken it,' she said, ' for seven years, and we have only been there one ; and we shall always find it difficult to let a house which is only one story high, so we had better return there ; lunatics do not escape every day.' As she urged it, her brothers wished nothing better, and the family returned to Cumberland. From there being no upstairs in the house it was impossible to make any great change in their arrangements. The sister occupied the same room, but it is unnecessary to say she always closed her shutters, which, however, as in many old houses, always left one top pane of the window uncovered. The brothers moved, and occupied a room together, exactly opposite that of their sister, and they always kept loaded pistols in their room.

" The winter passed most peacefully and happily. In the following March the sister was suddenly awakened by a sound she remembered only too well—srcatch, scratch, scratch upon the window, and, looking up, she saw, climbed up to the topmost pane of the window, the same hideous brown shrivelled face, with glaring eyes, looking in at her. This time she screamed as loud as she could. Her brothers rushed out of their room with pistols, and out of the front door. The creature was already scudding away across the lawn. One of the brothers fired and hit it in the leg, but still with the other leg it continued to make way, scrambled over the wall into the churchyard, and seemed to disappear into a vault which belonged to a family long extinct.

" The next day the brothers summoned all the tenants of Croglin Grange, and in their presence the vault was opened. A horrible scene revealed itself. The vault was full of coffins ; they had been broken open, and their contents, horribly mangled and distorted, were scattered over the floor. One coffin alone remained intact. Of

CROGLIN LOW HALL

that the lid had been lifted, but still lay loose upon the coffin. They raised it, and there, brown, withered, shrivelled, mummified, but quite entire, was the same hideous figure which had looked in at the windows of Croglin Grange, with the marks of a recent pistol-shot in the leg ; and they did the only thing that can lay a vampire—they burnt it."

It is to be added, from personal observation, that there is no place styled Croglin Grange. There are Croglin High Hall and Low Hall. Both are farm-houses, very like one another, and not in any particulars resembling the description given. Croglin Low Hall is probably the house indicated, but it is at least a mile distant from the church, which has been rebuilt. The churchyard contains no tomb which by any stretch of the imagination could be identified with that described by Mr. Hare.

The following story, often styled " the best authenticated ghost-story on record," by which a premium is put upon the word of a Bishop, to the depreciation of that of any mere layman, is told in the Memoirs of Samuel Wilberforce, Bishop of Winchester—the well-remembered " Soapy Sam " of nearly two generations ago. The tale, which might well be entitled " The Phantom Monk," belongs to the period when Wilberforce was yet only a Canon. He had been always a very strong and emphatic disbeliever in ghosts, until this experience befell him.

The believer in supernatural visitants will be further interested to learn that the Canon was at the time in his usual robust state of health, and not at all in that condition which opponents of ghost-seeing declare to be conducive to seeing visions.

The following, then, is a brief account of the story :

Canon Wilberforce was staying with a well-known Catholic family in the village of —— (the identity of it decently veiled) in Hampshire ; and, as the dinner-hour approached, he went up to his room in the usual way to prepare himself for the meal.

The hour was about seven o'clock, one December evening ; and as the Canon emerged from his bedroom and was going down to dinner, he passed a monk going towards the library. As the family were Roman Catholic, he took no notice of him, thinking he was a guest. The dinner had begun some time, and as Wilberforce did not see the monk there, he casually asked a lady next him if the monk was staying at the house.

The lady turned deathly pale, and then in a stifled way told the Canon that he had seen the family ghost.

The family ghost, it appears, was that of a monk, who appeared periodically, and not particularly in the dead hours of the night. He had been a former father confessor to the family, and, it was remembered, had died rather suddenly and apparently in some distress of mind.

Naturally, the Canon was somewhat startled at the time, but the incident passed off and nothing more was said about it. About 11.30 that night, however, Wilberforce, as was his custom, was reading in the library. Everybody else had gone to bed, when the door opened and in came the monk. A brave man at all times, the Canon kept quiet, but was really very frightened, and he noticed the monk go to a bookshelf, search high and low for something or other, and, not apparently finding it, take a hasty glance round the room, and then go out, slamming the door after him.

As soon as the scared Canon could sufficiently recover his senses, he went to bed, his disbelief in the unseen world already under revision. Next evening he determined to solve the mystery, and was sitting in the library as usual, when a creak on the stairs told him someone was coming. Then the door opened, and there the monk was again.

More than a little frightened, Wilberforce was nevertheless able to keep his head cool, and when the monk went, as usual, to the bookshelf, by a great effort the Canon asked him what he wanted.

The monk turned round, and, with a smile, said he was very glad that someone had spoken to him, as he was tongue-tied, and dared not speak to anybody before being spoken to. He went on to say that he had come to look for a bundle of incriminating papers he had left on the top of the bookcase before he died, and that the idea had so haunted him that he would never rest peacefully until he had found them. The Canon then volunteered to get them down for the monk, and mounted the step-ladder to do so. Sure enough, at the top of the bookcase, he found a large bundle of papers, which he handed down to the mysterious stranger. He then came down and asked the monk what he wanted done with them. With a weird look in his eyes, the apparition said they must be burned, as they contained important secrets about members of the family to which he had been father confessor. If revealed, they would no doubt have caused considerable unhappiness to their descendants.

So the two of them put the papers on the fire and watched them burn. As soon as the last sheet disappeared in the flames, the monk took his leave, and was never seen again.

The incident recalls the much older one that took place at Powis Castle, the seat of the Earl of Powis, near Welshpool, in 1780. " Castell Coch," or Red Castle, as it is called by the Welsh, from the hue of its red sandstone walls, is a great frowning building, still outwardly a mediæval fortress, although modernised for residential purposes within. If gloom be the sign of a haunted house, then certainly Powis Castle should be inhabited by a veritable house-party of ghosts. Indeed, many tales have been told of it, but we will select one only.

It is to a Mr. John Hampson that we are chiefly indebted for the preservation of this singular tale of over a century and a quarter ago. He was a locally celebrated preacher of the then new sect of Wesleyan Methodists, and, hearing that one of his communion, a poor old spinster of the neighbourhood, who supported herself chiefly by hemp-spinning and the like home industries, had seen the ghost that was well known to have haunted the Castle for years, he made it his business to obtain the facts from her, and to put them on record.

She said that, applying at Powis Castle for employment in spinning, she found the Earl and the family were away from home and the Castle in charge of the steward and a small staff of servants. The wife of the steward, however, found her sufficient work to keep her

employed for some days, and she was given a bedroom
in the house. This proved to be an apartment which
had for some time past been the scene of inexplicable
disturbances, and had acquired the name of " The
Haunted Room." The steward's wife had given her the
room with the object of experimenting upon her and
the apparition, and the rest of the servants were keenly
interested in the cruel trick.

The old woman, in narrating this strange story, told
how the room was grandly furnished and had a genteel
bed in one corner of it. The servants had made her a
good fire, and had placed her a chair and a table before
it, and a large lighted candle upon the table. They told
her that was her bedroom, and she might go to sleep
when she pleased. Then, wishing her good night, they
withdrew, pulling the door quickly after them, so as to
hasp the spring-sneck in the brass lock that was upon it.

When they were gone, she gazed awhile at the fine
furniture, under no small astonishment that they should
give such a room to so poor a person as herself. She was
abashed at being the tenant of so grand an apartment
and so fine a bed, with the added convenience and comfort of a fire, and could not quite understand the servants
so numerously escorting her to the place, and so hurriedly
withdrawing. She could not know, poor soul! that
this was the Haunted Room, and that she was placed
in it by way of experiment or practical joke.

Down she sat, and in her pious way took out the
small Welsh Bible she always carried with her, and of
which she always read a chapter before she said her
prayers and went to bed.

While she was thus reading she heard the room door
open, and, turning her head, saw a gentleman enter,
clothed in a gold-laced suit and hat. He walked down
by the sash-window to the corner of the room, and then
returned ; resting his elbow on the bottom of the first
window, and the side of his face upon the palm of his
hand. In that posture he stood some time, with his
side partly towards her. She looked at him earnestly
to see if she knew him ; but he appeared to be a stranger.
She supposed afterwards that he stood in this manner

to encourage her to speak ; but, as she did not, after some little time he walked off, pulling the door after him, as the servants had done before. She began now to be much alarmed, concluding it to be an apparition, and that the servants had put her in this room on purpose, which was really the case. The room, it appears, had been disturbed for a long time, so that nobody could sleep in it, and as she passed for a very serious woman, the servants took it in their heads to put the Methodist and the spirit together, to see what they would make of it.

Startled at this thought, she rose from her chair and kneeled down by the bedside to say her prayers. While she was praying the apparition returned, walked round the room, and came close behind her. She had it on her mind to speak, but when she attempted it she was so greatly agitated that she could not speak a word. He then walked out of the room again, pulling the door after him as before. She begged that God would strengthen her, and not suffer her to be tried beyond what she was able to bear ; and then she recovered her spirits, felt more confidence, and determined, if the apparation should again appear, to speak to him if possible.

He presently came in again, walked round, and came behind her as before ; whereupon she said, " Pray, sir, who are you, and what do you want ? "

The ghost put up his finger and said, " Take up the candle and follow me, and I will tell you."

She got up, took the candle, and followed him out of the room. He led her through a long, boarded passage, till they came to the door of another room. which he opened and entered. It was a small room, or what might be called a large closet.

" As the room was small, and I believed him to be a spirit," said she, " I stopped at the door. He turned and said, ' Walk in, I will not hurt you,' ; so I walked in.

" He said, ' Observe what I do.' I said, ' I will.'

" He stooped and tore up one of the floor boards, and there appeared under it a box with an iron handle in the lid.

" He said, ' Do you see that box ? '

POWIS CASTLE

" I said, ' Yes, I do.'

Then he stepped to one side of the room and showed me a crevice in the wall, where, he said, a key was hid that would open it.

" He said, ' This box and key must be taken out and sent to the Earl in London. Will you see it done ? '

" I said, ' I will do my best to get it done.'

" He said, ' Do ; and I will trouble the house no more.'

" He then walked out of the room and left me. I stepped to the room door and set up a shout. The steward and his wife, with the other servants, came to me immediately, all clinging together, with lights in their hands. It seems they had all been waiting to see the issue of the interview betwixt me and the apparition. They asked me, ' What was the matter ? ' and I told them the story and showed them the box. The steward dared not meddle with it ; but his wife had more courage and, with the help of other servants, tugged it out and found the key." The old woman said the box seemed pretty heavy, but she did not see it opened, and therefore did not know what it contained : perhaps money, or writings of consequence to the family, or both. They took it away with them, and then she went to bed and slept peaceably till the morning.

The box was duly sent to the Earl, and that nobleman returned a message to inform the poor woman that if she would come and reside in his family she should be comfortably provided for all her days ; or that if she wished to live elsewhere she should still be looked after.

This and similar stories of apparitions haunting places for a specific purpose which cannot be even hinted at until some spectator finds courage to speak, would seem to indicate that personal interests exist beyond the grave ; and, indeed, among the many theories seeking to account for ghosts and hauntings is found an application of the Biblical adage, " Where your treasure is, there will your heart be also." It has often been thought that the affections of the dead survive their death, and dwell long upon the people and the places they have loved in life. It is a beautiful thought, but carries with it, of necessity, the appalling corollary that if it be possible for the

CRESLOW MANOR HOUSE

affections to survive, it is equally likely that hatreds
are similarly immortal : and thus, in the inimical forces
in that case ranged against us in the unseen world, we
would have some foundation for the once universal belief
in evil spirits.

The ancient manor-house of Creslow, long since become
a farm, stands six miles north of Aylesbury, on the road
to Buckingham. Not readily visible from the highway,
you find it most easily by passing through the picturesque
village of Whitchurch and, about half a mile north, looking out for a not very prominent white-painted gate on
the right hand, leading to a rough road or farm-track
which, traversing three pastures, brings you at last to
the romantically-situated old house, almost entirely surrounded by noble trees and spacious rick-yards. No
explorer in beautiful Buckinghamshire should on any
account fail to visit Creslow : to come early to it and
stay long, for it is not only picturesque, and the subject
of vague ghostly legends, but is also possessed of an
exceedingly romantic history ; and, moreover, has not
been made the subject of any modern, ill-judged attempts
at restoration. Many are the pilgrims, by horsed vehicles,
motors, cycles, or on foot, who, with sketch-book or
photographic materials, turn off the high road, to be
warmly received by the farmer.

Among the peculiarities of Creslow is the odd fact
that, standing solitary as it does, the farm is still a
separate and complete parish, with a population returned
in many a census past as five. Surrounding the farmstead are the famed " Creslow pastures," still and for
many centuries past celebrated for their exceptional
fertility ; and once, when Crown property, the land
whereon grazed the cattle that supplied the households
of English monarchs from the times of Queen Elizabeth
to those of Charles the Second. Creslow, which derives
its name from Christ's Low, *i.e.* Christ's Meadow, and
still has a pasture known as " Heaven's Low," is the
smallest parish in Buckinghamshire, and has the largest
field : the " great pasture," containing 327 acres.

Approaching the house, a weathered and worn old
building on the left hand first attracts attention, with

RAMHURST MANOR HOUSE

its blocked-up door of fine Early English, or very late
Transitional Norman, character. This, now a stable, was
once the chapel attached to the manor-house, and what
is now the farmyard was once, in part, the graveyard,
as discoveries made in trenching during recent years
have proved.

Beyond the chapel the worn gables and the battle-
mented tower of the huge, rambling old house rise, more
like the creation of an artist's dream than actual brick
and stone. You wonder who it was, or who they were,
who built and lived so romantically in the long ago :
and the history of Buckinghamshire duly tells you.
They were the Knights Templars, who acquired the land
in 1120, and their successors, the Knights Hospitallers
of St. John of Jerusalem. Much has been destroyed
since their day, and much else built, notably the gabled
Elizabethan additions, but an octagonal turret, with walls
six feet thick, and a groined crypt with finely moulded
ribs, is of their time, together with a neighbouring crypt,
known locally as " the Dungeon," and of which the
customary tale of a subterranean passage is told. With
the confiscation of monastic property under Henry the
Eighth, Creslow passed from the Knights Hospitallers
to the Crown, and the alterations we perceive to have
been effected were the result of that change from semi-
ecclesiastical to entirely secular ownership.

Much excellent panelling remains in the different
parts of the house, with characteristically Tudor plaster
decorations in the hall. A second period of alteration
seems to have set in during the time of Charles the First,
when many large windows were cut, replacing the smaller
ones of ancient times. In the division of plunder among
the rebels and regicides following the execution of Charles
the First, Creslow came into the hands of Cornelius
Holland, to whom it was granted by Parliament in 1653.
That equally fortunate and impudent person subsequently
petitioned Parliament for a grant towards repairing and
improving the house—and was duly awarded it ! It was
he who desecrated the chapel. Holland's prosperity lasted
until the Restoration, in 1660 ; and then ended with
quakes and tremors indeed, for he was not only ejected

but attainted as a regicide. The property then reverted
to the Crown, but was leased, two years later, to Sir
Thomas Clifford, and conveyed in fee simple to his
successor, Lord Clifford, in 1673.

Although the haunted reputation of the old manor-
house of Creslow survives in print, no later manifestations
than those narrated " about 1850 " have been recorded.
About that time, it was narrated, a gentleman who had
been, not many years earlier, High Sheriff of the county
of Buckinghamshire, rode over to a dinner-party at
Creslow from his own house, a few miles distant ; and, the
night becoming exceedingly dark and stormy, he was
urged to stay over until the morning—if he had no
objection to sleep in the " haunted chamber."

He appears to have been one of your born investigators (like ourselves, respected readers), and he welcomed
the opportunity of sleeping, or seeking sleep (as *we* would)
in a room with such a reputation. But it was not with
him, at any rate, an affair of courageous parleying with
ghosts. He did not believe in the supernatural, and
being a man of powerful build, rather rejoiced at being
given an opportunity of contending with a suspected
practical joker.

The room was prepared for him. He would have
neither fire nor night-light, but was provided with a
box of lucifers, that he might light a candle if he wished.
Arming himself in jest with a cutlass and a brace of
pistols, he took a serio-comic farewell of the family, and
entered his formidable dormitory.

In due course morning dawned ; the sun rose, and a
most beautiful day succeeded a very wet and dismal
night. The family and their guests assembled in the
breakfast-room, and every countenance seemed cheered
and brightened by the loveliness of the morning. They
drew round the table, when the host remarked that
Mr. S——, the tenant of the haunted chamber, was
absent. A servant was sent to summon him to breakfast, but he soon returned, saying he had knocked loudly
at his door, but received no answer, and that a jug of
hot water left there was still standing unused. On
hearing this, two or three gentlemen ran up to the room,

and, after knocking and receiving no answer, opened it and entered. It was empty. Inquiry was made of the servants : they had neither heard nor seen anything of him. As he was a county magistrate, some supposed that he had gone to attend a meeting held that morning at an early hour.

But his horse was still in the stable, so that could not be. While they were at breakfast, however, he came in, and gave the following account of his last night's experiences : " Having entered my room, I locked and bolted both the doors, carefully examined the whole room, and satisfied myself that there was no living creature in it but myself, nor any entrances but those which I had secured. I got into bed, and, with the conviction that I should sleep soundly as usual until six in the morning, was soon lost in a comfortable slumber. Suddenly I was awakened, and, on raising my head to listen, I certainly heard a sound resembling the light, soft tread of a lady's footsteps, accompanied with the rustling as of a silk gown. I sprang out of bed, and, having lighted a candle, found that there was nothing either to be seen or heard. I carefully examined the whole room. I looked under the bed, into the fire-place, up the chimney, and at both the doors, which were fastened just as I had left them. I then looked at my watch, and found it was a few minutes past twelve. As all was now perfectly quiet again, I put out the candle, got into bed, and soon fell asleep.

" I was again aroused. The noise was now louder than before. It appeared like the violent rustling of a stiff silk dress. A second time I sprang out of bed, darted to the spot where the noise was, and tried to grasp the intruder in my arms. My arms met together, but enclosed nothing. The noise passed to another part of the room, and I followed it, groping near the floor to prevent anything passing under my arms. It was in vain ; I could do nothing. The sound died at the doorway to the crypt, and all was again still. I now left the candle burning, though I never sleep comfortably with a light in the room, and went to bed again, but certainly felt not a little perplexed at being unable to detect the cause of the noise, nor account for its cessation when the candle was lighted."

There is a something in the name "Manor-house" that presupposes ghosts. Thus it is that, looking upon the picturesquely-seated Ramhurst Farm, at Leigh (which is locally styled "Lye ") near Tonbridge, you only begin to think of ghostly possibilities when you learn that it was once a manor-house of the ancient Culpepper family. According to Hasted, the historian of Kent, the manor passed from them to the Saxbys. Ann Saxby married Richard Children, and here for many years they lived. Richard died in the old house in 1753, aged eighty-three, being succeeded by his son, John Children, of Tonbridge. In 1816, however, the family experienced a succession of misfortunes and were obliged to sell Ramhurst.

It then passed through several hands, and at length, in 1857, was let to the wife and family of a distinguished officer serving in India. Mrs. R—— had no sooner settled there than the house became continually disturbed by voices, noises, and mysterious footfalls. The cook was terrified by the sound of a silk dress passing her when no one was visible, and the lady's own brother, an athletic young officer, a sceptic in things occult, was disturbed by noises and the sounds of people talking. On two occasions, at the unearthly hour of three o'clock in the morning, a voice resembling that of his sister rose to a scream ; he hastened, armed with a shot-gun, to her bedroom, but found her peacefully sleeping.

They had not long been at Ramhurst when Mrs. R—— drove over to Tonbridge railway station to meet a friend, Miss S——, whom she had invited to visit her. This young lady had from early childhood often seen apparitions ; and no sooner had she been driven from Tonbridge to Ramhurst, reaching the old house at four o'clock in the afternoon, when she saw on the threshold the spectral figures of an elderly couple dressed in the style of a bygone age. Not wishing to disturb her friend, Miss S—— made no remark at the time, but frequently, within the next few days, and always in daylight, saw the same figures, apparently encircled with a grey haze.

On the third occasion they spoke to her and said they had been husband and wife and that their name was Children. They appeared melancholy, and when Miss S—— inquired the cause, they said they had in life taken great pride and pleasure in their house, and now it troubled them to know it had passed away from their family.

It is to be observed at this point that neither Mrs. R—— nor Miss S—— knew anything of the history of the old house, nor had they ever heard of the unusual name of Children. Miss S—— told her friend of this conversation, and Mrs. R—— herself some weeks later had a ghostly demonstration. She was hastening down from her bedroom to dinner, and was occupied with anything but spiritual thoughts, when she observed in the empty space of the open door the figures seen and described by her friend : clearly, and in detail, even to the brocade silk and the antique lace collar of the old lady's dress. No word was uttered, but in luminous letters in the grey haze above the woman's figure appeared the words " Dame Children," together with a statement, imperfectly recollected by Mrs. R——, to the effect that her hopes and fears having been entirely of this earth, she was " earth-bound."

Down below, in the dining-room, was Mrs. R——'s brother, calling out that he was tired of waiting for dinner. Closing her eyes, she rushed through the apparitions, and downstairs, exclaiming to her friend, Miss S——, " Oh, my dear, I've walked through Mrs. Children ! "

Never again did Mrs. R—— see the ghosts, but her friend, who appears to have been an excellent medium, often observed, and even held conversations with them, by which it appeared that the husband's name was Richard, and that he had died in 1753.

Inquiries were set on foot. None of the servants had ever heard the name of " Children," although the nurse, the oldest among them, had lived in the neighbourhood all her life. Sophie, the servant in question, had, however, relations living at Riverhead, and during a visit there mentioned these ghostly appearances to one who had, many years earlier, actually been in service at Ramhurst. She, in her turn, knew nothing of the Children family, but recollected having, when herself at Ramhurst, heard a very old man say that when a boy he had been a helper in the kennels then kept at the manor-house by a family of that name.

At the close of 1858, Robert Dale Owen, himself interested in spiritual manifestations, and a friend of Mrs. R——, made inquiries at Leigh and Tonbridge. At Leigh he found a record of one George Children, who in 1718 left a bequest for a weekly dole of bread to the poor of the parish, and of an earlier George, buried at Tonbridge. Eventually, however, on referring to the pages of Hasted, he discovered the facts respecting Richard Children already detailed. They tallied exactly with what the apparitions had told Miss S——.

The tale is still current in the neighbourhood that the house will be haunted until the property comes back into the Children family ; but not for many years past has anyone been disturbed by ghostly sights or sounds. Oddly enough, however, the name of Children has reappeared in the district.

Northumberland and Durham, and the country of the Scottish borderland in general, are rich in reputed haunted castles and mansions. Among these is, or was, according to Augustus Hare, the Trevelyans' seat at Wallington.

"At Wallington," said Augustus Hare, who visited there in 1862, "are endless suites of huge rooms, only partly carpeted and thinly covered with eighteenth-century furniture, partly covered with faded tapestry. The last of these is the ' ghost room,' and Wallington is still a haunted house : awful noises are heard through the night ; footsteps rush up and down the untrodden passages ; wings flap and beat against the windows ; bodiless people unpack and put away their things all night long, and invisible beings are felt to breathe over you as you lie in bed." But that was not quite so bad as in the haunted house in Warwick Gardens, Kensington—I forbear the number, lest any landlord with a grievance against me for taking away the character of his house should sue me for damages—where the ghosts were smelt

as well as felt, breathing over you. Vulgar, plebeian
ghosts these : their breath odorous of onions.

Mr. Hare frankly thought his bedroom at Wallington
" quite horrid." It opened into a long suite of desolate
rooms by a door without a fastening, so he pushed the
heavy dressing-table with its weighty mirror against it,
to keep out whatever might try to come in. We are not
told of anything or anyone making the attempt, and his
rest appears to have been unbroken, but it was an eerie
place and a strange *ménage*. His host, Sir Walter
Trevelyan, was the son of old Lady Trevelyan, " a very
wicked woman and a miser," and Sir Walter himself was
never known to laugh. He was " a strange-looking being,
with long hair and moustache and an odd, careless dress,
and enjoyed or endured the reputation of being a miser."
Another strange being in the house was a Mr. Wooster,
who fours years earlier had come to arrange a collection of
shells, and had never gone away. He looked " like a
church brass [a monumental brass, it may be presumed,
Mr. Hare meant] incarnated, and turned up his eyes when
he spoke to you till you saw nothing but the whites. He
also had a long, trailing moustache, and in all things
imitated, but caricatured, Sir Walter." In this strange
household, Lady Trevelyan was not the least of the
eccentrics. *Her* odd fancy was for sitting on the rug,
instead of upon a chair. This reminds a playgoer of
Mr. Pinero's *Trelawny of the Wells*, and the old judge's
remark to his sister, in a loud " aside," intended for the
ex-actress who (like Lady Trevelyan) preferred the rug :
" Have we no cheers, Trefalgy ? "

A remarkable story was told of a happening at the
little town of Woodbridge in Suffolk in the seventeenth
century. A Dutch naval lieutenant was walking along
the High Street with an English acquaintance when the
subject of ghosts came up. He said he had the faculty
of seeing ghosts in daylight, a thing his companion
scoffed at. " But I have seen them," retorted the
lieutenant, " and it is well worth while to get out of
their way."

Almost immediately he exclaimed, " I see one now. He
is coming towards us, swinging a glove in one hand and

with his head turned sideways and upwards. He will walk right into us if we don't take care."

So saying, he anxiously endeavoured to get out of the way, but his companion, holding his arm, prevented ; with the result that both were violently thrown down and badly injured. Inquiries proved that a tailor, who had the peculiarity of walking in Woodbridge streets swinging a glove in one hand and with the carriage of his head as described, had at that moment died.

A quaint seventeenth-century story from Ireland would seem to establish Sabbatarian leanings in inhabitants of the world of ghosts and spirits. The Earl of Orrery despatched his butler to buy some packs of playing-cards on a Sunday, but before that servitor had proceeded more than a few steps, several spirit forms appeared and sought to carry him away, lifting him bodily from the ground. It was with difficulty that he was rescued by Lord Orrery and others who came to his aid.

About the year 1847 it was stated that on a particular spot of a bedroom wall in Lulworth Castle, Dorset, a peculiar phosphorescent glow was observable when the room was darkened. This uncanny peculiarity was so objectionable that the room could not be used ; and the wall was pulled down and rebuilt. But the phosphorescence reappeared on the identical spot. Some observers, inclined to the marvellous, remembered the history of the building, and narrated with awe that the Castle was built with the stones of Bindon Abbey, demolished for that purpose by Thomas, third and last Lord Bindon, in 1590. The history of the Howards, Lords Bindon, would have pleased Sir Henry Spelman, who laboured earnestly in his *History of Sacrilege* to prove that the holders of what had been Church property were subject to a curse. A younger son of the third Duke of Norfolk was in 1546 presented with the lands of that Abbey, and assumed the title of Viscount Howard of Bindon. The third lord died without children in 1619, and the Castle and those lands passed to his cousin, that magnificent Thomas, Earl of Suffolk, who built Audley End. His grandson also died without issue, and the property was sold in 1641 to the

Weld family, who still own it. They are Roman Catholics, and perhaps immune ; but believers in the theory of a curse on sacrilege point with gloomy satisfaction to the extinction of those earlier holders. They conveniently forget that Humphrey Weld completed the Castle with some remaining portions of Bindon Abbey. But the work was scarce finished before the Civil War broke out. The Parliament troops occupied it and wrought great destruction here.

The great and stately mansion of Seaton Delaval, in Northumberland, has been a ruin for over a hundred years. The Delavals " came over with the Conqueror," as the old phrase runs, in the person of Hamo de la Val, who fought at the Battle of Hastings ; and the family, afterwards Blake-Delavals, long owned these manorial lands conferred upon their filibustering ancestor. Their ancient residence here remained, altered from time to time, until it occurred to Admiral Delaval in 1718 that he owed it to his wealth and dignity to rebuild the residence to which he had just succeeded. " I would be glad to divert myself a little in my old age," he wrote to his brother, " in repairing the old house, making a garden and planting forest trees, for which we may expect prayers when we are no more—praises, I should call it, for fear of being thought Popish." He sent for Sir John Vanbrugh, the foremost and most fashionable architect of that age, to suggest alterations, or perhaps entirely rebuild. Vanbrugh, of course, seeing an excellent job, suggested an entirely new house ; and in 1720 the old place was demolished and the present enormous mansion begun. It occupied eight years in building, and the Admiral was dead, from being thrown from his horse, before the completion. The works were finished in the time of his nephew and heir, Sir Francis Blake-Delaval. Sir Francis had a family of eight sons and five daughters, yet it was prophesied, by the family seer, that in the next generation there should be no heir male to carry on the name. Strange though it may seem, this was literally fulfilled. Sir Francis died in 1771, aged forty-eight. His children were already dead ; and his brother, Sir John, succeeded him. He became Lord Delaval, and died, aged

SEATON DELAVAL HALL

eighty years, in 1808 ; his only son, John, born 1756, having deceased in his twentieth year, in 1775. He was pressing unwelcome attentions upon a dairymaid, who kicked him so that he died.

When Lord Delaval had passed away, there was thus only one of the family left—Edward, a younger brother. When, in 1814, he died, Seaton Delaval went to the Astley family, represented by the Marquis of Hastings, the present owner.

In the park you may see the mausoleum built by Lord Delaval the year after the death of his son, the last hope of his race. It is a large and stately building, with all the brooding melancholy of Seaton Delaval as a whole. Indeed, the great mansion itself is monumental and imposing, and it never can have been joyous in appearance.

Vanbrugh's vast and palatial building, in the heavy style with which he has made us familiar in his Blenheim Palace and Castle Howard designs, never can have been homelike ; and the mansion and its wide-spreading arcades and wings are crested with those sculptured stone urns and plumy masses of stone which suggest the decorations of an old-fashioned hearse, or a mausoleum. Long, solemn avenues (those trees planted by the Admiral) radiate from it ; and all is now silent, save for the encroachment of colleries and industrial villages. For, a century since, January 3rd, 1822, a fire completely gutted Seaton Delaval Hall, and it has never been restored ; nor ever is likely to be. The present owners, the family of Lord Hastings, sometimes stay in the summer in the west wing, but that age is past and not likely to return when families lived in the state for which this great pile was built. The interior of the great hall, left exactly as it was after the fire had swept through it, still displays the Greek and Roman magnificence with which it was endowed. There, in their recesses in the walls, are yet the fine statues that originally were placed in them, still calmly smiling through the ravages of the conflagration that blasted them, and the passing of over a century, which has weathered them. Monumental is Seaton Delaval, and full of eerie thrills, for the visitor.

Rushbrooke Hall, three and a half miles from Bury St. Edmunds, the interesting domain of the Jermyns, was sold in 1922, after having been in the market for a considerable period. It was for some time thought that no purchaser would be found, and that the Hall would have to be demolished. But Lord Islington bought it. The old furniture and the portraits, for which the house was famous, have all been sold. Rushbrooke is a red-brick Elizabethan house, with a splendid staircase, and surrounded by a wide moat. Queen Elizabeth was " feasted " there by Sir Richard Jermyn. Henry Jermyn, Earl of St. Albans, was in love with Queen Henrietta Maria, to whom he was said to have been privately married. The estate passed by marriage to the Herveys, and in 1806 Colonel Rushbrooke obtained it by an exchange with Lord Bristol for the Saxham property. He took the contents of the house, and Lord Bristol was indeed miserable when he found that he had carelessly parted with two magnificent cabinets which had belonged to Henrietta Maria. The " White Lady," ghost of the unfaithful Agnes de Rushbrooke, wife of a former owner, is said to float about the moat occasionally in the night. She was thrown into the moat by her enraged husband.

Another East Anglian hall, that of Raynham, near Fakenham, the stately but now largely despoiled seat of the Marquess Townshend, has a spectre : the " Brown Lady," who on very rare occasions—supposed to be on the approaching death of the Marquess—pervades the house.

London, for ever renewing its youth, is a sorry field for the amateur of haunted houses. More and more, London lives in the present and forgets the past ; and in the rebuilding of whole neighbourhoods there remain few darksome neglected spots for spirits to harbour in. Alas ! poor ghosts !

" The " Haunted House " in Berkeley Square, however, still stands ; but even that is no longer haunted, nor even empty. Years ago, it was indubitably unoccupied and sufficiently forlorn ; but there are those who declare it was never haunted, and that the story was, indeed,

THE "HAUNTED HOUSE," BERKELEY SQUARE

WALPOLE HOUSE, CHISWICK MALL

invented by a more or less popular novelist of years ago.
However that may be, the famous " haunted house in
Berkeley Square " was long one of those things that no
country cousin, come up from the provinces to London on
sight-seeing bent, ever willingly missed ; but truth to
tell, its exterior is now a trifle disappointing to the casual
seeker after horrors.   Viewed in the afternoon sunshine,
with the milkman delivering the usual half-pint, or quart,
as the case may be, it is just as respectably commonplace
as any other house of similar late Georgian period, and
even at the weird stroke of twelve, when the midnight
policeman comes and thrusts a burly shoulder against the
front-door, and tries the area-gate or flashes a gleam over
the kitchen windows from his bull's-eye, there is nothing
at all hair-raising about it.   But there *was* a time when
No. 50—for that is the number of it—wore an exceedingly
uncared-for appearance.   Soap, paint, and whitewash
were unused for years, and grime clung to brickwork and
windows alike.   The area was choked with wasted hand-
bills, wisps of straw, and all the accumulations that
speedily made a derelict London house the very picture of
misery ;   and every passing stranger stopped the first
errand-boy and asked various questions, to which the
answer was, generally, " 'aunted 'ouse " ;   or, if the
question happened to be " Who lives there ? " the obvious
reply was " Ghostesses ! " or " Gose ! " according to their
especial type of illiteracy.

There is quite a literature accumulated around No. 50,
and even in the staid pages of *Notes and Queries* the questions of " Haunted or not haunted ? and if so, by what
or whom ? " have been debated.   It seems that a Something or Other, very terrible indeed, haunts, or did haunt,
a particular room.   This unnamed Raw Head and Bloody
Bones, or whatever it is, has been sufficiently awful to
have caused the death, in convulsions, of at least two fool-
hardy persons who have dared to sleep in that chamber.
The story is told of one who was not to be deterred by the
fate of an earlier victim.   He was sceptical and practical
as well.   Before retiring to bed he gave some parting
·instructions to those who occupied the rest of the house.
" If I ring once," said he, " take no notice, for I might

perhaps be only nervous, without due cause ; but if I ring *twice*, come to me."

They bade him good night. When the clock struck twelve they heard a faint ring, followed by a tremendous peal, and on opening the door they found the unfortunate man in a fit. He died, without ever being able to reveal what It was. A shuddery pendant to this story is that which tells how, a dance being given at a house next door, a lady leaned against the wall dividing the Haunted House from its neighbour, and distinctly felt an inexplicably dreadful shock. Apparently that haunted room is tenanted by the ghost of an electrical battery ! Apparently, also, the ghost has run down and not been recharged, for the house is now tenanted.

There are legends that tell how tenants were at last found for this uncanny house which at first no one would take. The first year, it seems, the incoming tenant was paid to take it ; the second—if not previously frightened away—he lived rent-free ; the third, he paid a certain sum, which increased up to the seventh year, when the ordinary rental would be reached.

The secret of the house, according to Mr. Stuart Wortley was that it belonged to a Mr. Du Pré, of Wilton Park, who shot his lunatic brother in one of the attics. The captive was so violent that he could only be fed through a hole. His groans and cries could be distinctly heard in the neighbouring houses.

The house was eventually let on the very curious terms of £100 for the first year, £200 the second, and £300 the third ; the tenant to forfeit £1,000 if he left within that period.

Among other reputedly haunted houses of London is the well-known Walpole House, in Chiswick Mall, itself a thoroughfare with romance written large upon it. Walpole House is the finest of the old seventeenth-century houses now left upon this, in many ways, delightful river-side road. As " Miss Pinkerton's Academy for Young Ladies," it appears in *Vanity Fair* as Becky Sharp's school ; but away back in 1709 it was the scene of the death of Barbara Villiers, Duchess of Cleveland, who ended in her sixty-ninth year, from dropsy, which

had "swelled her gradually to a monstrous bulk."
Tales have been told of how a vision of her used to be
seen, under favourable circumstances—i.e. on moon-
lit, but stormy nights, with cloud-wrack scudding across
the sky—at a window, with supplicating hands entreating someone unknown to "give me back my lost
beauty!"

Alas! for poor Barbara. No one can do so much ;
and the only traces of that beauty are those to be found
in the finely-engraved portraits of her, after that courtly
painter, Lely, and others. Whether she were really
beautiful, who shall pretend to say ? For if we are to
believe Pepys, Lely did not hesitate to sacrifice truth to
courtliness. "Pretty, but not like," was Samuel's
criticism of the portraits of those ladies of easy
unconventionality who graced the Court of Charles
the Second and are widely known as the "Lely
Beauties."

If they be the wicked who cannot rest in their graves,
but must wander uneasily upon the earth, Barbara
Villiers has every cause to haunt her old home ; for she
was perhaps the most completely depraved of a dissolute
number of women whose accommodating lack of morals
was the scandal of even that easy age. Of her numerous
children, Charles the Second acknowledged five, and the
descendants of one of them hold the Dukedom of Grafton
to this day, and bear in their family name of Fitz Roy
the evidence of their origin.

In her old age Barbara Villiers, who had gone the
complete circuit of vice, and whose very title of Duchess
of Cleveland was a badge of her infamy, became a convert
to Rome : an event which drew from Bishop Stillingfleet
the remark that "If the Church of Rome has not gained
more by her than the Church of England has lost, the
matter will not be much."

It has already been remarked that London makes
a poor questing ground for ghosts ; but at this very
moment (April, 1907) the letter printed beneath,
which appeared in *The City Press*, seems to indicate
that the Uncanny is not extinct, even in the City of
London.

"A LONDON WALL MYSTERY

"*To the Editor of ' The City Press '*

" SIR,—

" On Sunday night, while walking home down London Wall, I passed by the old piece of ' London Wall' which is railed off from the road. Suddenly I was aware of a hand and arm stretched out from the railings to bar my passage. Being scared, I jumped off the pavement into the road, and for a moment turned my back to the railings. On looking round, I saw a man dressed in dark clothes, walking back to the wall. He was wearing no hat when he reached the wall, and seemed to walk right into it. I could hear no sound of steps, and on close investigation after he had disappeared I could see no man and no hole in the wall. I went on Monday to look at the place, and I cannot throw any light on the subject. Possibly some of your readers have seen the same thing. I shall be very interested to hear if they have.

" I am, etc.,

" A READER."

But there the matter ended.

A wonderful modern ghost-story obtained much publicity at the close of December, 1913. It is probably the first appearance of a taxicab as a spectral adjunct ; but one may be very sure it will not be the last. The principals were said to be people of the highest social position.

The vicar of a Kensington church was leaving the church after choir practice when a lady stepped out of the aisle and asked him in agitated tones to come with her at once to an address near by.

" A gentleman is dying there," she said. " He is extremely concerned about the state of his soul and anxious to see you before he dies."

The clergyman followed her to a waiting taxicab, and a short drive round the corner brought them to a mansion. The lady, who seemed to be extremely agitated, urged the vicar to hurry. He sprang out of the cab, rang the bell, and a butler appeared.

" Does Mr. ── live here ? "

" Yes, sir."

" I hear he is seriously ill and has sent for me."

The butler seemed astonished almost beyond words. He expostulated that his master was not ill, that as a matter of fact he was in the best of health.

" But this lady—— " exclaimed the vicar, as he turned round, and then an expression of blank astonishment came over him.

The taxicab and the lady had completely disappeared.

But they can do that, however, without any supernatural implications.

The butler looked on the clergyman as either a madman or a practical joker, and was about to slam the door when his master came along the passage and inquired what it was all about.

" Are you Mr. —— ? " asked the clergyman. " I heard that you were seriously ill, that you were concerned about your soul, and that you had sent for me."

He described the lady who had brought him, and the " dying " man said he could not identify her ; that he had no such friend or acquaintance. The discussed this matter on the doorstep for a few moments, and then the clergyman was invited to come inside.

" It is very strange," said Mr. ——, " that you should have been sent on such an errand in such a mysterious way. As a matter of fact, though I am perfectly well, I have been troubled lately about the state of my soul, and I have been seriously contemplating calling upon you to discuss the matter with you. Now that you are here let us brush aside this strange incident, and if you will give me the time, we will discuss what has been on my conscience."

The clergyman stayed for an hour or so, and it was then arranged that his new acquaintance should come to the church the next morning and they would continue their discussion after service. He did not appear at the church, and the vicar, very much interested, called to see what was the matter. He was met at the door by the butler, *who told him that his master had died ten minutes after he left the house on the previous evening.*

They went upstairs to the bedroom where the dead man lay, and on a table in the middle of the room stood a portrait of the lady who had brought the clergyman in the cab from the church.

" Who is that ? " asked the astonished clergyman.

" That, sir," replied the butler, " is my master's wife, *who died fifteen years ago.*"

CHAPTER V

SOME RECENT INSTANCES

The Tenant of Silverton Abbey—The Strange Case of Ballechin
House—Bayhall Manor-house.

A CORRESPONDENT, writing to *The Standard* some years
ago, complained of having discovered a genuine haunted
house, much against his will and greatly to his pecuniary
loss. By his own showing, he was an Indian official, home
on extended leave, and was offered, and took, a five-
years' lease of a country mansion, "Silverton Abbey,"
at £200 a year. The place—he tells us this was not the
real name of it—had been empty for some years, owing,
it was reported, to the difficulty of coming to terms with
the landlord ; and it bore a look of long neglect. Weeds
three feet high choked the garden ; but they did not
daunt the would-be tenant, who thought the placing of
the garden in order would be a pleasant and interesting
occupation. He, at any rate, experienced no difficulties
with the landlord, and in due course came to terms and
entered into possession. Neither he nor his staff of
servants had any idea of the place being haunted ; but
the first suspicion of something being wrong was early
coming, for they had not long been settled in the house
before the maids were frightened one evening by a
Something—it is more terrible and mysterious when
you print it with a capital S—violently rattling the
windows. Then the governess complained that as she
lay awake one night a tall, dark lady, with heavy black
eyebrows, came toward the bed and made as if to strangle
her. The old Scotch housekeeper, with nerves of iron,
had her blood almost turned to water and her iron-clad
nerves severely wrung one night by a blood-curdling
shriek ; and the master of the house himself, lying awake,
once distinctly saw the bedroom door-handle turned and

the door pushed open, and *nothing* come in. This must
have been the worst of all. I think, for my part, I would
rather see the Something that had done it. Indeed,
I have a very vivid recollection of seeing and hearing a
door-handle turn without any visible agency ; but it was
a case of the handle being caught and suddenly releasing
itself. All the same, it was in the meanwhile, before that
explanation, a particularly hair-raising sight.

After these several manifestations, the tenant of
" Silverton Abbey " slept—when he *could* sleep—with
a lighted lamp and a loaded revolver beside him. When
he and his servants complained, the country-folk at length
found their tongues, and owned to having long known
the house to be, by repute, haunted. He naturally felt
aggrieved that no one should have hinted anything of the
kind before he was committed to £200 a year for five
years, and in writing to the Press bewailed the fact that
the law would not, on account of these supernatural
occurrences, help him be rid of his unfortunate bargain.
" The English law," his solicitor told him, " does not
recognise ghosts."

Some sceptical friends pooh-poohed the idea of the
uncanny, and ascribed the happenings to rats or draughts.
" But," objected the writer of the letter, " *whose* footsteps sound in ' Silverton Abbey ' at dead of night ?
' Rats,' say some. Rats do not turn door-handles.
' Draughts,' I am told. Rats and draughts do not raise
unearthly yells in corridors."

This unfortunate tenant at last found the place
unendurable, and could obtain no better offer for the
house and fourteen acres of paddock, than £50 a year.*

This may fitly introduce the story of Ballechin House,
that, owing to the close and patient investigations of the
sounds heard and the shapes seen in and around it, bids
fair to become the prime modern instance of hauntings.

One of the most fully ascertained and abundantly
witnessed modern instances of hauntings is that exemplified in the strange case of Ballechin House, Perthshire,

* Goldington Grange, after many vicissitudes, was demolished
in August, 1924, and the land is being developed in a Bedford
housing scheme.

duly set forth in a substantial volume entitled, *The
Alleged Haunting of B—— House,* of which a second
edition was published in 1900. Ballechin House does
not look a romantic building, and has none of the *stigmata*
of the abodes of ghosts. It is not deserted ; the roof
appears to be sound, the windows are in good repair, and
there is no look of the uncanny anywhere about it. The
house is not ancient, and does not even stand upon the
site of the old manor-house, demolished when the present
building was erected, less than a century ago.

The Stewart family, who own the estate, have been
in possession since the sixteenth century. At the time
when the present owner, Captain Stewart, let the mansion and the shooting for the season in August, 1896, to
a wealthy family, the house already had the reputation
of being haunted ; but this repute had not been made
known to the world at large, and was only a matter of
local gossip. It, however, acquired a wider notoriety
when, after a residence of some seven weeks, the tenants
who had intended to remain for months were driven
from the place by the supernatural sights and sounds
that constantly disturbed them. When tenants flee
from a house, and are even prepared to forfeit the considerable price (paid in advance) at which they hired it,
there must obviously be something out of the common
in connection with it.

These facts then came to the notice of the late Marquis of Bute, who was keenly interested in spiritualism
and was a member of the Psychical Research Society.
He conceived the idea of the question being thoroughly
examined, and to that end he, in conjunction with Major
Le Mesurier Taylor and other members of the Society,
hired Ballechin House for the express purpose of an
inquiry being conducted on the spot. This appears to
have had the approval of Captain Stewart himself. It
should be stated at once that there is no indiscretion
committed here in publishing these names and facts,
because, although the names are withheld in the title
and in the contents of the book already mentioned, they
are, as a matter of fact, already public property, the
names being freely divulged in the communications on

the subject made to *The Times* in June, 1897, by a correspondent, and in the somewhat heated correspondence that followed.

Some mention of the more modern portion of the Stewart family history must here be interpolated. Ballechin House had been the property, and the residence, of Major Stewart from 1834 to 1876, when he died, and was succeeded by the second son of his sister Mary, who on inheriting assumed the name of Stewart. " The old Major," as he is still known at Ballechin, appears to have been a very eccentric person. He had a profound belief in spirits, and spoke frequently of his own intention to return after death. He was very fond of dogs, and kept a large number of them in and about the house ; and often declared his belief in the transmigration of souls, and his intention of making his post-mortem reappearance in the body of a particularly favourite black spaniel. These oft-repeated intentions so greatly impressed his relatives and heirs that when the Major died, in 1876, they took especial care that all his dogs, fourteen in number, not forgetting the black spaniel, should immediately be shot. This seems conclusive evidence that the Major's spiritual society was not desired.

But the mere execution of these unfortunate dogs does not seem to have been sufficient. Disembodied spirits would appear to have more resources at command than generally suspected, and would certainly seem (if we are to believe the evidence of the hauntings of Ballechin House) to be able, not only to inhabit animals, but to bring the ghosts of animals in evidence to the senses of sight, smell, and touch. The supernatural manifestations began not long after the Major's decease. The wife of his nephew was one day making up her household books in the room that had once been the old man's study, and was thinking of anything rather than of the past, when the old familiar doggy scent the room had once worn came overpoweringly back, and she felt herself distinctly pushed by some invisible force, resembling that of an animal.

Other incidents occurred from time to time : knockings, and sounds like explosions, or people quarrelling ;

but the great era of hauntings did not set in, as already stated, until 1896. But the death of the old Major's nephew and heir, in January, 1895, was attended by some unusual circumstances. He was talking, on the morning of a departure for London, to his agent, in his business-room, when three raps were heard, loud enough to interrupt the conversation. He was no spiritualist, and, not seeking to interpret the raps, set off for London, where he was knocked down in the street by a cab, and killed. It appears to have been the opinion of the late Marquis of Bute that the raps were warnings, and that, had they been "interpreted" by the usual methods of spiritual-istic séances, the street accident would in some way have been averted. The reasoning seems cloudy.

But to come to the tenancy of the experimentalists in spooks. Lord Bute, Major Taylor, and Miss Goodrich-Freer assembled thirty-five guests in this country house, most of whom knew nothing of its reputation, and considered themselves to be only an ordinary country-house party. The idea was, it will be perceived, to exclude any suspicion that the object in view was to declare a belief in the supernatural manifestations said to be constantly occurring. It was determined that there should be no suspicion of collusion or suggestion, the object of the inquiry being merely to observe and not to proclaim either a belief or a scepticism in the existence of ghosts. Thus, there is no attempt at fine writing in the book, nor any appearance of advocacy for or against ; and mere readers of the ordinary "ghost-story" may feel disappointed in its pages ; but they have some thrills and creepy passages, notwithstanding the cold, dispassionate language and the formal tabulated statements of the places, dates, and hours of the sounds and appearances recorded. We may pass over the daily and nightly dish of detonating sounds in the corridors, the shuffling of slippered feet, the voices of an invisible man and woman in dispute, in which the words were indistinguishable, the sound as of someone reading aloud, and the like, which although set down by stolid persons of phlegmatic temperament to owls, hot-water pipes, servants' tricks, and collusion among the guests themselves, were proved to have been caused by none of these agencies. Parties of gentlemen sitting up at night armed with sticks, pokers, and revolvers, would effectually have dissuaded practical jokers ; and it is to be remarked that but one guest among so many refused to believe in supernatural forces and was disposed to suspect tricks on the part of unknown humorists.

Besides, as one of these investigators remarks, if these manifestations were part of a joke, a joke which persists for over a quarter of a century, as this by that time had done, would itself be a psychological phenomenon worthy of investigation.

But such incidents as resounding bangs against bedroom doors, " as if a very strong man was hitting the panels as hard as ever he could hit," were clearly proved to have been caused by some mysterious force exercised by other than human beings ; for on those violently assaulted doors being opened nothing could ever be seen.

The bowed and bent figure of a spectral hunchback, gliding upstairs, seen by two witnesses, was unnerving, but the most startling phenomenon was undoubtedly the frequent appearance of a spectral black spaniel, seen alike by those who had heard the story of the old Major and by many who had not. One of these last was a guest who, suffering one day from a severe headache, was trying to pass the time with setting up a camera in one of the rooms. He, strange to say, had a black spaniel of his own in the house, and thought he saw it run across the room. It looked larger, he thought, than his own dog ; and then he saw *his* dog run into the room after it and wag its tail and seem pleased at the meeting. Casual mention of the incident elicited the fact that there was no other corporeal spaniel in or about the place.

For guests to be pushed and snuffled at by invisible dogs was a common occurrence, and sounds as of dogs' tails striking, in being waggled, on doors and wainscots, were continually heard ; while real undoubted dogs, with no suspicion of anything ghostly about them, would frequently be observed watching the movements of persons or things invisible to merely human eyes. But one of the most unnerving experiences was that of one of two ladies who were sharing the same bedroom. She was wakened in the middle of the night by the frightened whimperings of a pet dog sleeping on the bed, and, looking round in the direction of the animal's gaze, she saw—what think you ?—nothing but two black paws on a table beside the bed !

An equally disturbing experience was that of a gentleman who saw a detached hand in the air at the foot of his bed, holding a crucifix ; but these were not all. With a board called by the author of the book " Ouija " —which seems to have been a contrivance very similar to, if not identical with, the well-known " planchette "— the company assembled at Ballechin House procured what is known to spiritualists as " automatic writing," in answer to questions. One of these questions propounded the name of a lady represented in an eighteenth-century oil-painting hanging in the hall. The written answer was " Ishbel " and " Margharaed " : Gaelic forms of the names Isabel and Margaret.

Among the less frequent apparitions in human form were those of sometimes one and on other occasions two nuns in black, in the grounds or in the house. The first recorded of these was a solitary nun seen weeping in a snow-covered glen. On another occasion there were two, observed simultaneously (but independently of each other) by two ladies, and at the same time by a usually quiet dog with them, which ran up to the figures, barking violently. It is to be remarked here that a sister of Major Stewart's had died as a nun in 1880.

Ballechin House is to be found at Logierait, Perthshire, half a mile from Ballinluig station.

Great Bayhall Manor-house, long years ago become a farm, and now deserted, has in recent years been the scene of manifestations in the ghostly kind. These mystical sights and sounds were duly narrated in the newspapers, and it is quite probable that they lost no circumstances of the marvellous and horrible thereby. According to one account : " The old manor, with its moss-grown roof, its broken doors and windows and its old moat, can be traced back to the reign of King John. For several weeks past persons residing in the immediate

BALLECHIN HOUSE

neighbourhood have been startled by unearthly noises and groans, and many of the villagers have been heard to declare that they have seen ghostly figures walking about. Such has been the sensation caused in Tunbridge Wells that a number of well-known gentlemen have visited the house and heard what they believe to be ' true spirit noises.' The investigators were armed with heavy sticks, and for upwards of an hour awaited the first sound which was to signalise the presence of ghosts.

" According to the story told by one of them, they were straining eye and ear when suddenly a rumbling noise like the dragging of some heavy body across the floor broke the silence of night. One or two of the explorers were paralysed with fear, but the rest were sufficiently courageous to enter the house. In the cellar below there was a succession of thuds, followed by groans, and the result was that the party beat a hasty retreat. Visits have been paid by other parties, who have reported the groans as ' terrible.' Meanwhile, the village is besieged daily by visitors from all parts of the country, and several men have been posted round the ruins to prevent damage being done."

This interesting place is situated near Pembury Green, and is reached by three-quarters of a mile of exceedingly steep and rough pathways leading through hop-gardens. When at last the spot is gained, the old manor-house, built of stone, in a heavy, gloomy classical style, about two hundred and fifty years ago, is seen to lie in a lonely hollow, neighboured only by two modern brick cottages. Melancholy pine-trees and a forbidding pond, eminently suitable for suicides, are fitting accompaniments of the scene of ruin.

The property belongs to Lord Camden, who was obliged to prosecute many of the rowdy and destructive people who made havoc here when the ghost-story was in full vogue eleven years ago.

The unquiet spirit supposed to haunt this spot and to bring a trail of mystery with it is locally said to be that of a lady whose tomb in Pembury old churchyard is the common talk of the neighbourhood. It stands by the porch, and is an altar-tomb bearing the epitaph :

GREAT BAYHALL MANOR-HOUSE

To the Memory of
MRS. ANN WEST, late of Bayhall,
In this Parish, who Died April 13th, 1803.
Aged 34 Years.

A large orifice is pointed out, and the story told is that
the lady, having been once nearly buried alive, went in
a not unnatural dread ever afterwards ; and made
especial arrangements by which she was to be buried in
a coffin without a lid, with a hole in the brickwork of the
vault, so that, in case of her being really alive and recover-
ing, she could call for assistance. An amplified version
of this story declares that she willed her fortune to a
man-servant on condition that he placed bread and water
on her coffin for twelve months after her presumed
decease.

Iron bars are fixed across the opening of the tomb,
and it has long been a pastime with country lads to drop
stones through, to hear them " drop onter ther cawfin,
mister."

As sheer matter of fact, you cannot taste this fearful
pleasure, because the vault is closed and the opening is
only that of a small air-chamber. But there are many
evidences, in the shape of half-burnt matches around
the grille, and in the stones pushed through, and the
plaster picked out of the church walls, that the story is
well known and the place plentifully visited.

It should be added, for the guidance of intending
pilgrims, that Great Bayhall Manor-house is quite three
miles from Pembury old church, Pembury Green being
a modern hamlet.

PEMBURY CHURCHYARD : TOMB OF MRS. ANN WEST

CHAPTER VI

TALES OF THE POLTERGEISTS

The Legend of Boggart Hole Clough—The Cauld Lad of Hylton—
The Demon Drummer of Tedworth—The Haunted House at
Sampford Peverell—" Button Cap " at Barnack Rectory—
The Epworth Ghost.

THE annals of haunted houses—or of houses alleged to
be haunted—are full of the pranks and escapades of
spirits filled with the mischievous impulses of schoolboys.
Deception, in the shape of human trickery, whether for
purposes of gain, or simply from a wanton love of mischief or notoriety, has been frequent, and has led many
worthy folk to be utterly sceptical of all such demonstrations ; but there have been equally numerous instances
that not the most searching investigations could convict
of being produced by tricksters. In short, the mischievous human beings who have played such pranks
—such, for instance, as the two women servants who
in 1838 for a whole fortnight set Aberdeenshire marvelling
by the commotion they raised at the farm-house of
Baldarroch—have their similarly mischievous counter-
parts in the spirit world. These are the spirits known
to the Germans as " poltergeists " : literally, " boisterous
spirits "—the irresponsibles of the Unseen. They are
in the same category as the brownies, sprites, and elves
of English legend, and greatly resemble the " boggarts "
of Lancashire folk-lore. The following story is characteristic of the kind.

Among the many striking legends that once abounded
in the now almost wholly commercialised Lancashire
districts was that of Boggart Hole Clough, once a
romantic dell between Manchester and Middleton, with
an old farm-house that had been occupied " once upon a
time " by one George Cheetham. The " boggart " lived

indifferently in the Clough (a name paralleled in the Transvaal by the Boer word " kloof ") or in George's house, and made himself thoroughly objectionable, crying at night with a voice like a baby's penny trumpet, and even in daytime snatching away the children's bread and butter, or dashing down their porringers of bread and milk. In the dead o' night the boggart would walk about with a heavy tread, like that of a person wearing wooden clogs, or would pull the bed-curtains, or even sit on the chests of people in bed, almost suffocating them. At rare intervals this demoniac visitor would relent, and churn the milk overnight, or scour the pots and pans ; but these kindly interludes did not suffice George Cheetham and his tormented family, who decided to remove to some other spot. Everything was packed up, and they were wending their way to the new home, when they met a neighbour. " So ye're gaun ? " exclaimed the neighbour.

" Yes," said George ; " the worry o't hev onmost killed my poor dame."

Instantly there came a voice from a churn : " Ay, ay, neighbour, we're flitting, yo see."

" 'Od rot thee ! " exclaimed the unhappy George ; " if I knowed thou'd bin flitting too, I wadn't ha' stirred a peg. Nay, 'tis no use, Molly, we may was well turn back agen to th' owd house."

So much for the race of " boggarts." Another, and less objectionable, type of spirit is the industrious kind that (in legends) churns the butter overnight, washes the plates and dishes in the scullery, and generally tidies up the domestic department ; and is usually represented in folk-lore as being highly offended when these services are in any way acknowledged or rewarded. Hylton Castle, now nothing but a ruined gatehouse, near Sunderland, was long said to be haunted by a spirit called " the Cauld Lad of Hylton," in which, although he has attributes special to himself, we have no difficulty in recognising the type.

The Cauld Lad was more often heard than seen, but was generally understood to be a naked spirit. He hunted the kitchens and their subordinate departments, and was of the true industrious brownie type, delighting in placing everything in perfect order, and enraged when he found no work to his hand. On such occasions he would employ himself in creating a scene of destruction : smashing the breakables, mixing the salt, pepper, and sugar ; overturning the milk, emptying the ashes into the flour-bin, and generally comporting himself like a lunatic. The servants were not long, it may be supposed, in humouring the Cauld Lad's singular passion for work ; and soon learned the trick of pleasing him. Why it should ever have been sought to banish so useful a sprite cannot be discovered, but it was found that the way to be rid of him was to present him with a suit of clothes. The suit was accordingly made—a handsome suit of Lincoln green, including cloak and hood—and set before the fire ; and the servants sat up to the witching hour of midnight, to see how their amiable unpaid helper received the gift. Punctually at twelve the Cauld Lad appeared and stood warming himself by the dying fire. Then he saw the clothes—Queen Mab's own green livery —tried them on with delight, and then gambolled about the kitchen until the hour before the dawn, when, drawing his cloak about him, he exclaimed :

> Here's a cloak, and here's a hood :
> The Cauld Lad of Hylton will do no more good.

At times the Cauld Lad would reappear. The reason of these reappearances is not stated ; but it may be hazarded that it was for as good a reason as any that may be imagined—because the suit was worn out and he wanted another.

The wings built on to the ancient castle gateway in 1735 were the scene of the Cauld Lad's hauntings ; but they have long since been demolished and the poor Lad has now no home, and is not known ever to have appeared in the still-existing Gatehouse Tower. He was a cleanly sprite, and as such is not likely to revisit Hylton, now the once fair scene has been defaced by the opening of coal-pits.

By some accounts the Cauld Lad was supposed to be the ghost of a young stable-lad, one Roger Skelton, killed in 1609 by his master, Robert Hylton, a hasty-tempered man, who, infuriated at his horse not being brought round, hurried to the stable and struck the lad so violently with a hay-fork that he died. Hylton then flung the body into a pond. The narrative goes on to tell how he was convicted of murder, but pardoned.

An amusing story is told of one of the Cauld Lad's vagaries. There was once at Hylton Castle a servant who was very fond of stealing into the dairy and sipping slyly at the cream, unobserved, as she supposed. One day, while thus engaged, she heard a reproachful voice over her shoulder : " Ye sip, and ye sip, and ye sip ; but ye never give the Cauld Lad a sip " ; whereupon she fled in terror.

It is perhaps a little startling to find, in these days when even agricultural labourers and the peasantry of remote places have ceased to believe in spirits, that so eminent a scientific man as Dr. Alfred Russel Wallace is a firm believer. Among the cases of prankish spirits in which he places credence is the famous instance known as the "Drummer of Tedworth," in which a demon (similar in some respects to the Epworth ghost, but more pertinacious and more mischievous) haunted Mr. Mompesson and his family, of Tedworth in Wiltshire, in 1661, for nearly two years.

This extraordinary affair is written of at considerable length by Joseph Glanvil, in his contemporary work on witchcraft entitled *Sadducismus Triumphatus*. It seems that in March, 1661, Mr. Mompesson committed to Gloucester Gaol, as a rogue and a vagabond, a beggar who had been wandering about the county playing upon a large drum, and soliciting alms, to the great annoyance of quiet people. The man's drum appears, in Mr. Mompesson's absence in London, to have been, for some unknown reason, sent to his house at Tedworth, on the borders of Salisbury Plain ; and when that gentleman returned home, he heard that the family had been greatly disturbed by the most extraordinary noises, at first thought to have been caused by thieves. But thieves do not make any noise, if it can be helped, and so that theory was abandoned. Three nights after his return,

Mr. Mompesson himself heard the noises, which appeared
to be that of " a great knocking at the doors, and at the
outside of the walls." This changed presently to a
" thumping and drumming on the top of the house, and
then by degrees went off into the air."

It was some time before Mr. Mompesson connected
these disturbances with the drummer he had sentenced,
but the drumming during the succeeding month became
so noticeable that the suggestion became inevitable. To
make the connection more certain, it invaded the room
where the drum itself had been placed, and during four
or five nights in every week would beat military tattoos,
from bedtime until the small hours of the morning.
Later, the demon turned its attention to the children,
" beating their bedsteads with so much violence that
everyone expected they would fall in pieces." It would
then shake the children, lift them up in their beds, and
scratch under the beds, as with iron talons. " On the
5th of November it made a mighty noise ; and a servant
observing two boards in the children's room seeming to
move, he bid it give him one of them. Upon which the
board came (nothing moving it that he saw) within a
yard of him. The man added, ' Nay, let me have it in
my hand ' ; upon which the spirit, devil, or drummer
pushed it towards him so close that he might touch it."
" This," continues Glanvil, " was in the daytime, and
was seen by a whole roomful of people. That morning it
left a sulphurous smell behind it, which was very offensive.

" At night, the minister, one Mr. Cragg, and several
of the neighbours, came to the house on a visit. Mr.
Cragg went to prayers with them, kneeling at the
children's bedside, where it then became very trouble-
some and loud. During prayer-time the spirit withdrew
into the cockloft, but returned as soon as prayers were
done ; and then, in sight of the company, the chairs
walked about the room of themselves, the children's
shoes were hurled over their heads, and every loose thing
moved about the chamber. At the same time, a bed-
staff was thrown at the minister, which hit him on the
leg, but so favourably that a lock of wool could not have
fallen more softly."

On another occasion, the blacksmith of the village, a fellow who cared neither for ghost nor devil, slept with John, the footman, that he also might hear the disturbances, and be cured of his incredulity; when "there came a noise in the room as if one had been shoeing a horse, and somewhat came, as it were with a pair of pincers," snipping and snapping at the blacksmith's nose the greater part of the night. Next day it came panting, like a dog out of breath; upon which some woman present took a bed-staff to knock at it, "which was caught suddenly out of her hand, and thrown away; and company coming up, the room was presently filled with a bloomy noisome smell, and was very hot, though without fire, in a very sharp and severe winter." It seems, in short, to have been quite as objectionable as a motor-omnibus.

The notoriety of these happenings spread to such an extent that the King, Charles the Second, sent down a Royal Commission to inquire, but so long as the Commissioners were at Tedworth nothing happened. So soon as they had taken their departure, the infernal drummer recommenced his antics, in the presence of hundreds who came to hear and marvel. Mr. Mompesson's servant declared he caught a sight of the demon, as it came and stood at the foot of his bed. "The exact shape and proportion of it he could not discover; but he saw a great body, with two red and glaring eyes, which for some time were fixed steadily on him, and at length disappeared." Innumerable were the antics it played. Once it purred like a cat; beat the children's legs black and blue; put a long spike into Mr. Mompesson's bed, and a knife into his mother's; filled the porringers with ashes; hid a Bible under the grate; and turned the money black in people's pockets.

In the meanwhile the drummer, the supposed cause of all the mischief, passed his time in prison at Gloucester. Being visited one day by some person from the neighbourhood of Tedworth, he asked what was the news in Wiltshire, and whether people did not talk a great deal about a drumming in a gentleman's house there? The visitor replied that he had heard of nothing else; upon

which the drummer observed, " I have done it ; I have
thus plagued him ; and he shall never be quiet until he
hath made me satisfaction for taking away my drum."

The drummer was eventually tried at Salisbury on a
charge of witchcraft and sorcery, and found guilty and—
in a very lenient fashion for those times, when wizards
were commonly put to death—sentenced to transporta-
tion. According to Glanvil, the noises ceased immediately he was sent beyond the seas ; but by some occult
means, " by raising storms and affrighting the seamen,
it was said," he managed to return, and the disturbances
continued at intervals for several years.

Furious controversies have raged around this story
of the Demon Drummer of Tedworth, and even in the
superstitious age when these manifestations occurred
those were not few who refused to believe in supernatural agency. Mr. Mompesson himself was suspected
(quite unreasonably) by some of being concerned in the
mystification ; but so late as 1672, ten years after the
events narrated above, he wrote solemnly denying any
knowledge of how the disturbances had been created.
" If the world will not believe it," he concluded, " it
shall be indifferent to me, praying God to keep me from
the same, or the like, affliction."

Tricksy spirits of this kind, or of the Cauld Lad
type, should render the houses they favour with their
presence the very paradise of clumsy-fingered servants,
whose breakages could easily be accounted for by supernatural agency : the usual excuse of " Please, m'm, it
come to pieces in me 'an's," or " The cat did it," becoming " Please, m'm, the Cauld Lad's bin at it again " ;
while every satanic crash could be ascribed to " that
there somethink wot ornts the scullery."

It was doubtless a poltergeist of unusual endurance,
or a company of poltergeists, who relieved one another
in the work, who originated and continued for more than
three years the infernal shindies at Sampford Peverell,
near Tiverton, long since become classic, in the Rev.
Caleb Colton's *Narrative of the Sampford Ghost.*

April, 1810, was the date when the Sampford ghost
became active in a house in the village tenanted by Mr.

THE "GHOST HOUSE," SAMPFORD PEVERELL

IN THE VILLAGE OF SAMPFORD PEVERELL

John Chave. The apparition of a woman had been seen at an earlier date by an apprentice, who had also declared he heard inexplicable noises at night ; but the one was set down to the lying depravity of youth, and the other to rats. Conceive the disgust of a self-respecting ghost, or even a romping poltergeist, at being mistaken for rats ! And it really seems as though the demonstrations that followed were designed to convince the most sceptical that, whatever caused the hullabaloo, it was not rats. The chambers of the house were filled, even in daytime, with thunderous noises, and upon any persons stamping several times on the floors of the upstairs rooms, they would find themselves imitated—only much louder—by this mysterious agency, which caused the very flooring to vibrate and send up smart spurts of dust, sufficient to half blind the experimentalists.

These malicious spirits grew more daring as time went on. A number of women servants in the house— Mary Dennis, senior and junior, Martha Woodbury, Ann Mills, Mrs. Pitts, and Sally Case—were very spitefully used, as they lay in bed o' nights, being beaten by invisible hands until they were black and blue. According to Mr. Colton, who claimed to have heard upwards of two hundred violent blows in one night delivered upon a bed, the sound was like that of a strong man striking with all his might, with clenched fists. They must have been the spooks of professional bruisers, for on a memorable occasion Ann Mills received what can only be described, in the beautiful language of the Prize Ring, as a " one-er " on the cheek which left a swelling " at least " as big as a turkey's egg upon her face. Mr. Colton then proceeds to talk of " visible marks " left by the spirits. Visible, indeed ! Ann Mills " voluntarily made oath that she was alone in the bed when she received the blows from an invisible hand " ; and Mrs. Dennis and Mary Woodbury swore before three witnesses that they were beaten until they were benumbed, and were sore for many days after. It is not remarkable that these tormented domestics refused any longer to use the room where they had been so severely handled. They were thereupon allowed to seek shelter in the room occupied by Mr. and Mrs. Chave ; but, even so, they had little peace. The candles had been put out and quiet had reigned for half an hour, when a large iron candlestick began walking rapidly about. Mr. Chave, trying to ring the bell, then narrowly escaped being hit on the head by the candlestick, which came hurtling at him in the dark.

The Reverend Caleb Colton narrates how he " often heard the curtains of the bed violently agitated, accompanied with a loud and almost indescribable motion of the rings. These curtains, four in number, were, to prevent their motion, often tied up, each in one large knot. Every curtain of that bed was agitated, and the knots thrown and whirled about with such rapidity that it would have been unpleasant to be within the sphere of their action. This lasted about two minutes, and concluded with a noise resembling the tearing of linen, Mr. Taylor and Mr. Chave, of Mere, being also witnesses. Upon examination, a rent was found across the grain of a strong new cotton curtain."

Sounds of a something like that of a man's foot in a slipper coming downstairs and passing through the wall were heard. " I have been in the act of opening a door," the narrative continues, " when a violent rapping was produced on the opposite side of the same door. I paused a moment, and the rapping continued : I suddenly opened the door, with a candle in my hand, yet I can swear I could see nothing. I have been in one of the rooms that has a large modern window, when, from the noises, knockings, blows on the bed, and rattling of the curtains, I did really begin to think the whole chamber was falling in. Mr. Taylor was sitting in the chair the whole time ; the females were so terrified that large drops stood on their foreheads."

The Sampford ghost had not the shy retiring nature of the Tedworth Drummer, which often refused to perform when special witnesses appeared ; and one memorable night, when two independent witnesses, one of them the governor of the County Gaol, sat up to see what would happen, they saw strange doings indeed. They had brought with them a sword, and placed it at the

foot of a bed, with a huge folio Bible on it, and, to their
astonishment, saw both flung through the air, and dashed
against the opposite wall, seven feet away. Mr. Taylor,
coming into the room, upon hearing the shrieks of the
women, observed the sword, suspended in the air, pointing towards him. In another minute it fell with a clatter
to the floor.

The owner of the property, a Mr. Talley, found the
reputation it had gained had rendered it an undesirable
residence. He alleged that the manifestations were
chiefly produced by a cooper banging tubs with a broom-
stick and a bludgeon, and that the object of it all was
that Mr. Chave, the tenant, should be enabled to purchase
the property at a ridiculously low figure. The result
was that Mr. Chave, besides being worried by supernatural agencies, was baited by the people of Sampford
Peverell and of Tiverton, five miles away, and very
severely handled. It was reported that, if a choice had
been possible between his human assailants and the ghost,
he would infinitely have preferred the ghost.

Mr. Colton, in the notes to a poem of his own, published at the time when the affair was still attracting
attention, declared it " might puzzle the materialism of
Hume, or the immaterialism of Berkeley. Here we have
an invisible and incomprehensible agent, producing visible
and sensible effects. The real truth is that the slightest
shadow of an explanation has not yet been given, and
that there exists no grounds even for suspecting anyone.
The public were given to understand that the disturbances
had ceased, whereas it is well known to all in this neighbourhood that they continue, with unabating influence,
to this hour. We were told, by way of explanation, that
the whole affair was a trick of the tenant, who wished
to purchase the house cheap—the stale solution of all
haunted houses. But such an idea never entered his
thoughts, even if the present proprietors were able to
sell the house ; but it happens to be entailed. At the
very time when this was said, all the neighbourhood
knew that Mr. Chave was unremitting in his exertions to
procure another habitation in Sampford, on any terms.
And, to confirm this, these disturbances have at length

obliged the whole family to make up their minds to quit the premises, at a very great loss and inconvenience. If these nocturnal and diurnal visitations are the effect of a plot, the agents are marvellously secret and indefatigable. It has been going on more than three years, and if it be the result of human machination, there must be more than sixty persons concerned in it. Now I cannot but think it rather strange that a secret by which no one can possibly get anything should be so well kept ; particularly when I inform the public, what the newspapers would not, or could not, acquaint them with, namely, that a reward of £250 has been offered for anyone who can give such information as may lead to a discovery. Nearly two years have elapsed, and no claimant has appeared. I myself, who have been abused as the dupe at one time, and the promoter of this affair at another, was the first to come forward with £100, and the late mayor of Tiverton has now an instrument in his hands, empowering him to call on me for the payment of that sum to anyone who can explain the cause of the phenomena."

The following extracts from a letter I owe to the courtesy of the Rev. Philip C. Rossiter, of Sampford Peverell, will prove interesting :

" The Sampford Ghost House is still in existence— though no doubt it is very much altered from what it was in 1810. The disturbances which then took place were never explained, but the man now living there tells me some of the walls are double, with a passage between, and of course this made [would have made] disguise and retreat much more easy. Mrs. Chave was alive when we came here many years ago [1874], but she could not explain anything : only relate what took place. My own idea is, the noises were caused by smugglers ; for when I was at Beer in 1876—taking the duty—I used to visit a very old smuggler—a delightful old man —and he told me many tales of the days of smuggling : how they used to land the spirits on very dark nights, and if pursued by the Revenue Officers take them inland, on pack-horses. I asked how far they took their load, and he—not in the least knowing where I came from—said, ' Sometimes we took them as far as Sampford Peverell, and hid some of them in the old tree in the churchyard.'

" There is an old Elm Tree here which is a great size, and perfectly hollow, with no entrance except from the top of the trunk.

" If they took some of their spirits to the Old Ghost House, they would wish to frighten the people, to account for their noise in storing them ; and sailors in those days were up to all sorts of mischief. It appears at the time that there was a rector here whose brother was Rector of Seaton (adjoining Beer) ; and perhaps they helped the smugglers, as it is a well-known fact that many gentry and parsons in those days did so."

It will be seen that the gentleman quoted above takes no stock in *poltergeists*.

The village of Sampford Peverell remains very much what it was when the mysterious affair already narrated was in progress—one of the many Devon, Somerset, and Dorset Sampfords (which derive their name from " Swampford "). It is. a large village of cob-built cottages with whitewashed walls, and is almost entirely devoted to dairy-farming. The " Ghost House " is at the extreme north-western end of the village, and is now occupied by a grocer and general dealer, who also carries on a baker's business under the same roof. Not even the grocer believes in the supernatural character of the disturbances that once rendered his house notorious. " I 'spect 'twadden a ghost," says he, in his rustic Devonshire way.

There is a lack of conclusiveness, but a plentiful and deplorable exhibition of levity, exhibited by the Reverend Charles Kingsley in his account of the ghost that was reputed to haunt Barnack Rectory when he was a boy. The fine rectory house of Barnack, in Northamptonshire, stated by Mrs. Charles Kingsley, in the *Life* she wrote of her husband, to have been built in the fourteenth century, has, or had, a " Haunted Room," troubled by a ghost commonly known as Button Cap. Charles Kingsley, when a little boy, and suffering from brain fever, had been put in this room of strange noises ; and the wonder

would seem to be, ghost or no ghost, that his illness did
not thereupon grow worse and carry him off. The ways
of parents towards their children in 1825, or thereabouts,
seem to the present age extraordinarily callous, and
would certainly nowadays draw down a severe reprimand.

This is how Charles Kingsley, in after years, wrote of
Button Cap :

" He lived in the Great North Room at Barnack.
I knew him well. He used to walk across the room in
flopping slippers, and turn over the leaves of books to
find the missing deed, whereof he had defrauded the
orphan and the widow. He was an old Rector of Barnack.

BARNACK RECTORY

Everybody heard him who chose. Nobody ever saw him ;
but, in spite of that, he wore a flowered dressing-gown,
and a cap with a button on it. I never heard of any
skeleton being found, and Button Cap's history had
nothing to do with the murder : only with avarice and
cheating. Sometimes he turned cross, and played
poltergeist, as the Germans say, rolling the barrels in
the cellar about with surprising noise, which was undignified. So he was always ashamed of himself, and
put them all back in their place before morning. I
suppose he is gone now. Ghosts hate mortally a certifi-
cated National schoolmaster, and (being a vain and
peevish generation) as soon as people give up believing
in them, go away in a huff—or perhaps someone has

been laying phosphoric paste about, and he ate thereof and ran down to his pond, and drank till he burst. He was rats ! "

But I don't believe he *was* rats ; and, whatever Kingsley may have thought in his mature years, I don't believe that as a child he believed any such simple theory.

We come now to the celebrated case of the Epworth ghost, which tormented the Reverend Samuel Wesley and his family.

In the midst of the monotonous levels of the district of Lincolnshire known as the Isle of Axholme stands the decayed market-town of Epworth. Here the famous John Wesley was born, at the old rectory, June 17th, 1703, his father being the Reverend Samuel Wesley, rector. The rector was not a favourite with the majority of his parishioners, who were convinced supporters of the by that time utterly ruined cause of the Stuarts, while he was an equally bigoted supporter of the Revolution, William the Third, and the Hanoverians. So embittered did feelings grow that the infuriated people burnt the rectory about the ears of Mr. Wesley in 1709, as the most practical form of protest they could imagine.

In the month of December, 1716, began the famous series of unaccountable disturbances ascribed to " the Epworth Ghost," known to the family as " Old Jeffrey." The rectory had been restored by that time, and political animosity did not run so high ; but there have been those who ascribed the manifestations that occurred here to a continuance of partisan spite, or to a malicious ingenuity similar to that which originated the " supernatural " pranks that frightened away the Parliamentary Commissioners from Woodstock Palace in 1649, and to that famous deception, the " Cock Lane Ghost " of 1762.

Unquestionably, however, the Reverend Samuel Wesley, and his wife and family, not excepting the famous John himself, were convinced of the genuine character of the spirit that troubled them ; and Southey, who in his *Life of Wesley* gives an extended narrative of the occurrences, undoubtedly believed, remarking in a deprecatory way, " An author who, in this age, relates such a story and treats it as not utterly absurd, must expect to be ridiculed ; but the testimony upon which it rests is far too strong to be set aside because of the strangeness of its relation."

The chief source of information as to the Epworth Ghost is the long account written by the Reverend John Wesley for *The Arminian Magazine*, and in its turn based partly upon the diary kept by his father, and upon the conversations he had upon the subject with the Reverend Mr. Hoole, Vicar of Haxey, who had been present when the spirit was creating a disturbance. John Wesley himself, who was not much more than twelve years of age at the time, and was away from home, was dependent upon these sources for his account.

He begins by stating that " on December 2nd, 1716, while Robert Brown, my father's servant, was sitting with one of the maids, a little before ten at night, in the dining-room, which opened into the garden, they both heard someone knocking at the door. Robert rose and opened it, but could see nobody. Quickly it knocked again, and groaned. ' It's Mr. Turpine,' said Robert ; ' he used to groan so.' He opened the door again, twice or thrice, the knocking being twice or thrice repeated ; but still seeing nothing, and being a little startled, they rose up and went to bed. When Robert came to the top of the garret stairs, he saw a handmill, which was at a little distance, whirled about very swiftly. When he related this, he said, ' Naught vexed me but that it was empty. I thought if it had been but full of malt he might have ground his hand out, for me.' When he was in bed he heard, as it were, the gobbling of a turkey-cock close to the bedside, and soon after the sound of one tumbling over his shoes and boots ; but there was none there ; he had left them below.

" The next day he and the maid related these things to the other maid, who laughed heartily, and said, ' What a couple of fools you are ! I defy anything to fright me ! '

" After churning in the evening, she put the butter in the tray, and had no sooner carried it into the dairy than she heard a knocking on the shelf where several puncheons of milk stood ; first above the shelf, then below. She took the candle and searched both above and below, but, being able to find nothing, threw down butter, tray, and all, and ran away as if for life.

"The next morning, my sister Molly, then about twenty years of age, sitting in the dining-room, reading, heard as if it were the door that led into the hall open, and a person walking in who seemed to have on a silk nightgown, rustling and trailing along. It seemed to walk round her, and then to the door, then round again ; but she could see nothing. She thought, ' It signifies nothing to run away, for, whatever it is, it can run faster than I.' So she rose, put her book under her arm, and walked slowly away. After supper, she was sitting with my sister Sukey (about a year older) in one of the chambers, and telling her what had happened. Sukey made light of it, telling her, ' I wonder you are so easily frightened. I would fain see that would frighten me.'

"Presently a knocking began under the table. She took the candle and looked, but could find nothing. Then the iron casement began to clatter. Next, the catch of the door moved up and down without ceasing. She started up, leaped into the bed without undressing, pulled the bedclothes over her head, and never ventured to look up until next morning.

"A night or two after, my sister Hetty (a year younger than my sister Molly) was waiting as usual between nine and ten to take away my father's candle, when she heard someone coming down the garret stairs, walking slowly by her, then going slowly down the best stairs, then up the back stairs, and up the garret stairs ; and at every step it seemed the house shook from top to bottom. Just then my father knocked, she went in, took his candle, and got to bed as fast as possible. In the morning she told it to my eldest sister, who told her, ' You know I believe none of these things ; pray let me take away the candle to-night, and I will find out the trick.' She accordingly took my sister Hetty's place, and had no sooner taken away the candle than she heard a noise below. She hastened downstairs, to the hall, where the noise was, but it was then in the kitchen. She ran into the kitchen, where it was drumming on the inside of the screen. When she went round, it was drumming on the outside, and so always on the side opposite to her. Then she heard a knocking at the back kitchen door. She ran to it, unlocked it softly, and, when the knocking was repeated, suddenly opened it ; but nothing was to be seen. As soon as she had shut it, the knocking began again. She opened it again, but could see nothing. When she went to shut the door, it was violently knocked against her ; but she set her knee and her shoulder to the door, forced it to, and turned the key. Then the knocking began again ; but she let it go on and went up to bed. However, from that time she was thoroughly convinced that there was no imposture in the affair.

" The next morning, my sister telling my mother what had happened, she said, ' If I hear anything myself, I shall know how to judge.' Soon after, she begged her mother to come into the nursery. She did, and heard, in the corner of the room, as it were the violent rocking of a cradle ; but no cradle had been there for some years. She was convinced it was preternatural, and earnestly prayed it might not disturb her in her own chamber at the hours of retirement : and it never did. She now thought it proper to tell my father. But he was extremely angry, and said, ' Sukey, I am ashamed of you. These boys and girls frighten one another ; but you are a woman of sense, and should know better. Let me hear of it no more.'

" At six in the evening he had family prayers, as usual. When he began a prayer for the King, a knocking began all round the room, and a thundering knock attended the ' Amen.' The same was heard, from this time, every morning and evening while the prayer for the King was repeated. As both my father and mother are now at rest, and incapable of being pained thereby, I think it my duty to furnish the serious reader with a key to this circumstance.

" The year before King William died, my father observed my mother did not say ' Amen ' to the prayer for the King. She said she would not, for she did not believe the Prince of Orange was King. He vowed he would never cohabit with her until she did. He then took his horse and rode away, nor did she hear anything of him for a twelvemonth. He then came back, and lived with her as before. But I fear his vow was not forgotten before God."

In acquiring complete information, John Wesley visited Mr. Hoole, of Hazey, who stated that the Reverend Samuel Wesley had sent his servant, Robert Brown, over to request his company. "When I came," said Mr. Hoole, " he gave me an account of all that had happened, particularly the knocking during family prayer. But that evening (to my great satisfaction) we heard no knocking at all. But between nine and ten a servant came in and said, ' Old Jeffrey is coming (that was the name of one that had died in the house), for I hear the signal.' This, they informed me, was heard every night, about a quarter to ten. It was towards the top of the house, on the outside, at the north-east corner, resembling the loud creaking of a saw, or rather that of a windmill when the body of it is turned about in order to shift the sails to the wind. We then heard a knocking over our heads, and Mr. Wesley, catching up a candle, said, ' Come, sir, now you shall hear for yourself.' We went upstairs, he with much hope, and I (to say the truth) with much fear. When we came into the nursery, it was knocking in the next room : when we went there, it was knocking in the nursery ; and there it continued to knock, though we came in, and particularly at the head of the bed (which was of wood) in which Miss Hetty and two of her younger sisters lay. Mr. Wesley, observing that they were much affected—though asleep, sweating and trembling exceeding—was very angry, and, pulling out a pistol, was going to fire at the place whence the sound came. But I snatched him by the arm and said, ' Sir, you are convinced that this is something preter- natural. If so, you cannot hurt it, but you give it power to hurt you.' He then went close to the place and said sternly : ' Thou deaf and dumb devil ! why dost thou fright these children who cannot answer for themselves ? Come to me, in my study, that am a man ! ' Instantly it knocked his knock (the particular knock which he always used at the gate) as if it would shiver the board to pieces, and we heard no more that night."

This clerical defiance of the demon was the beginning of further disturbances. Until then, the Reverend Samuel Wesley had not himself been molested. "But the next evening," John Wesley goes on to say, "as he attempted to go into his study (of which none had the key but himself), when he opened the door it was thrust back with such violence as had liked to have thrown him down. However, he thrust the door open, and went in. Presently, there was a knocking, first on one side, then on the other, and, after a time, in the next room, wherein my sister Nancy was. He went into that room and, the noise continuing, adjured it to speak, but in vain. He then said, ' These spirits love darkness ; put out the candle, and perhaps it will speak.' She did so, and he repeated the adjuration ; but still there was only knocking, and no articulate sound. Upon this he said, ' Nancy, two Christians are an overmatch for the devil. Go, all of you, downstairs ; it may be when I am alone he will have courage to speak.'

"When she was gone, a thought came into his head, and he said, ' If thou art the spirit of my son, Samuel, I pray knock three knocks, and no more.' Immediately all was silence, and there was no more knocking at all that night. I asked my sister Nancy (then fifteen years old) whether she was not afraid when my father used that adjuration. She answered she was sadly afraid it would speak when she put out the candle, but she was not at all afraid in the daytime, when it walked after her ; only she thought, when she was about her work, he might have done it for her, and saved her the trouble."

The haunted Wesleys at length grew so accustomed to " Old Jeffrey " that they took, as a rule, little notice of him. His presence was generally announced by a gentle tapping at the head of the children's bed, beginning usually between nine and ten at night. " If they heard a noise in the night," says John Wesley, " they commonly said to each other, ' Jeffrey is coming : it is time to go to sleep.' And if they heard a noise in the day, and said to my youngest sister, ' Hark, Kezzy, Jeffrey is knocking above,' she would run upstairs and pursue it from room to room, saying she desired no better diversion."

After some two months of this persecution, accompanied by many strange, inexplicable noises of things being flung violently about, the Wesleys were implored to leave the house. " But he constantly answered, ' No ; let the devil flee from me : I will never flee from the devil.' "

Fortunately, this deadlock came to an end by the devil, the spirit, or whatever it was, ceasing its attentions. The tricks it had performed were of the mischievous kind generally associated with merely human agents, but the behaviour of the mastiff dog kept in the house points to more esoteric agency. The Reverend Samuel Wesley, after recording how he was " thrice pushed by an invisible power, once against the corner of my desk in the study, a second time against the door of the matted chamber, a third time against the right side of my study door, as I was going in," goes on to tell of the behaviour of the mastiff, which " came whining to us, as he did always after the first night of its coming ; for then he barked violently at it, but was silent afterwards, and seemed more afraid than any of the children." Animals, and especially dogs, have always been more susceptible to the unseen than human beings, and are more likely to be enraged than terrified by the practical joker. We must therefore always, in estimating the genuineness, or otherwise, of the Epworth Ghost, bear in mind this recorded behaviour of the dog ; while the evidence of the Wesley family, as to all these things having really happened, will generally be regarded as above suspicion.

It is remarkable that so many ghost-stories are staged in the homes of the clergy ; in the old rectories and vicarages ; because the clergy are, incidentally, professional exorcists. They can, if you like to believe in their alleged supernatural powers, not only bid a ghost " Begone ! " but dismiss him or her (or It ?) to the depths of the Red Sea. Rather than risk a treatment so contumelious, they would, it might reasonably be thought, give the clergy a wide berth. But they do not : they never have.

One of the most completely authenticated ghost-stories is that of the ghost of an old college friend of the rector of Souldern, in Oxfordshire. It happened—that spectral visit—long ago ; but good ghost-stories, like good wine, improve with age ; and later years have given us no better vintage in the spectral sort than this. It was so long ago as 1706 that when, one evening, the Rev. Mr. Shaw, the rector of Souldern and Fellow of St. John's College, Cambridge, was taking his ease in his library, there appeared to him the spectre of Mr. Naylor, who had died five years earlier. The rector, in his account of the affair, declared he was not alarmed. The ghost made himself companionable and chatty. He did not merely sit down : he drew up a chair and conversed with Mr. Shaw for an hour and a half. Asked how matters were with him in the Beyond, the shade of Mr. Naylor declared, with a happy smile, that all was well ; but that he missed his old college friends. That, however, would soon be remedied. Mr. Arthur Orchard, spoken of in this account as a person of some fame—but who is not known to us—would soon be with him ; " and you," added the ghost, cheerfully, " not long after."

Mr. Shaw spread his story about among his fellow-clergymen, and it was quite famous in its day. No one ever has bettered it ; not even Dr. Jessop.

Three persons at East Rudham Vicarage, Norfolk, in December, 1908, declared they had seen the " ghost " of the vicar of the parish, who was at the time in Algiers.

The vision appeared to the housekeeper, a maid-servant, and the acting vicar, the Rev. R. Brock, who gave particulars of the singular occurrence in a letter to *The Times* of December 28th.

The vicar, the Rev. Dr. Astley, the " living ghost," had suffered injury in a recent railway accident in Algeria, and as a consequence he was at the time in the English hospital at Algiers.

The housekeeper, Mrs. Hartley, seen, said that late on the Saturday afternoon she went to close the shutters in the study when she saw the vicar, Dr. Astley, come across the lawn to the window.

" He had no hat on and was smiling," she said. " He

held a piece of paper in his hand. I thought he had come home unexpectedly and opened the French windows for him to come in. He beckoned to me with the paper and then went into a little recess outside the window. I could not make out why he did not come in."

She then called a servant and asked her if she saw anyone. "Why," said the girl, "it's Dr. Astley!" She then called Mr. Brock.

The acting vicar, an elderly man, who had seen Dr. Astley only once, said:

"When I was called into the study, I clearly saw the figure, which I recognised as that of Dr. Astley. He seemed to be sitting in a chair with some books before him. I noticed his Cuddesdon collar, and his way of wearing his watch-chain straight across his waistcoat high up. The figure had the appearance of a reflection in a mirror. The time was about 4.40. With no light in the room I could see the figure quite clearly. It gradually vanished."

A curious fact was that if Dr. Astley had been sitting in his usual place in his study with a light in the room, a reflection would have appeared in the window, making him appear exactly as Mr. Brock described.

Dr. Astley with Mrs. Astley had left England on December 10th, intending to take up the chaplaincy at Biskra for the winter months. The train in which he was travelling on December 16th from Algiers came into collision with a goods train, and the car in which Dr. and Mrs. Astley were seated was thrown over an embankment. Dr. Astley was severely bruised and Mrs. Astley had a leg broken and an injury to her face.

"The case is of engrossing interest," said Mr. Dudley Wright, compiler of the *Annals of Psychical Research.* "There are few cases so well attested of an apparition, or 'phantasm of the living,' appearing to more than one person at the same time."

But patient investigation of ghost-stories and haunted houses generally results in disappointment. There was in 1913 a very circumstantial account of poltergeist activities at Asfordby Rectory, in Leicestershire; and the Rev. F. A. Gage Hall, the rector, was stated to have at last put into practice his technical exorcising attributes, and with due ceremony to have commanded the spirit, or spirits, to depart, " in the name of the Father, the Son, and the Holy Ghost." The inhibition was successful, and Asfordby Rectory was troubled no more. No longer do residents, visitors and servants find their bedclothes torn away from them in the middle of the night by a spirit whose physical powers defy mortal resistance. The old mansion—for such it is—has peace. But the present writer, who curiously inquired at the Rectory, of Mr. Gage Hall's successor there, met with the usual disclaimer. In fact, the then rector described it as " all nonsense," and added that it was due to Mr. Gage Hall's own freakish imagination. There were, it was true occasional easily explicable noises, but they were such as would be heard in most old houses. He entirely deprecated any talk or public mention of ghosts at Asfordby Rectory merely because such gossip made it difficult to obtain or keep servants. The Rectory is a very large mansion of the eighteenth century.

At the time it was reputed to be actively haunted, the Rev. C. H. Strudwick, vicar of Whetstone, a neighbouring parish, slept for several nights in a haunted room, and related that on the very first night he was alarmed by a violent tugging at his bedclothes. He held on as tightly as he was able, but in vain. The ghost won the tug-of-war, and stripped the vicar of his covering.

" All I could see," he said, " was a heap of disordered bedclothes on the floor. There was nothing else to indicate that anything unusual had occurred. I searched the room thoroughly, and everything was in order. The door was locked on the inside, and no one could have entered. But when the same thing happened the very next night I was glad to change my room."

A sister-in-law of the rector subsequently slept in the same room, and had the same alarming experience to narrate to a small knot of scared folk in the middle of the night.

CHAPTER VII

HOUSES WITH SKULLS AND SKULL LEGENDS

Burton Agnes Hall—Wardley Hall—Bettiscombe Manor-house—
Warbleton Priory—Tunstead Farm—Higher Chilton Farm.

" To be knaved out of our graves, to have our skulls
taken, are tragic abominations," said Sir Thomas Browne,
whose own skull has, by a most extraordinary freak of
fate, been so knaved away, and has for many years been
preserved as a sight for the curious in a casket at the
Norfolk and Norwich General Hospital.

There are some singular instances of skulls being
preserved in old houses and becoming the subjects of
weird legends. Burton Agnes Hall is the chief of them.
This beautiful mansion, now the property of Mrs. Wickham
Boynton, is one of the stateliest homes in England. In
this case there is no element of doubt as to whose skull
is preserved here. The story has always been free from
the slightest suspicion of vagueness.

Burton Agnes is situated in the East Riding of Yorkshire, between Bridlington and Driffield, and the Hall,
a noble building in those phases of Renaissance architecture known as Elizabethan and Jacobean, stands on
a gentle eminence overlooking the village. The estate,
owned anciently by the De Somervilles, came at length,
in the reign of Edward the First, into possession of
the Griffith family, which, after many generations, was
reduced, in the last years of Queen Elizabeth, to three
co-heiresses, daughters of Sir Henry Griffith. They were
wealthy ladies, and on succeeding to the property conceived the idea that the old Hall, dating back many
centuries, was altogether out of date and unsuitable for
people of their position in the county. They were by no
means singular in their ideas, as the extraordinary number

of still-surviving country mansions built at that period
upon the site of older, and generally fortified, houses
clearly proves.   It was an age when the stern realities of
civil war and general insecurity seemed to be ending,
and when to dwell in castles and embattled and moated
granges appeared unreasonable.   In short, in every way,
in art and architecture, and in the graces of life, an Era
of Renaissance.

No one of the three sisters was so keenly interested in
the building of their new home as was Anne, the youngest.
She was possessed by the idea, and concerned herself
with the working out of it, day by day.   Money was no
object, and no expense was spared to render Burton Agnes
Hall as fine as architect and craftsman could make it.
Inigo Jones (the Gilbert Scott, in ubiquity, of his age)
was chosen architect :   although, to be sure, the work
resembles that of Thorpe ;   and Rubens is stated to have
executed some of the decorative work.

However that may be, the Hall is certainly a very
noble structure.   You approach it through an archway
in a highly elaborate gatehouse, bearing the royal arms
flanked with strange caryatidal figures, and then perceive
before you a great red-brick building with two projecting
gabled wings, and a recessed centre with two minor
projections—all plentifully supplied with large windows,
from which, in some instances, the mullions have been
removed and replaced by commonplace sashes, in the
debased taste of the early nineteenth century.   The
interior is handsome with rich panelling, but is chiefly
remarkable for the fine staircase and the Great Saloon.

Anne Griffith saw this delightful home growing to
completion with unaffected enthusiasm.   It was never
out of her thoughts, and even when it was finished she
was always devising little additional touches.   She
seemed to live for the house.

Soon after she and her sisters had taken up their
residence, Anne went one day on a visit to some neighbours and friends, the St. Quintins, at Harpham, only
one mile distant.   The times were not altogether safe
for an unprotected girl on a country road, and Yorkshire
in especial was then infested by ancestors of our modern

tramps, known as Wold Rangers—mendicants who had formerly been fed and roughly lodged at the gates of the monasteries, but who had in the years succeeding the dissolution of the religious houses grown desperate, and, while not prepared to work, were ever ready to rob. Yielding so far to her sisters' fears as to take a pet dog with her, she set forth, but had not proceeded farther than St. John's Well when she saw two beggars of that kind resting by the roadside. As she approached, they rose and asked charity. Helping them from her purse, a valuable ring she was wearing attracted their attention, and they demanded it with threats.

Alas ! poor sister Anne. She declared it was an heirloom, and had belonged to her mother ; but little the ruffians cared for that, and attempted to snatch it from her finger. The pet dog barked, but was not otherwise of much use, and the unhappy Anne shrieked ; whereupon one of the men struck her over the head with a cudgel and so knocked her senseless. They then made off with the ring, and when assistance at last arrived no one but the stunned girl was to be seen.

She was carried to Harpham Hall, and next day was removed to Burton Agnes ; but although she lingered during five days, never recovered, and presently died. In her last conscious intervals she besought her sisters, for the love she bore their home and the affection they owed her, when she was dead to sever her head from her body and to preserve it within the walls of the mansion, there to let it remain to all future time. " Never," she implored, " let it be removed ; and make this, my last wish, known to any who may come into ownership. And know, and let those of future generations know, that if my desire be not fulfilled, my spirit shall, if it be permitted, render the house uninhabitable for human beings."

The sisters considered this gruesome wish to be merely a part of her wandering faculties ; but promised to obey, in order to quiet her entreaties : and then she died.

A few days later her body was interred in the family vault, with her last wish disregarded, and the surviving

BURTON AGNES HALL

sisters settled down with their sorrow. But not for long.
Not many days had passed when those living at the Hall
were startled, as they were proceeding to bed, by hearing
a loud crash in one of the upstairs rooms ; and although
a thorough search was made, no fallen object could be
discovered. A few nights later the sleeping household
were awakened by the reverberating slam of doors ; but
although they rose and searched through the house with
lights—and duly armed with pokers and other lethal
weapons, you may be sure—nothing could be seen. For
some days afterwards the house resounded with weird
and inexplicable noises, and the corridors echoed at night
with groans, as of the dying.

The thoughts of the sisters then turned to their
broken promise, and they consulted the vicar, as presum-
ably an expert in spiritual matters, as to what had best
be done. He advised them to have the coffin reopened
and the head brought into the house, so that the dead
and the living alike might have peace. This suggestion
was acted upon. According to the ghastly stories told
for centuries past, the body was found perfect, but the
head had by some mysterious agency been severed, and
was already a grinning skull. When it had been duly installed in the Hall, the noises ceased, and no supernatural
manifestations occurred until many years after, when, the
ancient tale having become somewhat discredited in the
lapse of time, a maidservant, mischievously inclined, one
day threw the skull out upon a passing farm-cart. The
effect was like that of the famous Hand of Glory upon
surrounding objects : the horse and cart remained stubbornly fixed, and not all the whipping in the world would
remove it. The behaviour of the terror-stricken maid-
servant indicated what had happened to cause the trouble,
and the unpleasant relic was taken indoors again : whereupon the cart went upon its way.

When the Boynton family succeeded to the estate,
they, like everyone else who had not already experienced
the supernatural vagaries of " Owd Nance," as the
country-folk rather flippantly style her, made light of
what they considered to be a stupid belief, and promptly
had the skull buried in the garden ; but there was no luck

about the house until it was returned to its accustomed place.

The Boyntons of Barmston, originally of Boynton near Bridlington, own Burton Agnes by right of their descent from Sir Matthew Boynton, who married the last surviving of the three sisters, and was created a Baronet in 1618. The portraits of the three, in one large oil-painting, hang on the staircase of the Hall, and a very quaint trio they are, in their seventeenth-century ruffs and farthingales. Anne Boynton, the ill-fated, stands on the right hand, and certainly wears a rueful expression of countenance. The group would seem to have been painted after Anne's death, for she is very strikingly represented in black.

The skull, formerly placed upon a table in the Great Saloon, is now built in behind the great carved screen that came from Barmston.

A tale of hauntings was told of Burton Agnes Hall in the '60's, by which it appears that one John Bilton came down from London, visiting a cousin, Matthew Potter, gamekeeper on the estate, living in the then apparently otherwise unoccupied Hall. Bilton was asked to stay the night, but was warned that the house was haunted, and told that, if he were afraid of ghosts, he had better sleep elsewhere.

Bilton was a brave man. *He* was not afraid of ghosts, he declared. Going upstairs to bed, the gamekeeper held the candle up before the portrait-group of the three sisters, and was telling the story, when—Pouf ! out went the light. Draughts ? Possibly. But why could the candle not be re-lit ?

Keeping very close together on their way to the bed-room, they went to bed in the dark, and shared the same bed, for sake of security ; but not in peace, for there came a shuffling of feet in the passage, like that of a considerable crowd.

" What's that ? " asked the startled visitor.

" Jenny Yewlats," returned the gamekeeper, with a yawn, giving the local Yorkshire name for owls.

" But owls don't wear hob-nailed boots and bang

doors," returned the visitor, ducking his head under the clothes as the noises increased.

" Bats, then," said the gamekeeper.

" Bats be blowed," remarked his friend, with more force than politeness.

" Aw, then, 'tis Owd Nance," said the gamekeeper unconcernedly, and went to sleep ; but the stranger to these things thought it was more like Old Nick, and lay long awake, listening to the unearthly tumult. He did not sleep another night at the Hall.

The legend (or legends, as there are several versions) of Wardley Hall and its ghastly relic is one of those many old Lancashire folk-tales that have been exploited in modern times by writers of irresponsible books on Lancashire traditions, in which the originally highly interesting and really dramatic story has been worked up in the form of more or less unconvincing fiction.

Even the old legend of Wardley Hall, before novelists laid hands on it, was almost entirely without foundation in fact. It told how Roger Downe, the last male representative of his race, earned for himself the character of one of the most dissolute among the swashbuckling blades who formed the greater part of the Court of Charles the Second, and was one of those " scourers " whose delight it was to pervade London streets and provoke quarrels with unarmed and defenceless persons, to the end that they might earn the opportunity of slitting a few noses, or slicing off an ear or two, with little risk to themselves. The watch—being generally of the Dogberry kind, feeble and incapable, and only too eager to let all rogues and turbulent folk alone— were generally the sport of these fine fellows, and many a pleasant night Roger Downe and his companions were said to have enjoyed ·in beating those infirm old men within an inch of their lives.

Unfortunately, according to the legend, he happened at last upon a more than usually stalwart and courageous preserver of the public peace. The encounter took place on London Bridge, and the watchman defended himself so well with his halberd that the head of Roger Downe was presently severed from his body and fell in the gutter.

ANNE GRIFFITH (IN BLACK, ON THE RIGHT HAND) AND HER TWO SISTERS
From the painting at Burton Agnes

THE WARDLEY HALL SKULL

The wild young man's sister was living at the time at Wardley Hall, and to her the head of her brother was despatched, packed in a box. Let us hope she had been advised of the contents of that box before she opened it. She placed the head on the staircase, where it has ever since remained, except on those very rare occasions when attempts have been made to move it.

The first of these occasions was when she thought of giving the gruesome relic proper Christian burial. It was duly committed to earth, but that night a terrible tempest shook the house, until it seemed about to fall, and all the barns and outhouses were unroofed. All the household were terrified nearly out of their wits, and spent the dark hours of that unquiet night stuffily and uncomfortably, with their heads tucked under the bed-clothes—as you and I, dear reader, would certainly also have done. When morning was come, and the blessed sunshine streamed in at the windows, and everyone got up and felt themselves all over, to make sure they really were alive, they were not unnaturally surprised to find that the unpleasant relic had come back, and lay, with a sardonic grin, on the staircase.

After one or two more such disturbing experiences, it became quite evidently the intention of the head to remain in the house, and so, to keep the pestilent fellow quiet, a little hatch, or recess, was made in the wall for it, and there, ages ago resolved into a grinning skull, it has remained ever since.

This is all very well, as a tale of horrors, but the real history of the skull, which still stands in its glazed recess in the wall, is very different, and by no means less interesting. Wardley Hall was, in the early part of the seventeenth century, in the possession of the Downe family, to whom it had come by marriage. It was already an ancient house, and was about that time very largely remodelled, in accordance with the ideas of comfort then prevailing. Roger Downe, a barrister-at-law and member of Gray's Inn, and sufficiently well thought of in Lancashire and Cheshire as to have become Vice-Chancellor of Cheshire and a Member of Parliament, then resided here. He died, aged fifty-seven, in 1638, and his wife,

WARDLEY HALL

Penelope, four days later, this circumstance giving rise
to the belief that they must have been victims of one of
the many pestilences then from time to time ravaging
the country. This Roger Downe was succeeded by his
son, Francis, born in 1606. He also was a barrister, and
was cut off untimely, dying in 1648, to be followed by
his brother John, who died the same year, leaving a
widow, a daughter, Penelope, and one infant son, Roger,
the last of his race—the Roger Downe of the legend.
The old story is in some few particulars near the truth
as regards this Roger, for he was in fact a gay young
man about town in the reign of Charles the Second, and
met his death in 1676 in just such a scuffle with the
watch as already narrated : only the details are different.
It seems that he was, with Lord Rochester and others,
engaged in tossing in a blanket some fiddlers who had
refused to play for them, when a barber called the watch,
who interfered, to put a stop to the disturbance ; whereupon my Lord Rochester made as if he would run one
of the watch through with his sword. Seeing the imminent danger of the man, Roger Downe laid hold of
the sword, and in doing so no doubt saved the man's
life ; but in the darkness and confusion, another member
of the watch came up from behind and struck Downe
on the head with his staff, splitting his skull. He died
a few days later, aged twenty-eight, leaving his sister,
Penelope, sole heiress to Wardley Hall and £1,500 a year.
Penelope Downe in due course married Richard Savage,
fourth Earl Rivers, and left in her turn one daughter,
Penelope, to succeed.

We are not concerned with the further descent of
Wardley Hall, except to note that it is now the property
of the Earl of Ellesmere ; and will turn to Wigan for a
moment, to note that there, in the church, Roger Downe
was buried. His coffin was opened in 1779, when his
head was duly found upon his shoulders, only the top
part of the skull, above the eyebrows, having been sawn
off, for some surgical post-mortem purpose. Clearly,
therefore, it is not his skull that is preserved in his old
home. Whose, then, is it ? "

To show whose, we must draw attention to the fact

that, although in Queen Elizabeth's time the Downes
had been Protestants, they reverted by degrees to the
old faith, chiefly by force of circumstances, many of
their connections being, through the reign of James the
First, and Charles the First, and through the Commonwealth, Popish recusants, steadfast in hearing Mass in
secret, and in harbouring and comforting Romish priests.
An intimate friend of Francis and John Downe was
Alexander Barlow, son of Sir Alexander Barlow, of the
neighbouring Barlow Hall. This scion of an ancient race,
professing the Roman Catholic religion, was born in 1585,
and educated for that proscribed priesthood at Douai.
In the reign of Charles the First he resided in these
Lancashire districts, more or less covertly officiating as
priest among the gentry, who here were still very largely
affected towards Rome. For years he thus continued,
and being well known and liked locally, the offence of
practising the forbidden religion was very generally
condoned. Now and again, however, he was informed
against, and imprisoned for short periods in Lancaster
Castle, or fined. And so things might have continued,
had it not been for a sudden fury that seized the Puritan
minister and the congregation of Leigh on the Sunday
evening, April 25th, 1641. They were inflamed by an
announcement that " Father Ambrose," as Barlow styled
himself, was performing Mass at the neighbouring Morley
Hall, and forthwith rushed forth, a furious mob of four
hundred persons, armed with any weapons they could
lay hands upon, and, reaching Morley Hall, besieged the
chapel there. Breaking in the doors, they seized " Father
Ambrose," who, although pale and agitated, besought
his friends to make no attempt to rescue him. " I must
die at some time or other," said he, " and I could not
better die than in the act of defending my religion."
He was forthwith hurried off to a neighbouring Justice
of the Peace, and then sent with an armed escort of
sixty men to Lancaster Castle, whence, after trial and
conviction at the Assizes, he was drawn on a hurdle to
the place of execution, and hanged and quartered, on
September 10th, in the fifty-fifth year of his age. He
died courageously, walking twice round the gallows,

reciting the fiftieth Psalm, and rejecting the arguments of the ministers who endeavoured to dispute with him, saying " he had something better to do than hearken to their fooleries."

His head was impaled on the tower of the old church, Manchester, and was afterwards more or less secretly removed by a sympathiser and taken to Wardley Hall, where it has ever since remained, as already shown. The misleading legend as to its identity probably owes its origin to the very natural fear among the Downes and their immediate successors of being too intimately identified with this martyr for conscience' sake. Relics of " Father Ambrose " are treasured at Downside, and at the Benedictine convent of St. Mary, Stanbrook, where a hand is kept. " Father Ambrose " is on his way to being canonised, for in 1886 Leo XIII. conferred upon him the title of " venerable."

The skull is likely to remain in its accustomed place so long as Wardley Hall shall stand, for a clause is always inserted in leases of the house, forbidding its removal or concealment. Years ago, when the old house was down on its luck, and let out in tenements to poor colliers, an attempt was made to get rid of it, but, in the words of the marvel-mongers, " there was no peace in the house until it was restored." Once it was flung into the moat, which was drained in order to recover it ; and in 1897, when the Hall was restored, the skull was temporarily removed ; when, according to the foreman of works, a violent thunderstorm followed. To those who are not marvel-mongers, the incident recalls the story of the Jew eating ham-rasher for his breakfast, and of his remark, when a growl of thunder was heard, " Vat a futh about a little bit o' bacon."

The marks of a bloody hand and foot are among the cherished possessions of Wardley Hall, and are shown in one of the bedrooms.

Among the houses containing these gruesome heir-looms, Bettiscombe Manor-house is exceptionally famous. To find this house of ghastly legend, the House of the Screaming Skull, as it is called, you must go far, and seek in a very lonely part of the country : for it is situated

BETTISCOMBE MANOR-HOUSE

in a retired valley of rural Dorset, midway in that district
to which the tourist rarely penetrates, the rugged country
between Broadwindsor and Lyme Regis. No road
approaches Bettiscombe Manor-house, standing solitary
in its coombe overlooking Marshwood Vale : and access
to it is gained only through a field-gate, and by a half-
mile walk across meadows. The Manor-house, now, and
for many a long year past, a farm-house, with the parish
church, uninteresting since it has been rebuilt or " restored," and a few cottages, form the sum-total of the
place.

The situation is strikingly beautiful, under the shadow
of the hills, and embowered amid apple orchards. The
old house itself is, as the illustration will show, a fine and
characteristic example of domestic architecture, as understood in the reign of Queen Anne, and would appear to
have been built by one of the Pinney family, well known
in the district in the second half of the seventeenth
century. The Rev. John Pinney, of Broadwindsor, was
prominent among this family, and was held by his con-
temporaries to be a gentleman of a witty yet grave
character. In 1648 he became strongly affected with
Puritan principles, and continued in them through the
Commonwealth and on to the Restoration in 1660, when
his living of Broadwindsor was forfeited by the triumphant
Royalists and given to the Reverend Thomas Fuller, who,
however, had not the heart to disturb so estimable a
man, and left him in possession. But two years later
Pinney was turned out, and fled, to escape persecution,
to Dublin, returning to the old familiar scenes of Dorset
in after years. Dying December 6th, 1705, he was buried
at Bettiscombe.

His sons, John and Azariah, had meanwhile been
testifying to the faith that was in them. They lived
at Axminster, that stronghold of sturdy Nonconformity,
and became seriously involved in the ineffectual rebellion
of the Duke of Monmouth in 1685 : so seriously that both
were subsequently found guilty of high treason and
sentenced to death at Dorchester by the sanguinary
Judge Jeffreys, on September 10th of that year. John
was duly executed, but Azariah was sold, with others,

for a slave, and was shipped to the plantations in the West Indies ; remaining on the island of Nevis for some years, first in that abject condition, and afterwards rising to a position of some importance. He eventually returned, and died in London in 1719.

The skull that renders the house famous—we cannot well say attractive—is at this day preserved most unromantically in a cigar-box, thrust away in the rafters of the roof. It is, as a matter of fact, the upper part of a skull only, and is declared by physiologists who have examined it to be that of a negro. In that respect it agrees with the legend, which narrates that it is the last relic of a black servant brought home by Azariah Pinney from " foreign parts." According to this long-received account, the black servant declared his spirit would not rest until his body lay again in his native land. Other versions were that the skull is that of a black servant of a priest whom he murdered (or who was murdered by his master) : evidently hazy perversions of the original facts, which would seem to be that when Azariah Pinney returned from the West Indies, he brought with him to Bettiscombe a negro servant, who died here, doubtless from consumption. One has only to consider for a moment the effect likely to be produced among the ignorant and superstitious peasantry of Dorset in the early years of the seventeenth century by the appearance of a black man in their midst, to see that here we have, without any more foundation than this simple story, the basis of a very fine, blood-boltered legend.

Of course it did not come within the range of practicable things to convey the body of a negro servant back to his native home, and so it was buried at Bettiscombe. Hence the legend of the Screaming Skull, which, if we are to believe traditions, has in the past created the usual disturbances associated with these things—and more. Here, it will be observed, there is a very singular confusion of ideas. The black man's body was not, apparently, returned to Nevis, and so, by the terms of the legend, the disturbances should be constant. But the stories that cling about Bettiscombe change ground, and declare that it is only when the skull is removed from the house that uncanny manifestations begin. Then it will begin screaming, and will create such appalling disturbances and disasters that the occupants of the house are only too glad to get it back again, and save their cattle from disease, their pigs from swine fever, their crops from becoming failures, and all the other ills to which farming (especially under ghostly influence) is subject.

These things are said to have happened in the past —and the past is full of marvels ; but they have not been known to occur of late years. For one thing, no one, even now, seems able to dare so greatly as to remove the skull.

It is decidedly hard upon the earnest investigator, whose one desire is the truth, to find this daunting attitude. He comes, after infinite pains, and in bounding anticipation, to Bettiscombe, and finds the good farming folk entirely unimpressed, to outward appearance, by the thing that shares the house with them. He sees a blooming damsel, carrying pails of new milk, issuant, emergent (as a herald might say) from this House of Mystery, and he opens fire with questions.

" Is the skull still here ? "

" Yes."

" May one be permitted a sight of it ? "

" Oh, yes, certainly " ; and a candle is lit in the beautiful hall of the house, and a procession of two goes up to the attic. It appears that the farmer and his family do not in the least mind the presence of the relic. They are healthy-minded people, and ignore it altogether, except when occasional curious visitors, sufficiently energetic to walk thus far in search of the uncanny, desire to see it. But they will not advance the cause of Truth, and permit the skull to be removed, even for the briefest space, into open air. They are like those good people who " do not believe in absurd superstitions," but at the same time will not walk under ladders ; who take no account of omens, but who will turn pale with apprehension when the " death-watch " beetle ticks upon the hearth ; when a " shroud " appears in the candle ; when a hollow coal—a " coffin "—bursts out

WARBLETON PRIORY

of the fire ; and when a dog howls at night. It is the old story : no one believes the tale, but, well—" there *might* be something in it, and ——" : and so the experiment is not made.

In the neighbourhood of Heathfield, Sussex, may be found the more or less famous haunted house of " Warbleton Priory," an ancient farm-house built upon the site of a still more ancient Augustinian monastery removed from Hastings by Sir John Pelham, in the time of Henry the Fourth.

Warbleton Priory is by no means near Warbleton village, and is discovered by in the first instance seeking Rushlake Green and then carefully asking the way. Rushlake Green is one of the prettiest hamlets in Sussex : a number of rustic cottages and a village shop or two and a post-office surrounding a genuine old English green such as is to be found more often in highly idealised pictures than in real life ; and with such useful and ornamental features as quacking ducks and hissing geese waddling across and disputing right of way.

The " haunted house " is situated in a spot especially suited for hauntings, deeds of mystery, and happenings in the hair-raising, blood-curdling sort, for it stands in a lonely spot, a mile from anywhere, in a meadow surrounded by woods and coppices. No road—only the roughest and muddiest of cart-tracks, muddy even in the height of summer—leads to it. Coming out of a very tunnel of greenery, you see the stout old farm-house standing in what looks like a clearing among the woods. It is built of stone from the long-vanished Priory, mingled with tile-hung walls, and is roofed steeply with red tiles. The remains of the chapel were long since converted into oast-houses and stables, but blocked-up Gothic arches, evidence of its former use, may yet be seen.

If the amateur of haunted houses visits Warbleton Priory in search of thrills, his time will be wasted, for nowhere are its supernatural experiences so scoffed at as here.

" Ghosts ? " asks the farmer's wife, amused at the stranger's inquiry ; " I've never heard nothing " ; and when you ask to see the two grinning skulls that used to be kept in the house, behold, they were stolen, the matter of two years ago, much to the wrath of the owner of the property.

These two grisly relics, said, on uncertain authority, to have been those of a former owner of the house and a man who murdered him, at some unspecified periods, were once jealously preserved in the building, and legends told, in the usual way, of the dreadful manifestations that had been known to take place on their being removed ; but certainly the profound quiet of the spot has been undisturbed since their final disappearance, and the cattle, that used to be afflicted when these relics were disturbed, appear to thrive and give milk in the ordinary course. The only relic in the house is the bloodstain on the floor of an upper room, a stain that refuses to be scoured out. The efforts of generations of experimentalists may be seen, in the floor-boards being distinctly worn down at that place, but the " damn'd spot " refuses to " out," even as it did in *Macbeth*.

Meanwhile, the farm-folk are very pleased to supply tea to parties of cyclists and others, who have the thrilful pleasure of sitting in a large bare room where the skulls used to be, and of gazing upon a huge empty stone fireplace, where relics in the shape of andirons, dated 1563, and an elaborate fireback, remain in company with an old coat of arms, painted on panel.

It is almost always impossible to trace these various skull relics to their true origin ; but where facts are wanting, legends do not lack. Near the remote little Derbyshire town of Chapel-en-le-Frith, at the hamlet of Tunstead Milton, there is an old farmstead commonly known as " Dickie's Farm," from the skull of one " Dickie " preserved there, for what length of time past, or for what reason, there is nothing to show. The present farm-house dates back in part to the early years of the eighteenth century, as the style of the architectural decoration shows. " Dickie " is quite a famous personality at " Chapel," as Chapel-en-le-Frith is locally known. Everyone knows of him, or her ; for the skull, now in three pieces, and incomplete, is said, notwithstanding the name, to be that of a woman. But even here we are not

on sure ground, for a legend tells how this is the last
memorial of one Ned Dixon, who, returning home from
" the wars," after many years, to enjoy his own, was
murdered by his cousin in the room where the pieces of
skull are still kept.

The inquirer after these things finds the farm perched
at the crest of a steep and rutty lane. " I charge two-
pence to see it," says the girl, when you ask if this is
not the home of the grisly relic ; and forthwith she
brings from the window-sill of the upstairs bedroom
where they are preserved the poor fragments in question ;
telling, probably for the thousandth time, the familiar
story of how, if they be removed, disasters will descend
upon the farm : the sheep becoming a prey to the rot,
the cows going dry, the horses breaking their knees, the
hens refusing to lay eggs, and even the domestic cat
acquiring the mange. Nay, more : to " Dickie's "
agency were attributed the difficulties experienced many
years ago in constructing that portion of the London and
North Western Railway to Manchester which runs close
by, through the farm lands. Engineers, in their mere
matter-of-fact way, ascribed to the local sands and bogs
the repeated failures to secure foundations for a bridge
they were building at this point ; but the people of
" Chapel " and of Tunstead knew better ; triumphantly
pointing out that the bridge was only successfully built
when another site was selected which happened to be
on another farm than " Dickie's."

Finally, we have the story of the skull still kept in
perfect preservation at Higher Chilton Farm, in the
village of Chilton Cantelo, Somerset. This is the head-
piece of one Theophilus Brome, who died August 18th,
1670, aged sixty-nine, and was buried in the north
transept of Chilton Cantelo church : the epitaph over
him declaring that he was " a man just in his actions of
this life, true to his friends, forgave those that wronged
him, and died in peace."

He came of the Bromes of Woodlowes, near Warwick.
The reasons that induced him to live down south, in the
county of Somerset, do not appear ; but it was always
understood that he had been engaged on one or other

TUNSTEAD FARM

side in the Civil War between Charles the Second and his Parliament, and was the victim of persecution from the party to which he was opposed. Collinson, in his *History of Somerset*, referring to Chilton Cantelo and Brome, says :

" There is a tradition in this parish that the person here interred requested that his head might be taken off before his burial and be preserved at the farm-house near the church, where a head—chop-fallen enough—is still shown, which the tenants of the house have often endeavoured to commit to the bowels of the earth, but have as often been deterred by horrid noises portentive of sad displeasure ; and about twenty years since (which was perhaps the last attempt) the sexton, in digging the place for the skull's repository, broke the spade in two pieces, and uttered a solemn asseveration never more to attempt an act so evidently repugnant to the quiet of Brome's Head."

It may be added to the foregoing extract, that Philip Higdon, a native of the parish, who died in 1826 at the advanced age of ninety-five years, stated that " it was always said that Brome was a gentleman who had lived in the middle counties in the troublous times, and had come therefrom to Chilton " ; but he had never heard any reason assigned for this removal, nor for the wish to have the head cut off and kept in this house.

The circumstances, however, of Brome's change of residence from one of the midland counties, coupled with the mention of the troublous times, and his age at the time of his decease, together with the directions given for cutting off his head before his burial, seem to favour the conjecture that he had been actively engaged in the civil commotions of the reign of Charles the First. It is a matter of general notoriety that at the time of the Restoration the bodies of many of the regicides, as well as others who had taken an active part against the monarchy, were, in a fruitless spirit of revenge, taken up from their burial-places, and their heads cut off and exposed in different places.

That Brome was a man of family, the arms borne by him at a time when such distinctions were less common

UPPER CHILTON FARM, CHILTON CANTELO

than now, sufficiently prove. They are : Sable, on a
chevron argent, three sprigs of broom, proper, and are
engraved on his tomb, surrounded by sepulchral emblems.
The inscription sets forth that " he was true to his friends,
and forgave those that wronged him," which would seem
to imply that he had in some respects considered himself an object of persecution : and though there is no
particular mention of his name in the history of those
days, it is not unreasonable to suppose that he had been
an active spirit in those contentions, and duly suffered
for his activity.

Higher Chilton Farm is a substantial and very
superior farm-house, long since the property of the Good-
ford family, whose arms are carved over the entrance,
together with the date of its restoration, or almost
complete rebuilding, in 1826. The truth of the story
that the skull preserved in the house is that of Theophilus
Brome was proved during the restoration of the church,
some forty-five years since, when Brome's tomb was
opened and the skeleton discovered, *minus* the head.
Until a few years since the skull was kept in one of the
living-rooms of the house, and, in spite of the legend
that disturbances would arise if it were even moved
a hand's breadth, was frequently given a new place.
Nothing, of course, happened. It now resides in a
cupboard or cabinet made especially for it, in an appropriately seventeenth-century style, and placed over a
door in the hall. Only the teeth are missing. When
the house was under restoration, the workmen filled the
skull with beer, and drank out of it : a ghastly freak in
which some will perhaps find the influence of heredity,
our very remote ancestors—and savages all the world
over—being accustomed to drink out of the skulls of
their deceased enemies. But the incident does not say
much for the intellectual development of the race in all
those centuries.

As a pendant to the foregoing comes the queer story
of the mansion at Hutton-in-the-Forest, near Penrith,
Cumberland, the seat of the Vanes. Lady Vane, widow
of Sir Henry Vane, Baronet, died at the close of 1916.
She used to tell of how she and her husband were

accustomed to hear the most unaccountable noises in the
walls of their old residence, as though someone were
trying to climb a chimney and kept falling down. At
last, growing weary of the disturbance, Lady Vane, in
the absence of her husband, had the wall nearest the
noise opened, when a lofty closet was discovered, narrow-
ing at the top to a funnel with a small opening in the
roof. In this cavity were found an ancient Bible, a
broken bottle, and some human bones. The bones were
gathered up and placed in a box which was taken to
Sir Henry Vane's room to await his return. He arrived
very tired, and Lady Vane decided to say nothing about
the matter until the morrow ; but soon after he had gone
to his room, to rest, a fearful noise was heard. Running
in, Lady Vane found him greatly agitated. He had seen,
he said, in the corner where the box had been placed,
the apparition of a woman. Lady Vane then told him
what had been done. From a date on the cover of the
Bible and a reference to ancient papers in possession of
the family, it was found that a woman had been walled
up in the aperture and apparently had perished
there. Sir Henry and his wife personally buried
the bones in the churchyard, and the house ever after
had peace.

It would seem, at times, as though there could be
few places that have not the reputation of being haunted.
Old or new, the " haunted house " is ever with us.
There are, for example, the not altogether disagreeable
manifestations of Carham Hall, along the English side
of the Tweed, near Cornhill and Coldstream. The two
separate and distinct evidences of something uncanny
which lend a note of the unusual to the ownership of
Carham are, firstly, a carriage which no one ever sees, an
equipage that may drive up by day or night. You hear
the noise of it : the horses breathing, their hoofs and the
wheels crunching the gravel ; but it is never visible, and
apparently nothing ever happens. Secondly, there is
the " Carham Light." This is a ball of light which at
night-time sometimes hovers about the trees and deludes
some people into the belief that it is a full moon. Many
folk, formerly sceptical of this phenomenon, are reported

later to have seen it, and thereafter to have become indignant with other secptics.

A favoured few report having seen the ghost of the aged Countess of Salisbury, who in 1541 was beheaded on Tower Hill. They have not seen her in the precincts of the Tower of London, but about the ruins of Lordington at Racton in Sussex : the mansion built by her husband, the father of Cardinal Pole. The wraith is said to pervade the ruins and the roads, showing a red line round her neck.

Then there used to be the ghost of Sir Thomas More, who was beheaded in 1535, for—to Henry the Eighth—the sufficient treason of not assenting to the King's assumption of supremacy in religious matters. His head reposes in the vaults of St. Dunstan's Church, Canterbury ; and if you like to see that gruesome sort of a sight, it is possible to view there the grinning skull, in its leaden box, securely placed in a niche of the wall and guarded by an iron grating. His daughter, Margaret Roper, caused it to be placed there. The ghost of Sir Thomas used, by repute, to issue in a carriage from his country house at Baynards in Surrey once a year and drive—some believed—to Loseley, which is near Guildford. But we have not heard from Sir Thomas for a long time past ; and Baynards has been so remodelled and modernised and has had such a succession of new owners, that a reactionary like More may well have quitted his jaunts and given up in disgust. The Loseley ghost—whoever *he* was—was supposed to drive out the next year, to Baynards, and repay More's courteous visit. But even the spook from Loseley seems to have given it up !

CHAPTER VIII

FAMILY CURSES

The Mystery of Glamis Castle and the Earls of Strathmore

UNQUESTIONABLY the most famous haunted house in Britain is Glamis Castle, in Forfarshire, and it is the more famous from the fact that the uncanny things connected with it and its secret chamber have ever been kept as inviolable secrets, and are no nearer solution now than they were hundreds of years ago. Thus, Glamis is not in the usual sense a haunted house : it is rather the abode of mystery, the home of some secret of which many have made light, but which those most nearly concerned have never been known to regard with indifference.

No other residence in the world, imperial or private, has been the subject of so much eager discussion as Glamis Castle ; and no secret has been so continuously assailed by investigators as that safe in the keeping of the Earls of Strathmore, the lords of Glamis. The identity of the man in the Iron Mask, and that of the writer of the *Letters of Junius* have been the subjects of furious controversies, in which the respective partisans have, every one of them, convinced themselves to be right ; but those once fertile subjects have long been abandoned, or at the most attract but feeble attention. The mystery of Glamis, however, still piques curiosity, and still defies the acuteness of investigators.

Glamis shares with Cawdor—but with more show of probability—the tradition of being the scene of the murder of Duncan by Macbeth, Thane of Glamis ; and the identical room in which that tragedy is supposed to have been wrought was long shown, together with the sword and the shirt of chain-mail worn by Macbeth !

Such are the lengths to which, everywhere, the desires of the seekers after gory landmarks and original blood-stained weapons that have done even mythical deeds, will lead the purveyors of marvels to go. Malcolm the Second, however, was certainly assassinated in the neighbourhood of Glamis : on Hunter's Hill, according to local tradition.

Although Glamis is very old and grim, it may well be doubted if anything quite so ancient as the times of Macbeth and Malcolm the Second remain to it ; and although those half-legendary, half-historic events are sufficiently tragical and have been sublimated by Shakespeare into the finest stage tragedy extant, they have no relation to the stories of unnamed horrors that reside in some undiscovered corner of the hoary pile. Those undesirable items date only from the coming of the Lyon family, in 1371. It was in this year that Sir John Lyon, Baron Fortevist, was given the lordship by Robert the Second, King of Scotland, whose daughter he had married. Among other honours conferred upon him was that of Great Chamberlain of Scotland, but he ended in a duel in 1383. It was this Sir John who brought with him to Glamis a kind of family curse, the famed " Lion Cup," an hereditary possession whose ownership is said to have caused many tragedies in the family. The plain man at this point naturally inquires why this accursed goblet was never thrown away, or at least sold, or given to some unsuspecting beneficiary against whom the Lyon family nursed a grudge, after the old Scots sort. But your plain man has no business here with family curses or spooks. Inquiry would, however, probably disclose the fact that the several disasters and violent endings of the Lyons were due less to the ownership of that item of gold plate than to the ferocity of themselves and their times.

The son of Sir John Lyon was one of those very few of the race for many centuries who died peacefully in their beds, and his son, created Lord Glamis in 1445, ended in the like natural manner. But a peculiarly horrible fate befell Janet, the young and beautiful widow of the sixth Lord Glamis, who with her son and other relatives was indicted for the practice of witchcraft, and for attempting the life of James the Fifth by the arts of magic and sorcery. Lady Glamis was found guilty on the perjured evidence of her own servants, among others, and was burned on Castle Hill, Edinburgh, in 1537. Her son John, at this time a boy of sixteen, afterwards seventh Lord Glamis, was put to the torture, and under it committed the infamy of falsely accusing his mother. He also was found guilty, but was respited until he should come of age, and was at length released and restored to his ancestral honours. His son, the eighth Lord Glamis, was killed in a chance meeting with the Lindsays, with whom the family of Lyon maintained a cherished feud.

An Earldom—that of Kinghorne—was conferred upon the castellan of Glamis in 1606, and another—that of Strathmore—in 1677. The recipient of this last honour was Patrick Lyon, who was born in 1642 and died in 1695, after having thoroughly restored the ancient castle of Glamis, and refitted it and its garden and policies according to the taste of that age.

The Earls of Strathmore at the present time own a remarkable multiplicity of titles, being also Earls of Kingborne, Viscounts Lyon, Barons Glamis, Tannadyce, Sidlaw, and Strathdichtie.

The third Earl of Strathmore died of wounds he had received at Sheriffmuir in 1715, and was succeeded by his brother as fourth Earl. The fourth Earl had five sons and three daughters, and of these no fewer than four sons succeeded to the title. Charles, sixth Earl of Strathmore, died in 1728, in a duel arising out of a quarrel at cards or dice.

It is with this Charles, sixth Lord Strathmore, that the chief of the uncanny stories of Glamis is concerned. There are, of course, many versions, but the most generally received is that of the fatal gaming party. By that it seems that the long-standing feud between the Lindsays and the Lyons had so far healed that the members of the two families dined, drank, and diced together, like the fine old Scottish gentlemen they were : bent upon some form of ill-doing, at any cost. Those ancient Scottish noblemen who were not up to some

devilry or another, from slitting the throat of monarch
or friend, conspiring against the State, or making off with
a neighbour's wife, down to mere ordinary sharp practices
and insane gambling, were few indeed, and even those
abstaining few did not generally receive the credit to
which their abstention entitled them. Such another set
of equally atrocious villains it would be difficult to find,
in any age or country.

The legend goes on to declare that the play, one fatal
night at Glamis, grew desperately high. The Earl was
suffering a run of ill-luck, and when he had gamed away
all his money, resolved if possible to win back his losses
in staking his estates. But the bad luck was still in
force, and, staking one property after another, he continued to lose, until Glamis itself stood at hazard upon
the turn of a card and was lost. Then the dazed and
infuriated Lord Strathmore, not able to understand such
extraordinary ill-fortune, lost his temper, and accused
his guest of cheating.

A blow was the only reply; swords were drawn,
and, after a few passes, the Earl was run through the
body. Thus died the sixth Earl of Strathmore; but it
would appear that it was not a Lindsay, but one James
Carnegie, of Finhaven, who killed him, as appears in the
trial that followed.

From this comparatively simple version, which
bears, in its broad aspects, the stamp of truth, many
wild varieties have been elaborated, in which the evil
characteristics of earlier lords of Glamis have been in-
corporated, to make tales of marvels. In these narratives
the chief actor is " Earl Beardie," or " Earl Patie," of
whom the real original would appear to be the first Lord
Glamis, who died in 1454, and whose actual or imaginary
ill deeds had rendered him for generations a kind of
traditional Bogy or Raw Head and Bloody Bones, the
terror of many a nursery in the country round about
Glamis.

According to these horrific imaginings, clearly evolved
in the minds of an ultra-Sabbatarian peasantry, Earl
Patie was not only a gambler, and a gambler who would
not merely play day and night and with his fellows, but

would continue on Sundays, and in default of any of his
own station, would play for bawbees with the veriest
scullion in his proud castle. It was on a dark and
stormy November Sabbath night (observe the excellent
stage-management of this legend!) that Earl Patie,
wearied of the empty day, called with his most startling
oaths for a pack of cards and for a partner in the game.
The cards were duly forthcoming, but it was not so easy
to secure a partner. My lord, with growing fury, invited
each individual member of his staff of retainers, but
without avail. Starting with the steward, and working
down to the meanest pot-walloper in the establishment,
he received refusals from all. Then he tried the rather
hopeless task of persuading the domestic chaplain to take
a hand, with the result that he not only got another
refusal, but found that any likely waverer among his
menials was scared out of obliging him by the threats
the chaplain proceeded to hurl against anyone who
should so desecrate the Lord's Day.

Earl Patie thereupon, consigning the chaplain and
everyone else to Helensburgh, and swearing if possible
worse than ever, took himself and his pack of cards away
to his own especial room, declaring himself prepared to
play with the Devil, if no other partner were forthcoming.

He had not sat long, before a knock came at the door,
and a deep voice without was heard asking if he still
wanted a partner.

"Yes," shouted the Earl; "enter, in the foul fiend's
name, whoever you are."

Thereupon there entered a tall, dark stranger,
wrapped mysteriously in a cloak. Nodding familiarly
to the Earl, he took his seat, without further ceremony,
on a vacant chair opposite, and the game presently began.
The stranger had proposed a high stake, and in accepting,
the Earl agreed, if he were the loser and found himself
unable to pay, he would sign a bond for whatever the
stranger might choose to ask. (What doited fools these
legendary gamesters always are!)

Fast and furious became the game. Loud and louder
were the oaths that resounded through the chamber and
echoed down the corridors, alarming the household.

Up crept the terrified servants, and listened at the door—after the manner of servants—wondering who this might be who should thus bandy words with their wicked master.

At last the old butler, who had served the family for two generations, and had peeped through many a keyhole in his time, applied his eye in the old familiar manner ; but he had no sooner done so than he fell back and rolled upon the floor with a yell of agony. In an instant the door was flung open, and the Earl, with furious face, instructed the servants to slay anyone who should pass, while he went back to settle with his guest.

But the guest was gone, and with him had gone the bond. It seems that while the game was in progress, the stranger had noticed the keyhole, and, throwing down his cards, had exclaimed, with a dreadful oath, " Smite that eye ! " whereupon a sheet of flame had darted directly to the keyhole, blighting the butler, and the stranger himself vanished. This would make an impressive tract for the conversion of Keyhole Peepers.

For five years after this dramatic scene, Earl Patie lived, and then was gathered into Abraham's—or someone else's—bosom. But every Sabbath evening afterwards the room where the two had played at cards resounded in the same boisterous manner, until at last, unable any longer to endure this Sunday evening tumult, the family had it built up. Of course the stranger, as the intelligent reader will already have perceived, was none other than the Devil himself, and the bond resulted in his winning the Earl's soul.

An even more thrilling version tells how the Earl declared, with many dreadful oaths, that he would play until the Day of Judgment ; and that on stormy nights the gamblers may yet be heard, quarrelling over their play.

The jealously guarded mystery of the secret room at Glamis may or may not be connected with this legend. There are, in fact, several " secret " chambers in the ancient fifteen-feet-thick walls, but these are neither more nor less a matter of secrecy than the so-called " secret " drawers that form so perfectly obvious a

feature of most old escritoires.   The one absolutely secret
chamber is never known to more than three persons at
one time : to the Earl of Strathmore for the time being,
to his eldest son (or to the next heir), and to the factor,
or steward, of the estate.   The solemn initiation ceremony takes place upon the coming of age of the heir, on
the night of his twenty-first birthday, when the three
are supposed to be armed with crowbars to break down
the masonry which walls up the mystic recess.   This rite
duly performed and the wall again built up, the factor
invariably leaves the castle and rides for home, no matter
how stormy the night or late the hour.   The Lyon family
is wealthy—the late Earl left over a million sterling—
and could easily reside elsewhere, but on the night that
witnesses the coming of age of the heir, its members will
be all gathered together at Glamis.

The theories as to what this terrible secret may be
embrace every possibility and impossibility.   An often-
repeated story is that which narrates how the unhappy
Lady Glamis, " the witch," who was burnt on Castle Hill,
Edinburgh, was really in league with the Devil, and that
her familiar demon, an embodied and visible fiend,
inhabits the spot !

With other people, greedy of the horrible, a favourite
theory is that there exists, in this dungeon, a hideous
half-human monster, of fearful aspect and fabulous age.
Another variety would have us believe that a monster of
the vampire type is born every generation into the
family, to represent the embodiment of a terrible curse
upon the house of Lyon.

Again, a tradition declares that in the old days of
feuds, when the Ogilvies and the Lindsays were for always
flying at each others' throats, a number of hunted Ogilvies
came to the doors of Glamis, imploring the Lord Glamis
of that day to shelter them from the fury of their enemies.
He was not on particularly friendly terms with either of
those warring clans, but he opened his door to the fugitives
and, under the pretence of securely hiding them, locked
and bolted the unfortunate Ogilvies in a remote dungeon,
and callously left them there to starve.   The tale goes on
to tell how the bones of those wretched fugitives strew

the floor of that dismal hold to this day, the position of
some of the skeletons showing that the captives died in
the act of gnawing the flesh from their arms.

Dr. Lee, who, in his *Glimpses of the Supernatural*,
shows himself prone to swallowing anything, however
startling, says : " On one occasion, some years ago, the
head of the family, with several companions, was deter-

GLAMIS CASTLE

mined to investigate the cause of inexplicable noises
heard at Glamis Castle. One night, when the disturbance
was greater and more violent and alarming than usual,
his lordship went to the Haunted Room, opened the door
with a key, and dropped back in a dead swoon into the
arms of his companions ; nor could he ever be induced to
open his lips on the subject afterwards."

Why the factor should be included in the triune

initiation into the mystery of Glamis is a question that has always excited highly interested conjecture. If the factor's office were hereditary, there would conceivably be reason for it, but this is not generally the case at Glamis. But whatever the reason of the factor being always taken into the confidence of the Earl for the time being, to the exclusion even of the Countess, it is certain that the trust reposed has never once been misplaced. Whatever it is the factor has seen, or whatever the ceremony in which he takes a part, the nature of it has never been divulged.

The revelation of the mystery has often in times past been promised by reckless young heirs to the title, sceptical as to its importance, but the twenty-first birthday has come and gone and the initiation into the secret has been performed ; and the promised revelation has never been made. Instead, the subject, mentioned by expectant friends, has with evident anxiety been avoided. To an inquirer the late Earl, who died in 1905, said, " If you could guess the nature of this secret, you would go down on your knees and thank God it were not yours."

Mr. Hare, who was a visitor at Glamis in 1877, speaks of the pleasant house-party then assembled there, and adds, " only Lord Strathmore himself has an ever-sad look. The Bishop of Brechin, who was a great friend of the house, felt this strange sadness so deeply that he went to Lord Strathmore, and after imploring him in the most touching manner to forgive the intrusion into his private affairs, said how, having heard of the strange secret which oppressed him, he could not help entreating him to make use of his services as an ecclesiastic, if he could in any way, by any means, be of use to him. Lord Strathmore was deeply moved ; he said that he thanked him, but that in his most unfortunate position *no one* could ever help him. He has built a wing to the castle, in which all the children and all the servants sleep. The servants will not sleep in the house, and the children are not allowed to do so."

Whatever the nature of this heirloom, the late Earl seems to have found it a subject for constant prayer.

A guest who had been staying at the Castle, and was leaving in the early morning, passed by the private chapel, and there he saw his host kneeling in prayer, and still wearing the evening clothes he had worn overnight.

Once, in the temporary absence of a former Earl of Strathmore, a party of guests, headed by the Countess herself, made an ingenious effort to discover the secret chamber. Starting on the supposition that it must have a window (but why ?) they hung towels out of every casement, concluding that any window which displayed no towel would be the mystic chamber. The attempt failed, and while it was in progress my lord returned, with unpleasant results. It was even said that Earl and Countess parted, never to meet again.

It will thus be seen that it is not from want of inquiry that the secret has been kept. Sir Walter Scott, Sir Augustus Rumbold, Augustus Hare, and many antiquaries have puzzled their brains over it, with the solution as far removed as ever. Lord Playfair, who was a distant relative of the Lyon family, had been on the estate as a boy, and was possessed with a furious zeal to pluck out the heart of the mystery. Lord Strathmore was not in residence, and young Playfair had the run of the place, his uncle being one of the trustees. " I naturally did my best," he says in his autobiography, " to discover the famous secret and the awful mystery connected with it. I drew my own conclusions, which were probably as erroneous as those which have been made by others in regard to this famous secret." He left the neighbourhood no wiser.

Fifty years passed, and he was again at the Castle. Lady Playfair was with him, and the then Countess of Strathmore conducted them all over the place. " She even showed me," he says, " *a* secret chamber, but not *the* secret chamber, which has defied so many keen inquirers." She could not, as we have already proved, have shown it if she would.

Of course many attempts have been made to show that the mystery is of merely commonplace origin, and the extraordinary activities of Patrick, first Lord Strathmore, in constructing secret rooms in his various residences,

have been pointed out. A secret staircase, which would
seem to have been built about 1670, and afterwards
bricked up, was discovered in 1849, during some alterations ; and a splendidly carved fire-place, whose existence
had not been suspected, was accidentally revealed, a few
years since, in the drawing-room.

Patrick, Lord Strathmore, left behind him an account
of his works, called by him the *Book of Record*, printed
by the Scottish History Society in 1890. In this he
gives very full details of the work done by him at Glamis
Castle. For instance, the construction of this back
staircase, so long forgotten, is distinctly described, and
from his references to certain leaden statues which he had
erected in the grounds, these works of art were recovered
from their undignified seclusion in some of the cellars,
and have been restored to their original positions. When
confronted with a mystery like that of the secret chamber,
one naturally turns to the *Book of Record* to see if it
contains any allusion to this apartment. The diligent
student of that remarkable book will find two curious
entries that seem to have some bearing on this subject.
Writing on June 24th, 1684, Lord Strathmore records
the following transaction : " Agried with the four
masones in Galmmiss for digging down from the floor
of the litil pantry off the Lobbis a closet designed within
the charterhouse there, for wch I am to give them 50 lib.
scotts and four bolls meall."

The work of constructing this closet or small chamber
was more serious than the Earl had contemplated.
Judging from similar chambers which he caused to be
made at his other residence at Castle Lyon (now Castle
Huntly) in the Carse of Gowrie, the closet was probably
dug out of the thickness of the wall.

On July 25th there is another reference to this closet,
which shows that its construction was an arduous undertaking : " I did add to the work before mentioned of a
closet in my charterhouse severall things of a considerable
trouble, as the digging thorrow passages from the new
work to the old, and thorrow that closet againe so that
as now I have the access off on flour [one floor] from the
east quarter of the house of Glammis to the west syde

fo the house thorrow the low hall, and am to pay the masones, because of the uncertainty yrof dayes wages, and just so to the wright and plasterer."

From these precise entries it becomes evident that in 1684 the first Earl of Strathmore caused a secret chamber or closet to be constructed, with an entrance from the charter-room. This was by no means an unusual thing, for many noble Scottish families have had frequent occasion to conceal documents that would have compromised them in times of war, and even a charter-room might not have been secure against the searches by enemies. The first Lord Strathmore himself was deeply implicated in a Jacobite plot with the Earls of Southesk and Callander in 1689; and though he afterwards became reconciled to William the Third, it would have been useful for him to have a secure hiding-place for treasonable papers. Several of his descendants were concerned in the risings of 1715 and 1745, and a chamber of this kind would be useful either to secrete documents or to afford shelter to a fugitive. By that time, it is urged, the masons who had constructed the secret chamber thirty years before would have passed away, and the lingering rumours of its existence would be linked in the popular mind with the "wicked" Earl. For obvious reasons, it is pointed out, the successive Earls of Strathmore would not seek to dispel this superstition, and thus the simple " closet designed within the charter-room " has been elevated to the dignity of a haunted chamber.

Such are the matter-of-fact deductions drawn from the unromantic entries in the *Book of Record* ; but they do not, it will at once be seen, meet and controvert the tales of magic and terror at all points.

CHAPTER IX

FAMILY CURSES (*continued*)

Thomas the Rhymer and the Erskines, Earls of Mar—The Brahan Seer and the Seaforths.

THE hereditary curse upon the Erskines, Earls of Mar, is a striking example of these ancient family dooms. According to the historians of their house, the title of Earl of Mar goes back to immemorial antiquity, and was originally the Pictish dignity of " Maormor," inferior only to that of King. There was a Marmor (or Mormaer as it is sometimes written) of Mar at the Battle of Clontarf, in 1014 ; and the present Earl of Mar is reckoned the thirty-third in descent from the chieftain who flourished in 1065.

There seems to have been quite a number of Marmors ; those of Fife, Moray, Ross, Athole, Sutherland and Argyle, among others, long ago converted into Dukedoms and Earldoms. In every case the original Gaelic families holding those ancient distinctions have become extinct, and the existing Earldom of Mar, although traced back to 1404 and connected with the original holders, is associated with them only by a very slender thread, on the female side.

The origin of the Erskine family name is the subject of an ancient legend which narrates the gory doings of a noble Scot in the reign of Malcolm the Second. This person appears to have gone into the Battle of Murthill without a name, and, fighting fiercely for his King and country, against invading Danes, to then and there have earned one. He is said to have seized a Danish chief named Enrique, or Hendrik, and to have cut off his head ; exclaiming, as, holding the head in one hand and his bloody dagger in the other, he approached the

King, " Eriskene," *i.e.* " On the dagger " ; and remarking
that he intended to do even better in future. The King
thereupon, according to this wonderful story, gave him
his Gaelic name of Eriskene and at the same time supplied
him with a French motto, " *Je Pense Plus*," a polyglot
performance that at once shakes our belief in the present
form of the story, which, like many another family
legend, has doubtless been generally evolved from some
slight basis of fact. The crest of the Earls of Mar still
shows a hand grasping a dagger, or rather a scimitar,
and their motto is the English version of the original
French, " I think the more."

The descent of the Earldom, and the arbitrary confiscation of the title rightly belonging to Robert, Lord
Erskine (properly fifteenth Earl Mar), by James the Third
of Scotland, are involved genealogical matters only
profitably to be followed by the professed genealogist ;
but, briefly, the rightful owners of the Earldom only
came to their own again after having been deprived of it
for over a century. The honours were restored to John,
Lord Erskine, who in 1565 succeeded as twentieth Earl
of Mar, and no misfortune would appear to have befallen
his descendants until one hundred and fifty years later.
But then, when the family curse began to work, it was
thorough, as we shall presently show. In the several
instances of the hereditary curses narrated in this volume
it is frequently to be noticed that the doomed families
were for generations lulled into a sense of false security
by this tardiness in operation, but that when the pent-up
doom began to operate it was resistless and complete.

The prophecy foreshadowing the varied fortunes of
the Erskines, Earls of Mar, is ascribed to two distinct
persons, who flourished at periods three hundred years
apart. The elder seer is said to have been that famous
thirteenth-century minstrel, Thomas the Rhymer, the
Scottish Merlin, known also as Thomas of Learmount,
and Thomas of Ercildoune (Earlston, near Melrose).
The other was the Abbot of Cambuskenneth, deprived of
his office by the Regent of Scotland, the Earl of Mar,
and his Abbey destroyed.

The Curse of Alloa Tower, as this warning of doom

was commonly known, was not—at any rate in its later incidents—one of those *ex post facto* " prophecies " that are more than sufficiently in evidence in these tales of the marvellous. The legend was current, not only by word of mouth, but in print, long before the final incidents in it became enacted, and its good faith is, in so far at least, beyond suspicion.

" Proud Chief of Mar : Thou shalt be raised still higher, until thou sittest in the place of the King. Thou shalt rule and destroy, and they work shall be called after thy name ; but thy work shall be the emblem of thy house, and shall teach mankind that he who cruelly and haughtily raiseth himself upon the ruins of the holy cannot prosper. Thy work shall be cursed and shall never be finished. But thou shalt have riches and greatness, and shalt be true to thy Sovereign, and shalt raise his banner in the field of blood. Then, when thou seemest to be highest—when thy power is mightiest, then shalt come thy fall ; low shalt be thy head amongst the nobles of thy people. Deep shall be thy moan among the children of dool. Thy lands shall be given to the stranger, and thy titles shall lie amongst the dead. The branch that springs from thee shall see his dwelling burnt, in which a king was nursed,—his wife a sacrifice in that same flame ; his children numerous, but of little honour ; and three born and grown who shall never see the light. Yet shall thine ancient tower stand ; for the brave and the true cannot be wholly forsaken. Thou, proud head and daggered hand, must dree thy weird until horses shall be stabled in thy hall, and a weaver shall throw his shuttle in thy chamber of state. Thine ancient tower—a woman's dower—shall be a ruin and a beacon, until an ash sapling shall spring from its topmost stone. Then shall thy sorrows be ended, and the sunshine of royalty beam on thee once more. Thine honours shall be restored : the kiss of peace shall be given to thy Countess, though she seek it not, and the days of peace shall return to thee and thine. The line of Mar shall be broken ; but not until its honours are doubled, and its doom is ended."

The personage indicated in the prophecy as " Proud

chief " was the restored Earl of 1565 ; and the prophecy itself would thus seem, by internal evidence, to be that of the incensed and ruined Abbot of Cambuskenneth, rather than of the thirteenth-century Thomas the Rhymer. There is too much passion in the diction of this " family curse " upon the descendants of " he who cruelly and haughtily raiseth himself upon the ruins of the holy " for it to be the work of a remote clairvoyant bard not stated to have been in any way injured by the thirteenth-century Earl.

Let us follow the successive clauses of the curse and its fulfilment.

" Thou shalt be raised still higher," it began ; and the twentieth Earl became Regent of Scotland during the minority of James the Sixth, and thus little less important than the King himself.

" Thy work shall be called after thy name. . . . Thy work shall be cursed, and shall never be finished." This indicates the building of a magnificent palace by the Earl, at Stirling : a project that he began with stones from the demolished Abbey, but which neither he nor any of his descendants completed. This fragment remains and is still, as ever, known as " Mar's Work." It is a singular building, supposed to be the finest example of Renaissance architecture in Scotland, and is adorned —if that be quite the word—with grotesque sculptures and moral maxims, set forth in distressing spelling, such as :

THE MOIR I STAND ON OPPIN HITHT
MY FAVLTIS MOIR SUBIECT AR TO SITHT.

I PRAY AL LVIKARIS ON THIS BIGING
WITH GENTIL E TO GIF THAIR IUGING.

I SAY SPEIK FORTH AND SPAIR NOTHT
CONSIDDIR VEIL AND CAIR NOTHT.

The prophecy then becomes a little vague, after the manner of all prophecies that ever were, from those in the Bible down to Nixon and Old Moore. It goes on to declare that " thou shalt be true to thy Sovereign, and shalt raise his banner in the field of blood." Unless

the prophet is read as referring to the house of Mar
in general, he was here very wide of the mark, for it
was the great-great-grandson of the Regent who in
1715 joined the rebellion in aid of the Old Pretender,
and raised his banner on the bloody field of Sheriffmuir.

" Then shalt come thy fall ; low shall be thy head
amongst the nobles of thy people. . . . Thy lands
shall be given to the stranger, and thy titles shall lie
amongst the dead." This refers to the forfeiture and
confiscation of the rebel Earl's title and estates, after
the failure of the rebellion ; when his lands were sold
and acquired by the Earl of Fife.

" The branch that springs from thee shall see his
dwelling burnt, in which a king was nursed,—his wife
a sacrifice in that same flame ; his children numerous,
but of little honour ; and three born and grown who
shall never see the light." This clause found its fulfilment in the time of the rebel Earl's grandson, John
Francis Erskine, resident in 1801 at the ancient family
residence of Alloa Tower, where James the Sixth, as
an infant, had been nursed. A careless servant leaving
a candle too near a bed, the place was soon in a blaze,
and Mrs. Erskine was so severely burnt that she died
of her injuries. There were three children, among a
numerous family, born blind, who remained so all their
long lives.

" Horses shall be stabled in thy hall, and a weaver
shall throw his shuttle in thy chamber of state. Thine
ancient tower—a woman's dower—shall be a ruin and
a beacon, until an ash sapling shall spring from its topmost stone." This was fulfilled in the early years of
the nineteenth century, during the alarm of a French
invasion, when all the regular and yeomanry cavalry of
the district were drafted into Alloa and a troop was
billeted in the old tower, the horses being stabled in
the once lordly hall. Following this, somewhere about
1810, a party of curious visitors found a weaver who
had been evicted from a house in Alloa town, for non-
payment of rent, established there, and plying his trade
in the old chamber of state ; and between 1815 and

1820, an ash sapling grew and flourished in the topmost
stone of the building.

That was the final portent; and many there were
who wondered if the " sunshine of royalty " would, as
predicted, beam on the unfortunate family once more.
That, too, came to pass; for in 1822 George the Fourth,
visiting Scotland, sought out those who had suffered in
the Stuart cause and restored many to their ancient
honours. Among them was Erskine of Mar, grandson
of the Earl who had figured in the rebellion. Great

" MAR'S WORK," STIRLING

were the rejoicings in Alloa when the title was restored.
Local poets celebrated the occasion in verse, and told
how Mr. Erskine was invested with the honours of the
Earldom:

> They placed a crown upon his head,
>   And on his breast a star, man;
> And our gude King has said that hence
>   We'll ca' him Earl of Mar, man.

His wife, although never presented at Court, in after
years met Queen Victoria by chance in Stirling Castle.
The Queen gave her the unsought " kiss of peace "

ALLOA TOWER

mentioned in the prophecy. The honours of the house
were doubled by grandsons of this restored Earl being
both Earls, one becoming Earl of Kellie. Then the
" line of Mar " was broken, for the family name of the
Earls of Mar became, in the descent of the title in the
female line, " Goodeve-Erskine."

Alloa Tower still stands. It is an ancient royal
stronghold, built about 1223, and exchanged in 1365 by
David the Second, King of Scotland, for the estates of
Strathgartney, Perthshire. It rises, stern and very
little ornamented in any part, to a height of eighty-nine
feet, and its walls are eleven feet thick. The growth of
the busy town of Alloa, which takes its name from the
ancient Gaelic words *Ath Luath*, the " swift ford," on
the river Forth, has robbed the surroundings of their
old-time picturesqueness, just as the growth of London
around the Tower has surrounded that ancient keep
with the commonplace ; but the old lair of the Earls of
Mar still stands amid the trees of the Glebe Park, the
last relics of ancient conditions. It has long been
uninhabited.

If you look upon the map of southern Scotland—
that region of Roxburghshire famous as the " Scott
Country "—Melrose is seen standing out prominently
where the Ettrick Water and the Tweed and the Allan
Water join their several streams and so go in company
down their long journey to the sea.

Melrose lies at the foot of the Eildon Hills, those
singular mountains whose triple peaks caused the Romans
to give them the name of " Trimontium." The old-
time monks loved such a situation as that in which
you will find the ancient little town of Melrose—in a
comfortable hollow—where, as the sardonic Byron said,
they could " shelter their devotions from the winds."
Abbotsford, the Gothic home built for himself by Sir
Walter Scott, lies only three miles away, and about the
same distance, east of Melrose, is the ancient mansion
of Bemersyde, among the hills.

Bemersyde holds much interest for us at the present
juncture of public affairs, for it has belonged ever since
the middle of the twelfth century to the Haig family.

General Sir Douglas Haig, created Earl Haig, Viscount Dawick, and Baron Haig of Bemersyde, in 1919, is now the owner, the property having been purchased and presented to him by public subscription.

There has ever been much interest in the holding of Bemersyde by this ancient race, for mansion and family were made the subject of a prophecy by a famous Scottish seer and clairvoyant long ago. "Thomas the Rhymer," the first Scottish poet, who was born at Ercildoune and died about 1286, was one of those prophets whose usual form was cursings and revilings and prophecies of disaster, but when he considered the Haigs he was in a mood to bless. This is what he said of them :

> " Tide what e'er betyde,
> Haig shall be Haig of Bemersyde."

There are many slightly different verbal versions of this, but the sense is the same. Those many versions derive from the fact that in those times few could read, and so, passing from mouth to mouth, there happened these different forms. I say it with all deference, but I think that, although Thomas could rhyme, he himself could not write any more than his own name. At any rate, he uttered this saying more than seven hundred years ago, and there are still Haigs of Bemersyde.

The Haigs of Bemersyde are the most ancient family in that region, and their mansion, the older part of which is an ancient Border peel-tower, stands on an elevated, rocky site, overhanging one of the most beautiful reaches of the Tweed, swiftly running between its bordering woods of oak and birch. The tower, on this rocky bluff, is, with its high-pitched roof and corbie-stepped gables, a building of the second half of the sixteenth century, remodelled as to its upper part in or about 1690. Antiquaries have been indignant that a small building should have been added to the east end, about 1796, and more indignant at the addition of a large wing to the west, in 1859 : the Haigs of those periods having, in this view, unreasonably desired a little more comfort than that which sufficed their sixteenth-century ancestors in their cold, defensible tower.

The earliest known of the Haigs was one who was sometimes written of in old documents as " De Haga,' and again as " Petrus de Hage." He is first heard of

BEMERSYDE, BEFORE RECENT ALTERATIONS

as witness to a deed of about 1162–1166. They were possibly a Norman family, from the neighbourhood of " La Hague," a cape in the peninsula of the Cotentin.

THE RHYMER STONE ON A WALL OF THE OLD PARISH CHURCH
AT EARLSTON

A huge dyke, or earthwork, four miles long, the " Hague-dike," runs across, near Beaumont town.

It is the second Peter de Haga, about 1200–1228, who is the first of the family identified with Bemersyde.

Thomas the Rhymer is supposed to have spoken his prophecy to the fifth of the Haigs—Sir John de Haga, 1280–1326—after the death of King Alexander the Third of Scotland, when everything seemed to be melting away in national disaster : the sense of the saying being that everything else Scottish might go into the melting-pot, but that the Haigs should still endure amid the surrounding wreck.

This is very comforting.

The first of the family to adopt the modern spelling was Sir Andrew Haig, the ninth of Bemersyde, 1388–1414.

And thus their race came down through the centuries, until at last it seemed almost as if the Rhymer's saying would prove false : James Haig, who died in 1854, being succeeded by his three sisters, Barbara, Sophia, and Mary, who had no direct heirs. However, they disposed of Bemersyde in 1878 to another Haig, their cousin, Lieutenant-Colonel Arthur Balfour Haig, and thus a new line of the old stock began.

Earlston, on the Leader Water, also about three miles from Melrose, is a place with a broad, empty-looking street. Its name is an entirely unauthorised corruption, and has nothing to do with earls, being properly " Ercildoune," which itself is a corruption of " Arcioldun," meaning " the look-out hill." Outside the village still stands the ruined, ivy-clad " Rhymer's Tower," which is supposed to have been the home of " True Thomas," the Rhymer. On a wall of the parish church also may still be seen the rough inscription, grotesquely spelt :

> " AULD : RYMR : RACE
> LYEES : IN : THIS PLACE."

That was a cruel fate that banished the Earls of Moray from their home at Darnaway Castle. All save the lord of Darnaway might safely repair thither, but when the Earl himself came to his great red stone castle on the Findhorn, his doom was pronounced. So sure as he came to his seat, he died ; so for many years the mansion that was built on to the ancient castle remained unoccupied. Now, however, the weird is dreed, and my lord may safely come to Forres and Darnaway.

The enduring malignance of the saints is not a very saintly attribute. " To err is human, to forgive divine " ; but when, somewhere away back in the seventh century, the then owner of Tilliecoultry, near Alloa, killed the favourite ram of St. Serf, the saint launched upon Tilliecoultry the curse that no heir born to the estate should ever come into possession. Whether the ban has been meticulously fulfilled, it would be difficult to say ; but within two hundred years the estate successively came into the hands of fourteen different families.

The Seaforth curse is one of the most dramatic of these ancient tales of dread. It seems that in the time of Charles the Second there dwelt an eccentric clairvoyant, one Coinneach Odhar Fiosaiche, *alias* the Brahan Seer, *alias* the Warlock of the Glen, at Strathpeffer, hard by the Earl of Seaforth's hideous castle of Brahan, near unto Dingwall town. He was a mystical native of the Western Islands, born at Baile-na-Cille, Uig, and greatly respected, and perhaps even more greatly feared, as a seer. Like all the brotherhood of seers, in all times and in all countries, the things he saw were rarely to the credit, and seldom calculated to add to the happiness, of those who, through him, looked into what was happening elsewhere, or what was to happen in the future. The wonder therefore remains that these prophets of woe and seers of discreditable and unpleasant things in remote places were so frequently consulted by people about their own affairs. It could be better understood if they had been resorted to for the purpose of learning the ills that were to afflict other people.

The Brahan Seer was a mere peasant, a hind in the employ of the Seaforths of Brahan ; but he had a full measure of those supernatural qualities of divination of which the Celtic races seem to have almost the monopoly. The amazing legends of his magical powers, and of the white divining stone with a hole in it, that was presented to him by beings not of this world, are still current in and around Dingwall and Brahan, and fulfilments of many of his still unfulfilled prophecies are looked forward to by the people with complete faith in their surely coming to pass, and with no little dread

BRAHAN CASTLE

in the prospect. Their faith is the natural outcome
of many of his foreshadowings of the future having
already been proved correct ; and their dread of those
yet to be is natural enough when it is said that the
predictions are chiefly those of disasters and bloody
wars. Among the calamities to come is that connected
with a standing stone, called in the Gaelic " Clach an
t-Seasardh," on Windhill, Beauly. Coinneach prophesied
that when a mountain-ash should grow out of the walls
of Fairburn Tower, and should grow large enough to
form a cart-axle, the time would be at hand for the
raven to drink from the top of Clach an t-Seasardh
its fill of blood of the Mackenzies, for three successive
days ; when the Mackenzies should be so reduced in
numbers that the sole remnant of them would be able
to cross over to Ireland (whence they had come originally)
in an open boat. This is not looked forward to, it may
well be imagined, with any pleasurable anticipation—
not, at any rate, by the Mackenzies. The time, however,
should be at hand, for the mountain-ash long since grew
from the walls of Fairburn Tower, as foretold.

Coinneach was in life, and is in death, as disturbing
to peace of mind as a modern penny newspaper, and it
is to be remembered that he is no myth, like Mother
Shipton, but a well-ascertained person, who died less than
two hundred and fifty years ago, and many of whose say-
ings were taken down from his mouth and preserved in
writing. Among many other correct prognostications, he
foretold the making of the Caledonian Canal, surveyed a
hundred years after his death ; but his principal achieve-
ment is the Seaforth Curse, which the Seaforths owed to
the mistaken cruelty of one of his clients, the Countess
of Seaforth. It is the merest folly to provoke a seer.

There are several versions of this affair, varying
in details, but agreeing in the main issue. It seems
that she summoned the warlock to Brahan Castle, to
amuse a large company she was entertaining, in the
absence of the Earl, travelling abroad ; and among the
feats of clairvoyance she asked the Seer to perform was
that of telling herself and her guests what her husband
was doing at that moment. This is always unwise ;

and in this instance Coinneach Odhar narrated a simple
tale which, if it amused the guests, had the effect of
enraging the Countess. He had been urgently pressed
to reveal the Earl's doings ; and, applying his divining
stone to his eye, had gazed earnestly into it, and merely
remarked that his lordship was pleasantly occupied and
in no hurry to return. But that was not sufficient. He
was reluctantly compelled to narrate what he saw, and
told how he perceived the Earl in Paris, on his knees before
a fair lady, his arm round her waist and her hand to his
lips. " *Quand on est à Paris* "—as the poet remarks.

The Countess violently abused the man, who, after
all, had simply obeyed instructions. " You have spoken
ill of dignities," she stormed, " you have maligned the
mighty of the land, have defamed a mighty chief in
midst of his vassals," and so forth, and presently ordered
him forth for instant execution.

It is quite evident that Lady Seaforth was no lady,
except in the conventional sense ; and it is also, when
you come to coldly consider it, not à little astonishing
that in Scotland, in the comparatively settled times of
Charles the Second, even so mighty a person as a Countess
could order off any person to execution, on her own
motion ; and see it done, too—for the Seer was properly
done to death. You cannot, however, help thinking that
his clairvoyance was—what shall we say ?—incomplete,
and that, if he had seen a little more clearly, he would
have refused this ill-omened invitation to the Castle ; or,
at the very least of it, would have described the absent
Earl as engaged in his devotions, or something innocent.
For warlocks die no more willingly than other men.

We must do the guests at Brahan Castle the merest
justice, and tell how, shocked at the violence of Lady
Seaforth's behaviour, they endeavoured to save the
unfortunate man. With no avail ; but, as he was being
led forth to his doom, he turned and, inspired by the
situation with the spirit of prophecy, foretold the doom
of the Seaforth posterity :

" I see far into the future, and I read there the doom
of my oppressor. The long-descended line of Seaforth
will, or ever many generations have passed, end in

extinction and sorrow. I see a Caber Feidh, the last of his house, both deaf and dumb. He will be the father of four fair sons, all of whom he will follow to the tomb. He will live bowed with care, and will die mourning, knowing, as he will know, that the honours of his line are to be extinguished for ever, and that no chief of the Mackenzies shall bear rule at Brahan or Kintail. Lamenting over the last and most promising of his sons, he himself shall sink into the grave, and the remnant of his possessions shall be inherited by a white-coifed lassie from the East, and she is to kill her sister. And as a sign by which it may be known that these things are coming to pass, there shall be four great lairds in the days of the last deaf-and-dumb Seaforth—Gairloch, Chisholm, Grant, and Raasay—of whom one shall be buck-toothed, another hare-lipped, another half-witted, and the fourth a stammerer. These shall be the allies and neighbours of the last Seaforth ; and when he looks round him and sees them, he may know that his sons are doomed to death, that his broad lands shall pass away to a stranger, and that his race shall come to an end."

The story has been sown with additional marvels. In one account we are told that Coinneach was hanged, and in another that he was burnt, with the approval of the Church, for witchcraft, being plunged head downwards in a barrel of molten tar, on the seashore at Chanonry Point, near Fortrose, quite thirteen miles away, where a flat stone, now covered with sand, in the neighbourhood of the lighthouse, is said to mark the spot.

The Countess—no lady, as we have already remarked —not content with summarily packing him off for execution, is said to have taunted him with the prospect of becoming the property of the Prince of Darkness in the next world ; whereupon he declared that when he died, a raven and a dove would be seen circling in the air, and would descend simultaneously upon his ashes. If the raven were to alight first, the words of his persecutor were correct ; but if the dove were first, his hope of salvation was well founded.

The birds appeared, as he had predicted, and the dove was first to alight.

THE LAST OF THE SEAFORTHS

Legends tell that the Seer flung away his magic stone in a puddle formed by the impression of a cow's hoof in the road, and that the water spread and hid the stone, and continued to spread until it formed Loch Ussie. And whosoever shall find that stone will succeed to the knowledge of the future once possessed by Coinneach.

It is rather unfortunate for the verisimilitude of this story that Loch Ussie is considerably over a mile from Brahan Castle, in the opposite direction from the way to the scene of his execution on the shore, and the Loch itself is rather large for an exaggerated puddle, being nearly three-quarters of a mile across.

All the disasters foretold by Coinneach befell the Seaforths, in the fullness of time, down to the minutest details; but we have to observe that, if this were revenge, or retribution, it simply missed its mark, and punished the wrong people. The old, unjust law that the children shall suffer for the sins of the fathers, of course. It was the wife of the third Earl who brought down this malison upon unborn generations. We do not hear that *she* suffered in any way for hanging the Seer ; and little enough can it matter to know that at some future time your remote descendants are to pay, at usury, for your misdeeds.

It was, in short, not until 1754—when more than seventy summers had flown (to speak in the language of romantic writers)—that the curse began to unfold itself. It is true that the Earldom, in default of direct heirs under the patent, became extinct ; but such lapses are infinitely more common than full-fledged curses in the annals of the Peerage. The junior Mackenzies, if they did not bear the title, at least kept the property—which, after all, is the chief thing ; for what is a title without an acre or a stiver to support it ? Why, even a Chicago pork-packer's daughter is nowadays beginning to feel a contempt for such unqualified emptiness.

And presently the junior line acquired a title also. They became Barons Seaforth, and Barons Mackenzie of Kintail, in 1797, in the person of Francis Mackenzie Humberston. But with him, born in 1754, the Seaforth doom was accomplished. He was that chief of the prophecy who was to be born deaf and dumb. The prophecy is a little loose here, for Mackenzie was not precisely born in that lamentable condition, but was at the age of twelve rendered permanently deaf by scarlet fever, and for a time only deprived of speech. That, however, is a slight inaccuracy to which even the most finished and cold-drawn of curses are liable.

Mackenzie looks, in his portrait, a fine robust fellow, and indeed seems to have been so. He is notable as having, in 1793, raised the 78th Regiment of Foot, the Ross-shire Buffs, now and long known after him as the Seaforth Highlanders. The family curse, already familiar in tradition, worked itself out only too completely in his time, before the eyes of expectant neighbours, among whom were the buck-toothed Sir Hector Mackenzie, of Gairloch, the hare-lipped Chisholm, the half-witted Grant, and the stammering MacLeod of Raasey.

The curse was a matter of common knowledge before its fulfilment was accomplished. Thus, Sir Walter Scott is found writing to his friend Morritt : " I do fear the accomplishment of the prophecy that when there should be a deaf and dumb Caber Feidh* the house was to fall."

The experiences of the unhappy Mackenzie were unutterably sad. He had four sons, as foretold. One died an infant, but the others grew to manhood. They all, however, died before their father, who, bereaved, and ruined partly by his own extravagance and in part by inevitable disasters, sank into the grave, heart-broken, in 1815. The title again became extinct, Kintail passed from his race, and the " white-coifed lassie from the East " who was to kill her sister was his eldest daughter Mary who, coming from India as the widow of Admiral Sir Samuel Hood, inherited the remnant of her father's lands, and was present with her sister in a pony-carriage when the ponies ran away and, pulling beyond her strength, overturned the carriage ; with the result that Miss Mackenzie was killed.

Lady Hood married again, and with her the Seaforth property was finally dispersed.

Among those who testified to having been acquainted with the prophecy before its fulfilment was Davison of

* " Caber Feidh " : Gaelic for " stag-head " ; in allusion to the family crest.

Tulloch, Lord-Lieutenant of Ross-shire. Writing to Mr.
Alexander Mackenzie, on May 21st, 1878, he said :
" Many of these prophecies I heard upwards of seventy
years ago, when many of them were not fulfilled : such
as the last Lord Seaforth surviving his sons, and Mrs.
Stewart Mackenzie's accident near Brahan, by which
Miss Caroline Mackenzie was killed."

There has been of late years a revival of the Seaforth
title, and it has again lapsed. Colonel Francis Humberston Stewart-Mackenzie was in 1921 created Baron
Seaforth of Brahan, at the age of seventy-six. He was
a distinguished soldier, having served in the Afghan War,
under Lord Roberts, and so efficiently that he was twice
mentioned in despatches. He married the daughter of
Edward Steinkopff, of 47, Berkeley Square, and sometime proprietor of the *St. James's Gazette*. Lord Seaforth
took his seat in the House of Lords wearing the robes of
his great-grandfather, who was the subject of the prophecy. The late Lord Seaforth died March 2nd, 1923,
and the title again is extinct.

The death in October, 1918, of their only son and only
child is a crushing blow to The Mackintosh of Mackintosh
and Mrs. Mackintosh, and reminds Scots folk painfully of
that curse of Moy which is the theme of a ballad in Scott's
" Minstrelsy." The Clan Chattan (of which The Mackintosh
is head) and the Clan Grant were at war, and a Mackintosh
of Moy treacherously murdered the father and the lover of
a girl of the rival house, and forced her to look upon their
mutilated bodies. For this she entreated heaven that—

> " Never the son of a Chief of Moy
> Might live to protect his father's age,
> Or close in peace his dying eye
> Or gather his gloomy heritage."

And the curse has worked to some extent throughout the
centuries, if not to the full extent of her desire. It is of
melancholy interest to remember that The Mackintosh
succeeded a brother who married the eldest Miss Graham
of Netherby and died a few months later before his child
was born. This proved to be a girl (later the wife of Sir
Godfrey Baring), and Mrs. Mackintosh in course of time
became the Lady Verulam through a second marriage.

CHAPTER X

FAMILY CURSES—(*continued*)

The Dalrymples, Earls of Stair—The Tichborne Family—The
Lambton Worm.

THE Dalrymples, Earls of Stair, were long thought to be
under a ban earned by the first Earl who, when Master
of Stair, and Secretary of State for Scotland under William
the Third, was one of those primarily responsible for the
infamous Massacre of Glencoe, whereby, on February 13th,
1692, thirty-eight members of the Macdonald clan were
shot down in cold blood by the soldiery, acting under the
peremptory orders of the Secretary. The wild Gaelic
curse of Jean Macdonald upon the authors of this atrocity
was translated as follows :

> May no prosperity or good fortune,
> May no blessing nor length of days
> Be the portion of the black murderers
> Who have made me poor and miserable.
> May their sleep by night be oft disturbed and unrefreshing ;
> May fear and terror haunt their pillows ;
> May their wives ever prove barren,
> And my thousand curses still alone attend them.

Dalrymple, although roughly handled by the Commission of 1695, which was appointed to inquire into his
part in the affair, and obliged by the force of public
opinion to resign office, was created an Earl in the reign
of Queen Anne. His eldest son was accidentally killed
when a boy, by being shot with a pistol handled by a
younger brother. The second Earl had no sons, and was
succeeded by a nephew ; who in turn was succeeded by
his brother ; who in his turn was followed by a cousin,
the fifth Earl. He handed on the title to his son, the
sixth and last of his line, who died in 1821 ; the Earldom
then devolving upon a remote branch of the family,

perhaps not regarded as responsible by even a thorough-going Gaelic curse.

It used to be said that a curse was laid upon the family : that no Stair should have three sons again. This happened to come true for eight generations, until the birth of the Hon. Hew Hamilton Dalrymple, third son of the tenth Earl. Breaking the spell, he came in for the whole of the property left to accumulate by the first Earl of Stair for the next son of his house who should have two elder brothers. The eleventh Earl of Stair, Sir John Hew North Gustave Henry Hamilton Dalrymple, Baron Newliston, Glenluce and Stranraer, in Scotland, and Baron Oxenfoord, Midlothian, in the peerage of the United Kingdom, died December 5th, 1914, and was succeeded by his son, the present Earl.

The remarkable story of the Tichborne family is another instance of the immortality of tradition and the belief in family legends. It all arose out of the Tichborne Dole. It should, however, be premised that the Tichbornes, although they have not risen beyond the condition of Baronets (" Barts. of the B.K." as the famous Claimant would say), are among the few genuinely ancient families of England who can trace their descent, with the Cruwys and the Coplestones, back to Anglo-Saxon times, and remain to this day on the identical broad acres whence they derive their name. The Tichbornes were seated, long before the Conqueror came a-conquering, on their land at Tichborne, near Alresford, in Hampshire, through which the immemorial " Ticceburn " of Anglo-Saxon times yet flows. They were knights, centuries before the Hogwards (or pig-keepers) became Howards and Earls and Dukes ; and were great landed proprietors long before the original John-at-town's-end left the last house of his particular town (wherever that was) and became Townshend, and commenced climbing up the social ladder that led his descendants into a Marquisate, and into quaint marriages and all kinds of odd predicaments.

It was in the reign of Henry the First that the circumstances took place out of which the Tichborne tradition arose. The Sir Roger Tichborne of that time married one Mabella, or Isabella, heiress to lands in the Isle of

Wight, and they lived, happily, we may suppose, many years. The only thing that would seem in any way to have troubled that good knight was the indiscriminate charity to which his lady was prone. After a long life, she drew at last to her end, and lay upon her death-bed. There she prayed her husband to keep her memory green in all that country-side by setting apart so much land as would suffice to establish a dole of bread for all comers to the gates of Tichborne on every Lady Day.

Sir Roger acted in much the manner of the famous Earl Leofric of Coventry, insisting on what seemed an impossible feat as a condition to granting the request. What stony-hearted men those antique husbands were !

In this case, Sir Roger took a blazing brand from the hearth and, looking with saturnine humour at the dying woman, promised her as much land as she could walk over while it continued burning. To his annoyance, we may safely presume, she accepted his challenge and, summoning attendants, caused herself to be carried out into the open. There she began creeping round in a large circle on hands and knees, and by the time the brand had expired in a final splutter, had in this manner enclosed no fewer than twenty-three acres. The land is known as " The Crawls " to this day.

Carried to her bed again, after this supreme effort, the Lady Isabella composed herself to die, warning all, with her last breath, that so long as the Dole thus secured was annually distributed, and no longer, the Tichbornes would prosper ; but should the charity be discontinued the fortunes of the house would fail, the name of Tichborne would be changed, and the family would become extinct. As a sign by which these disasters might surely be looked for, there would be born a generation of seven sons, followed by one of seven daughters.

The Dole thus established continued for many centuries to be distributed according to the Lady Isabella's directions ; for the penalty pronounced by her upon its lapsing seemed a very real contingency to generations that had not yet learned to discredit the force of powers they could not see, and to scoff at everything not material. From near and far on every succeeding Lady Day crowds

TICHBORNE HOUSE

came to partake of the famous Dole, which consisted of
1,900 small loaves. This annual occasion became the
excuse for an uproarious merrymaking, in the nature of
a fair, which was the real attraction : for it is not to
be supposed that even the poorest would journey long
distances for the sake of a penny loaf.

More than six hundred years had passed when at
length, towards the middle of the eighteenth century,
this assemblage of undesirables became such a nuisance
that representations were made to the family that a stop
ought to be put to these scenes of low revelry ; and at
length, in 1796, the then Sir Henry Tichborne discontinued
the time-honoured distribution ; substituting in its stead
gifts of equal value, given through the agency of the
Church to the necessitous poor of the parish. Earlier
generations would have hesitated thus to disobey the
positive injunctions of the Lady Isabella ; but that was
a material age, and took little count of traditions ; and
so Sir Henry Tichborne dared greatly. If anyone had
given the matter a thought, it would have been only to
declare how unlikely it was that the Tichborne family
should be in danger of extinction, for Sir Henry had a
numerous family. But when the number was increased
to seven, there were ominous shakings of heads at the
coincidence ; and something like panic when in the next
generation there was a family of seven daughters. At
the same time, despite these numerous sons, there was
such a remarkable failure of heirs that four of Sir Henry
Tichborne's sons succeeded in turn to the title and
estates. Of these, the second, Sir Edward Tichborne,
ninth Baronet, had in earlier years, before there had been
any prospect of his inheriting the family honours, assumed,
in addition to his own name, that of Doughty, under the
terms of the will of Miss Doughty, a distant relative, who
bequeathed her property to him on that condition.

Thus in his time the family name may be said to have
been changed, within the meaning of the prophecy.

Sir Edward was succeeded by his brother James, as
tenth Baronet, the only one of the seven sons of Sir
Henry Tichborne who left a male heir. Sir James was
father of two sons, of whom the elder, Roger, was the

cause of more trouble than befalls the generality of families. Through his disappearance originated the famous " Tichborne Case."

Roger Charles Doughty-Tichborne, the youthful heir, disappointed in love, determined to ease his sorrows by foreign travel and adventure. Accordingly, in January, 1852, he made a will, placed it in a sealed packet, and, after visiting his father and mother in Paris, sailed away for Valparaiso. Thence he wrote numerous letters, and in the last announced his intention of returning home, in a sailing-vessel, the *Bella*. This ship was presumed lost, for she never was again heard of ; nor was Roger Tichborne. All, except Lady Tichborne, were at last convinced that Roger was drowned ; but she refused to believe it, and for many years continued to advertise for news of him. Meanwhile, his younger brother, Alfred, had succeeded to the title and estates, as a matter of course, in 1866, on the decease of his father.

The advertisements for news of the missing Sir Roger Tichborne at last bore fruit. Roger was what commercial people used to style a " felt want " ; and as the want was so insistent, it was duly supplied by a claimant from Australia, who arrived in England, on the invitation and at the expense of the widowed Lady Tichborne, and was recognised by her ; although by no one else. The Claimant (as afterwards he became known, with a capital C, in the course of years of legal proceedings) was a man of massive proportions and so stout that he weighed some thirty stone.

The trustees of the Tichborne estates did not share in Lady Tichborne's recognition of the stranger, and " the Claimant " thereupon brought an action to gain possession.

On the 103rd day of the trial the Claimant elected to be non-suited. The presiding judge committed him to prison for perjury. Subsequently he was brought to trial on this charge. The hearing lasted from May, 1873, till February, 1874. The prisoner, in reality Arthur Orton, son of a butcher in Wapping, was sentenced to fourteen years' penal servitude.

The two trials involved a cost of £200,000, of which about half fell on the Tichborne estates. Arthur Orton died in 1898, having in 1895 admitted his identity, and

then retracted the admission. He was buried with a
brass plate claiming that he was " Sir Roger Charles
Doughty-Tichboure, 11th Baronet." It was a curious
circumstance, during the course of the two trials, not
only that a large number of people of position believed
in " the Claimant," some supporting his cause with
money ; but also that—for some obscure reasoning—the
Radical section of the British public very extensively
were convinced that a poor man was being " done out of
his rights " ; and the case became mixed up with politics,
chiefly through the eccentricities of " the Claimant's "
counsel, Dr. Kenealy.

It was remarked, years afterwards, when " the
Claimant " was released from prison, that, having lost all
his enormous superfluity of flesh, the tall and thin elderly
person who then again emerged into the world did indeed
have the appearance of an aristocratic gentleman.

Meanwhile, at the time when these celebrated " Tichborne Cases " were looming up, Sir Alfred Tichborne died,
early in 1866 ; and for a time it seemed that the Lady
Isabella's prediction was to be fulfilled. Apart from
" the Claimant," there was no heir. And then was born
the posthumous son of Sir Alfred : Henry Joseph Doughty-
Tichborne, the twelfth Baronet ; and the succession was
preserved. He became a sportsman and traveller in
foreign parts. It was while away on one of his expedi-
tions that he was fined £500 : having been absent when
High Sheriff, and thus not attending the Judge of Assize.
He died, aged forty-four, on July 27th, 1910, at Tichborne House, from a paralytic stroke, immediately on his
return from Africa. The present, the thirteenth, Baronet,
Sir Henry Joseph Bernard Doughty-Tichborne,has one son.

The famous and historic " Tichborne Dole," to which
an end had been put in 1796 by Sir Henry, the seventh
Baronet—as already mentioned—was restored, with some
modifications, by his son who, alarmed by having seven
daughters and no son, as had been foretold, and further
alarmed by a portion of the old mansion falling down in
1803, thus sought to avert fate.

There is no difficulty in taking a part in the annual
celebration of the Dole at Tichborne House, on March

25th—Lady Day. The Tichbornes are yet, as always they have been, Roman Catholics, and the distribution is attended by the family chaplain.

Tichborne is found at the distance of a mile and a quarter to the left from Alresford station in Hampshire as you go towards Winchester. It is advisable to reach Tichborne Park at about 10.30 a.m. Troops of country-folk will be found wending their way thither : some to take part in the distribution of flour to about 753 villagers, and others to look on.

The mansion will be seen as a typical country house of its period : the first year of the nineteenth century, when it was rebuilt, chiefly with the materials of the old one. Among the family relics is still preserved the flat, circular leaden weight with which the Dole in olden times was measured out. It is inscribed on one side " Tiche-borne Dole Weight," and on the other *Fundamentum Henrico Regnante Secundo*. In the dining-room hangs a curious seventeenth-century painting of the distribution of the Dole, with the older house in the background.

A ton and a half of flour is distributed to the parishioners : a gallon to each adult, and half a gallon each to the children ; each family being limited to two gallons. The distribution is preceded by prayers in Latin and in English, recited on the steps of the house by the Chaplain, who sprinkles the flour with holy water. What—if any—remains of the flour after those who have received the Dole, according to the list read out by the steward, have been duly satisfied, goes by traditional use to the Dowager Lady Tichborne.

Away on the hill-top, some distance from the house, is the ancient parish church, in which remain some fine monuments of the Tichbornes : notably that to Sir Benjamin Tichborne, 1629, and his wife, Amphillis, with effigies ; and a queer little recumbent figure in red robe, of Richard, son of Sir Richard, 1619 ; who, as the inscription quaintly says, died at the age of " one yere, six monethes, and too daies." The Sir Benjamin named above was the first Baronet. He it was who restored the fortunes of the family, which had been under a cloud after the execution of Chidiock Tichborne in 1586, for his part in that

Babington Conspiracy which had aimed at deposing Queen
Elizabeth and placing on the throne Mary Queen of Scots.

The legend of Lambton Castle, near Chester-le Street,
in Durham, is one of those fearful old folk-tales clearly
derived from Teutonic sources. The Lambtons, now
ennobled as Earls of Durham, have been seated at
Lambton Castle, beside the river Wear, for many centuries, and the family curse traditionally pronounced
against them has been expiated for nearly a century and
a half ; but the gruesome story gathered from the floating
traditions of the country-side by Surtees, and printed by
him, is still well remembered.

The original hero of this tale of the Loathly Worm of
the river Wear was John Lambton, Knight of Rhodes, an
ungodly head of the house, who died at last, penitent,
some time in the fifteenth century. The Lambtons were,
according to popular belief, " so brave that they feared
neither God nor man " ; and so impious that they
positively delighted in publicly desecrating the Sabbath.
John Lambton appears to have been the fullest-fledged of
these evil-living knights. On one memorable Sunday he
went forth, as usual, to angle in the Wear, but went un-
rewarded by even a single bite, although he whacked the
waters for hours. The wayfarers, passing on the road to
church, heard with dismay the fearful newfangled curses
he called down upon the river, the fish, the day, and anything and everything else a fluent fancy could comprehend.

But at last he felt a something tugging at his line, and
without a struggle landed a loathsome object of snake-
like appearance. He was so disgusted with his catch
that he flung it down a well that stood near by, and
with difficulty refrained from flinging after it a foolish
person who—after the manner of casual wayfarers with
anglers—had asked him, " Any luck ? "

But John Lambton repressed his natural impulse,
and merely remarked that he thought he had hooked
the Devil himself. " Take a look at it," he said.

It is not often one can see devils, and especially at
so favourable a remove as at the bottom of a well, and
so the stranger looked, and looking, crossed himself and
said the uncanny object boded ill.

LAMBTON CASTLE

Then, according to the legend, John Lambton, bidding farewell to his aged father, went abroad to the wars, and in foreign parts wielded his lance and broadsword for seven long years, against all manner of foes.

Meanwhile the worm, lizard, dragon, or devil he had caught was making trouble by Wearside. It had outgrown the well, and had taken up its residence near Fat field, where a hill three hundred yards or more in circumference is shown as the spot on which it loved to wind itself—like cotton upon a reel—on sunny days. Its body went thrice—and some accounts say nine—times round this hill ; but let us be moderate, and put it at three times !

There are many wonderful extinct monsters preserved at the Natural History Museum at South Kensington, but there are no lizards or dragons of the prime nine hundred yards in length to be found there.

It is not surprising to learn that this monstrous creature was the terror of the neighbourhood. Its appetite compared favourably with its measurements, and flocks and herds vanished down its throat with lamentable completeness, while its noisome breath blighted the pastures. At length all the cattle at a distance were devoured, and the Worm then took up his quarters closer to the Castle and preyed upon the herds, and even the people, there ; until the milk of nine cows was placed daily for him in a trough. Whenever there was a shortage in the quantity, the Worm resented it by tearing up the trees in the park. It is not surprising to learn that the many knights who sought to destroy this immensikoff among monsters were entirely unsuccessful. When it is remembered that the Worm, according to the measurements already given, must at the least have been one hundred times the size of a tall man, the only wonder is that there were found those brave enough to make the attempt.

> In days of old,
> When knights were bold,

as the song says, no knight could have found a bolder task than that of attacking the Lambton Worm.

The Worm, indeed, killed and ate not a few, and maimed more ; and even those who were fortunate enough to get a cut at him found their labour gone for naught, because the severed parts always re-united themselves.

When John returned from the wars, he found in the Worm a more considerable foe than any he had met abroad ; but, undaunted, he determined to rid the neighbourhood of the pest. In those days one embarked upon no considerable undertaking without consulting dealers in magic and the arts of sorcery ; and so John Lambton, before falling upon the enemy, resorted to a witch, who advised him on no account to attack the Worm until he had provided himself with a suit of armour set with razor-blades. Thus protected, and armed with his two-handed sword, he might venture ; but even then only upon vowing to slay the first living creature he should meet after the deed was accomplished. The penalty attaching to violation of this vow was that nine succeeding generations of Lambtons should not die in their beds.

John Lambton cheerfully registered this vow, for he had it in his mind to arrange that the first living creature to meet him should be his favourite hound ; and even then, he might have considered that the penalty for the breaking of the vow was not very serious, for how seldom did gallant knights in those days of continual warfare die in their beds, or otherwise than by the sword ?

But, however absurd the penalty may seem, the legend must be told as it has always been. John Lambton procured a complete set of armour according to speci-fication, and went forth to do battle with the Worm, leaving word with his father that when he had accom-plished the task, he would blow three blasts upon his horn. His greyhound was then to be released, and would thus become the sacrifice indicated.

And then the intrepid warrior went forth to the en-counter. He slashed it with his sword, and the Worm on its part sought to enfold him with its constrictor embrace. The affray seemed hopeless to the people who looked on, from a safe distance ; for no sooner did the knight's sword and razor-studded armour cut slices off his terrible antagonist than they re-united themselves, as before. But Lambton was not too busy to think. It occurred to him that if he stepped into the river, and fought there, the severed portions of the enemy would be carried away by the current before they had time to piece themselves together again ; and thus the victory would be his.

And so the battle was fought to a finish in the river Wear. The hero hacked and hewed throughout the livelong day, until the best part of nine hundred yards of Worm had floated down the stream by sections, and the remaining portion was dead. And then he winded three blasts upon his horn, and there came joyously to meet him—*not* the hound, but his father ! Him he could not slay ; and thus nine generations of Lambtons were doomed.

John Lambton himself died in the fullness of time, but the circumstances of his death are not related. He was the last of four brothers who had in turn succeeded to the Lambton estates, but he had a son, Robert, who was, however, drowned at the new bridge, Bridgford, the site of the chapel where his father had, years before, vowed his sacrifice in the event of victory. The last but one of those affected by the " doom " was Henry Lambton, who died while crossing the new bridge in his carriage, in 1761. His surviving brother, General Lambton, lived to a very advanced age, and, fearing that the prophecy might be fulfilled by the action of his servants, under the impression that he could not, by the terms of the curse, die comfortably in his bed, kept a horsewhip beside him in his last illness, to prevent them removing him ; and thus evaded the prediction.

Lambton Castle stands in a commanding and romantic position, but, although a place of much magnificence, is in these days neither old nor a castle, having been rebuilt about fifty years ago, in a " castellated " style. It was greatly injured by a subsidence, some years since, having, by some strange oversight, been built over a disused and forgotten coal-pit.

The hill upon which the famous Worm coiled himself is still shown, and the ringed marks made by him pointed out ! The utter impossibility of there ever having been such a creature has led many painstaking writers upon the legend to assume that the whole story is an elaborate allegory, in which Danish or Norse invaders, raiding the country in remote times, figure as the fabled monster.

CHAPTER XI

THE DOOM OF THE SACRILEGIOUS

Sherborne Castle and the Curse of King Osmund—Cowdray House and the Montagues—Newstead Abbey and the Byrons—Fyvie Castle—Moreton Corbet—Smithills Hall and the Martyr's Footprint.

SIR HENRY SPELMAN, in his *History of Sacrilege*, set himself the task, many years ago, of tracing the history of those families that were enriched—chiefly in the reign of Henry the Eighth and Edward the Sixth—by grants of lands and buildings that had long been the property of the Church. The work was undertaken with the object of showing how very many families had been gorged with the spoil of the monasteries, and how a very large proportion of them had suffered in consequence : and, this being the set purpose of the book, it is not surprising to find that (according to Sir Henry Spelman) disaster, in the vast majority of cases, overtook those sacrilegious beneficiaries. Of late years, a new and extended edition of the book has been issued, in the Roman Catholic interest, and the story of retribution, as may well be supposed, has not lost in the revision.

But the whole thing is an arrant piece of special pleading, and we do not, in actual fact, find that the most of the families thus endowed with Church properties were one whit the worse, spiritually, for it, while in a worldly sense they flourished, for the most part exceedingly ; for they were rich and fertile lands of which that Church was spoiled, and yielded fine, and now yield much finer, revenues. The Russells, Earls, and now Dukes, of Bedford, probably received more plunder of this kind than any other family, for the first Earl was in high favour at Court when fat manors by the score were to be had for the asking ; but although the rich lands of

Tavistock and other abbeys fell to him, and are still enjoyed by his descendants, it does not appear that the Russells have suffered by reason of the fact. It is true that a good many tragedies have happened to that race in the course of three hundred and seventy years, but that would be a singularly fortunate family history, even among those not guilty of sacrilegious possession of property, which numbered no misfortunes, and the house of Russell not only still flourishes exceedingly on stolen goods, but has grown into the likeness of an extensive clan, with new honours divided among them. Of course, if the theory which runs through the pages of Spelman's *History of Sacrilege* held good, the Russells, as being loaded above all other families with the goods of the Church, should long ago have sunk under repeated misfortunes, and have become extinct. As the grasping landlords of a large portion of central London, they have extinguished many a poor wretch, but their own prosperity has as yet seen no bounds put to it.

But in spite of this remarkable failure, there are some strange recorded instances in which complete disaster and extinction have befallen families holding old-time manors of the Church.

Some little distance away to the eastern side of the picturesque old Dorsetshire town of Sherborne, in the pretty village of Castleton, stands Sherborne Castle, which, with its surrounding park-lands, was originally given to the Church by Osmund, King of Wessex. By " the Church " we are in this case to understand the Bishopric of Sherborne, which was then, and so remained until 1078, an independent see ; when it was merged into that of Sarum.

The Saxon King Osmund, in endowing Sherborne with these properties, clinched his gift by calling down a curse upon any who should dare to alienate castle or lands from the Bishop of Sherborne. " Whosoever," he is declared to have said, " shall take these lands from the bishopric, or diminish them in great or in small, shall be accursed, not only in this world, but also in the world to come, unless in his life he make restitution thereof."

Osmund probably never contemplated the revision in

dioceses by which the see of Sherborne was abolished ; and we are not to suppose that the curse was started on its destructive career in 1078. After all, the lands were still in the Church, and what mattered it whether they were Bishops of Sherborne, of Sarum, or (later) of Salisbury who resided in state at Sherborne Castle !

But not long afterwards the gift was indeed alienated within the meaning of the sainted Osmund's malediction. In 1139 Bishop Roger of Salisbury, who nine years

SHERBORNE CASTLE

earlier had built himself a fine late Norman castle on the ruins of a smaller residential fortress, was so unfortunate as to be overtaken by the vengeance of King Stephen, whose cause he had consistently opposed in favour of Matilda. The King stripped the Bishop of his castles of Devizes and Sherborne and heavily fined him as well ; and thenceforward the Church lands of Sherborne became Crown property. Immediately afterwards, Stephen's party lost ground. Later, his eldest son, Eustace, his one hope, died, some said from poison ; and, ambition being thus foiled, the King made peace with his enemy, by which her son, afterwards Henry the Second, was given the succession.

For over two hundred years, until 1355, Sherborne Castle and its lands were thus alienated, and Osmund's curse slept. The troubles of the several sovereigns who reigned over England in this interval can scarcely be ascribed to this cause, and, moreover, continued just as tragically after the lands had been restored. The Crown, in the person of Edward the Third, granted the stronghold of Sherborne Castle and its demesne to Montacute, Earl of Salisbury : a grant which led at last to a humorous interlude, the Bishop of Salisbury (Robert Wyville, 1330–1375) proposing to fight the Earl for the property, in gage of single combat. The proposal, however, came to nothing, and in the end an arrangement was arrived at by which the whole was purchased by the Bishop for 2,500 marks.

Whether the Earl, in Etonian phrase, " funked it," and, thinking solemnly of that ancient curse, imagined the Bishop's steel would be as invincible as the sword of the Lord and of Gideon, who shall presume to say ? At any rate, Bishop Wyville, strenuous cleric, who feared neither the ordeal of the sword nor of the purse, duly entered into the gates of his predecessors of old.

There remains to this day in Salisbury Cathedral a very instructive monumental brass to the memory of this Bishop, which alludes to these events. In the midst of an astonishing castle, appears the figure of Bishop Wyville, properly habited in ecclesiastical vestments, while below is seen standing in the doorway the figure of the Bishop's Champion (a very big Bishop, and a very little Champion, by the way), armed only with a conviction of being in the right, a shield, and a something that looks like a coal-pick, ready to do battle with all and sundry. This is an allusion to Wyville's determin-ation to win back the ancient heritage of the Church ; and shows us that it was not scandalously, in his own proper person, that the good Bishop was prepared to fight, but by deputy, in the shape of one skilled in arms ! The quaint little figures of rabbits seen diving into their burrows at the foot of the brass were placed there to show that the Bishop was owner of the warren.

MONUMENTAL BRASS TO BISHOP WYVILLE, IN SALISBURY CATHEDRAL

If the Earl was jockeyed out of Sherborne Castle by any ghostly fears, he did wrong; for surely nothing much worse could have befallen him and his than what

they suffered *after* they were quit of it. Curses, like
torpedoes, deal destruction so indiscriminately after they
are once launched. The first Earl had an eye gouged
out in Scottish warfare ; and, warring in France, was
taken prisoner and ignominiously chained and trundled
in a cart through the country, the populace flinging filth
over him. He at last died from a blow at a joust. In
a similar knightly exercise, the second Earl had the
fearful misfortune to kill his only son. A Cirencester
mob beheaded the third Earl in 1400. Parliament
afterwards heaped on him the indignity of declaring
him a traitor ; but he probably did not much mind that.
The fourth and last Earl was slain ingloriously at the
siege of Orleans. Greeting the morning sun from a
window, a shot and fragments of stonework carried by
it wounded him so severely that in two days he died.
And with him the race of Montacute ended.

Until 1540, Sherborne Castle remained the property
of the Church, when it was granted, on the confiscation
of Church holdings, to the Lord Protector, the Duke of
Somerset, uncle of the King, Edward the Sixth. Thereupon, the curse seems to have again entered into its own,
for a series of tragedies ensued. Somerset was arraigned
and executed on a charge of high treason ; and after a
brief interlude, when Sherborne Castle was restored by
Queen Mary to the Bishop of Salisbury, it was once more
secularised, and was given to Sir Walter Raleigh, in 1591.

With this fatal gift, the prosperity of that gallant
and brave heart faded. Transient gleams of good
fortune shone upon him, and he built himself a large
and imposing mansion near the old castle, but failure
and sorrow dogged him persistently thereafter, and in
1618 he went the way that Somerset had gone, sixty years
before. James the First, whose foreign policy had cost
Raleigh his head, then seized the unfortunate man's
estates, and gave Sherborne Castle to his eldest son,
Prince Henry, who died in less than a year from the
date of that gift. Then the King's unworthy favourite,
Robert Carr, became the owner ; and he, after being
convicted of a guilty knowledge of Sir Thomas Overbury's
murder, was ruined and died obscurely in 1645. With

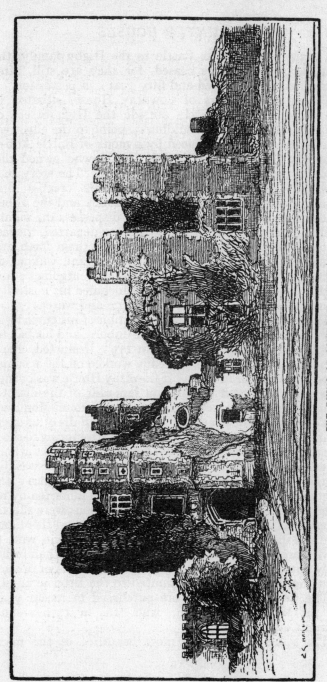

THE RUINS OF COWDRAY HOUSE

the grant of Sherborne Castle to the Digby family, the curse appears to have ceased, for they are still, after more than two hundred and fifty years, in possession.

The romantic ruins of Cowdray House, situated in the meadows immediately outside the High Street of the little Sussex town of Midhurst, point to the effectiveness of the curse pronounced by a monk of Battle Abbey upon the Brownes, the ancient family who owned this place in the reign of Henry the Eighth. The story tells how Sir Anthony Browne, afterwards created first Viscount Montague, was given the Abbey and the abbey lands of Battle, and made haste to dispossess the monks of that ancient establishment. As they departed, the last of them turned upon those who thrust them forth and cursed Sir Anthony Browne in sleeping and waking, in eating and drinking, in his incomings and outgoings ; and in this comprehensive malediction included his posterity, whom he doomed to extinction by fire and water.

The monk did not time the execution of his curse upon the unoffending generations as yet unborn, and his baleful prophecy long slept. At last, in 1793, it started, like a belated alarum clock, and speedily worked off the accumulated arrears ; for in that year Cowdray House was burned down, and the next month, yet ignorant of the disaster that had befallen his residence, the last Viscount Montague but one met his death by drowning in the Falls of Lauffen, near Schaffhausen, on the Rhine, when attempting to shoot the rapids in a boat. The next heir was a Roman Catholic priest, who died childless, despite the fact that he was dispensed from his vows in order that he might marry and continue the line. The estates were then inherited by his sister, Mrs. Stephen Poyntz, whose two sons were shortly afterwards drowned at Bognor. Her husband thereupon sold the ill-omened place to the Earl of Egmont, who, to have dared buy it, must have been a more than ordinarily courageous man ; unless, indeed, he was of opinion that the curse was strictly limited to the Browne family.

The Cowdray estates were purchased in recent years by Sir Weetman Pearson, who was in 1910 created Baron Cowdray.

The ruins, among the most beautiful of the many

ruined historic mansions of England, are those of a noble range of buildings erected about 1530 by Sir William Fitzwilliam, Earl of Southampton. The mouldering shield of arms of Sir Anthony Browne is still visible over the arch of the great gateway.

Meanwhile, the Webster family had acquired the dangerous lands of Battle Abbey and the ruins of the Abbey itself, where is that oft-altered mansion called after the ancient religious house. Thomas Webster made the purchase in the last year of the seventeenth century, and was created in 1703 a Baronet. The history of the Websters is long and chequered. Finally, in 1923, Sir Augustus Webster, the eighth Baronet, died in a nursing home at Hastings, when the title became extinct, there being no surviving heirs. The Websters ended in cumulative heaped-up disaster ; for Lady Webster was drowned while bathing in a lake near Powder Mill House, the residence of Sir Augustus, in the park, near the mansion of Battle Abbey in which he could not afford to live. It was on June 15th, 1917, that Lady Webster was drowned, and with her perished her younger daughter, Evelyn, aged twelve. The only son, and heir to the Baronetcy, Godfrey Vassal Augustus Webster, born September 2nd, 1897, was killed in action in the Great War, two months later, August 4th, 1917.

The Abbey of Newstead, founded by Henry the Second for a community of black Augustine Canons, in expiation of the murder of Thomas à Becket, came to an end in 1539. Its income was then £219 18s. 8d. per annum. The last Prior, John Blake, surrendered the place peaceably, and was granted a pension of £16 13s. 4d.

In May, 1540, the property, with other monastic lands and buildings, was sold to Sir John Byron of Colwick, who speedily set about building a fine residence adjoining the Abbey. This was formed partly from the existing domestic buildings of the monastery, but was greatly extended with the stone and other materials torn from the Abbey church itself, which he completely unroofed and thoroughly dismantled. The fine cloister walks and the noble, although sadly mutilated, West Front, with its empty window, are the most important portions left.

The history of the Byron family, after they had acquired Newstead, affords striking confirmation of the belief in the penalties supposed to await the sacrilegious.

Sir Richard Byron, who garrisoned the house in the cause of King Charles, was reduced to severe straits. His successor, who was made a Baron in 1643, died childless and in poverty, and his widow was granted a pension of £500 a year at the Restoration. The second Lord Byron, who had proposed to raise money by felling a thousand of the ancient oaks of Sherwood Forest, that had been presented to him by Charles the First, was granted a sum of money in lieu ; but still the family remained in very poor circumstances. He and the third Baron had each one son surviving them.

The fourth Baron thrice entered the " holy state." There were no children of the first marriage, and the three sons and one daughter of the second all died unwed, leaving the family honours to be perpetuated by the children of his third venture, among whom was the fifth Lord, grand-uncle of the poet. The fifth Lord Byron was put upon his trial in 1765 for killing Mr. Chaworth in what was represented by the charitable to be a duel. This was the famous, or infamous, " Devil Byron," whose sister so incensed him by figuring in a scandal that he refused ever after to speak to her, and was said to be haunted by her wailing spirit, crying, " O ! speak to me, my lord."

The father of the poet did not succeed to the title. He eloped with the Countess of Carmarthen, whose husband promptly divorced her ; and in after years he married Miss Catherine Gordon, for the sake of her great fortune, which he speedily dissipated.

The sixth Lord Byron, the poet, who is the only one of his race whose name is of any account, was at once a genius, a *poseur*, and a degenerate. Modern men of science would say that the first two of these attributes implies the third. However that may be, he was unfortunate enough to be afflicted by nature with the physical deformity of a club-foot, which his morbidly sensitive and self-conscious organisation rendered an ever-present infliction ; and he was unfortunate enough to succeed a great-uncle who was possessed by an insane fury for

NEWSTEAD ABBEY.

destroying his heritage, with the object of rendering it as little valuable as possible to those who in the course of nature should follow him.

It was in 1798 that the poet came into this dismantled possession. The noble woods that had surrounded it had been cut down, and the stumps left ; the lake was choked with mud and weeds, the house itself in a pitiful state of neglect and dilapidation. The damp came up from the floors, and the rain descended through the rotten roof, and the poet, coming into residence, was reduced to a small habitable corner, itself not altogether rain-proof.

Unable to maintain his inheritance, Byron sold Newstead in 1818 for £95,000 to Colonel Wildman, an old school-fellow. Wildman, at least, had plenty of money, and expended £100,000 on repairs. To reinstate all its plundered beauties was, however, a work that required not money alone, but time ; and although he planted extensively, it was not until comparatively recent years that woods of any size waved once more around the Abbey. Immensely wealthy when he entered into possession of Newstead, Colonel Wildman became reduced by the Emancipation of Slavery Act, which made away with most of his riches in the West Indies, to comparative poverty. After the death of Colonel Wildman, in 1861, the estate was again sold, and the park, except for the grounds immediately surrounding the house, was cut up into farms.

Mr. Webb owned Newstead in comparatively recent years, and suffered many domestic afflictions. The property passed at his death to his eldest daughter, Miss Webb, who married Lieutenant-General Sir Herbert Chermside. Lady Chermside died very suddenly, in Switzerland, at a comparatively early age ; and Newstead then passed to other Webbs : firstly, a sister of Lady Chermside, who held it four years, and died, very suddenly, at the Abbey. Her successor was her brother, Major Webb, who in the course of twelve months died suddenly, in East Africa. *In the same week,* the tenant of Newstead, Sir Arthur Markham, M.P. for Mansfield, born 1866, died suddenly, in 1916. The last of the Miss Webbs then succeeded. She was living at the time near

Inverness, in a mansion also reputed to be an " unlucky house." Newstead Abbey then became the residence of Major-General Sir Herbert Chermside.

" Newstead," triumphantly declare the Roman Catholic editors of Spelman's *History of Sacrilege*, "no longer belongs to the Byrons, and the present Baron has " (*therefore*, we may presume the argument to run) " six surviving children, of whom three are married."

The poet himself appears to have been impressed by some features of the family history. " I have been thinking," he wrote, " of an odd circumstance. My daughter, my wife, my half-sister, my mother and sister's mother, my natural daughter, and myself are, or were, all only children. . . . Such a complication of only children, all tending to one family, is singular enough, and looks like fatality almost."

Byron—of course there is but one possible Byron— loved Newstead with a peculiar romantic love that was not perhaps wholly reverent, for he buried his favourite dog, Boatswain, on what is said to be the site of the High Altar of the Abbey, and raised a monument to him there. There is an exquisite raciness in the following descriptive stanza from his poem on Newstead Abbey :

> An old, old monastery once, and now
> Still older mansion—of a rich and rare
> Mix'd Gothic, such artists will allow
> Few specimens yet left us can compare
> Withal ; it lies perhaps a little low,
> Because the monks preferred a hill behind
> To shelter their devotions from the wind.

But it is a fine poem throughout, and figures the beautiful ruins to perfection :

> A glorious remnant of the Gothic pile
> (While yet the church was Rome's) stood half apart
> In a grand arch, that once screen'd many an aisle.
> These last had disappear'd—a loss to art ;
> The first yet frown'd superbly o'er the soil,
> And kindled feelings in the roughest heart,
> Which mourn'd the power of time's or tempest's march
> In gazing on that venerable arch,
>
> Within a niche, nigh to a pinnacle,
> Twelve saints had once stood sanctified in stone ;

But these had fallen—not when the friars fell,
  But in the war which struck Charles from his throne
When each house was a fortalice, as tell
  The annals of full many a line undone—
The gallant Cavaliers, who fought in vain
For those who knew not to resign or reign.

.   .   .   .   .   .

But in the noontide of the moon, and when
  The wind is winged from one point of heaven,
There moans a strange unearthly sound which then
  Is musical—a dying accent driven
Through the huge arch, which soars and sinks again.
  Some deem it but the distant echo given
Back to the night-wind by the waterfall,
And harmonised by the old choral wall.

.   .   .   .   .   .

Amid the court a Gothic fountain play'd,
  Symmetrical, but deck'd with carvings quaint—
Strange faces, like to men in masquerade,
  And here perhaps a monster, there a saint :
The spring gush'd through grim mouths of granite made
  And sparkled into basins, where it spent
Its little torrent in a thousand bubbles,
Like man's vain glory and his vainer troubles.

In the cloister garden the monks' fishpond still remains. At one end, a grove of trees is neighboured by a number of leaden statues of fauns and wood-nymphs, once known to the gaping rustics as " the old lord's devils."

A variety of spectres are said to make Newstead their home. Chief among them is, or was, the Black Friar, a brother of the old monastery. Byron himself saw—or said he saw—him :

                    A monk arrayed
In cowl, and beads, and dusky garb, appeared,
  Now in the moonlight, and now lapsed in shade,
With steps that trod as heavy, yet unheard.

The Black Friar was the harbinger of ill to the family :

By the marriage-bed of their lords, 'tis said,
  He flits on the bridal eve ;
And 'tis held as faith, to their bed of death
  He comes—but not to grieve.

When an heir is born, he is heard to mourn,
  And when aught is to befall
That ancient line, in the pale moonshine,
  He walks from hall to hall.

His form you may trace, but not his face,
'Tis shadowed by his cowl ;
But his eyes may be seen from the folds between,
And they seem of a parted soul.

Byron declared he saw the Black Friar just before his marriage with Miss Milbanke, which he described as the most unhappy event of his career.

" Sir John the Little, with the Great Beard," the Sir John Byron of Colwick to whom the Abbey was granted in the sixteenth century, is supposed to haunt his old home ; and there was once a portrait of him which was said to descend from its frame at the midnight hour. Once even, a young lady visitor declared she saw him in daylight, reading a book by the fire. Washington Irving, too, tells of a cousin of the poet, another lady, to whom a White Lady appeared ; but Joaquin Miller's account of how he slept for several nights in Byron's haunted room is disappointing to the seekers after horrors, however much it may please those who prefer the humorous.

He says, of his first night's experience : " It was the loveliest night possible. The moon lay on the water like silver. Soon I undressed, and hastily blew out one of the candles, and set the other at the bedside, as I lay down. I did not dare to blow it out. It takes a great deal of courage to admit this ugly truth. The great, heavy, rich and tattered curtains of yellow silk were like tinder, and it was a dangerous thing to leave the candle burning, particularly after dinner. But it did not seem to me so dangerous, just then, as to blow it out ; and so, I think, I fell asleep. Suddenly I heard, or rather felt, the door slowly open. I looked straight ahead as I lay there, but did not move. A figure entered from the other door, but I could not see it. I felt it stop at the table. Then I felt it advancing upon me where I lay. I distinctly heard the clink of two candlesticks. Then I felt, or rather saw, that my light was being slowly and certainly withdrawn. I cautiously turned my head, and was just in time to see the patient footman, who had been waiting all the time outside, bearing away the lighted candle. Oh ! how ashamed I was ! "

FYVIE CASTLE

Fyvie Castle, the romantic castellated residence of
Lord Leith of Fyvie, situated beautifully upon the banks
of the river Ythan, in the north of Scotland, is associated
with a prophecy traditionally uttered by Thomas the
Rhymer :

> Fyvens riggs and towers,
> Hapless shall your mesdames be,
> Till ye shall hae within your methes,
> Frae harryit kirk's land, stanes three—
> Ane in Preston's tower,
> Ane in my lady's bower,
> And ane below the water-yett :
> And *it* ye shall never get.

The existing castle is built up around a hoary peel·tower,
erected so far back as the thirteenth century. It passed
from King Robert the Second to his son, Robert the
Third, who made a gift of it to Sir James Lindsay. In
1390 the tower was alienated to Henry de Preston, who
forthwith proceeded to enlarge the castle, and built the
still-existing " Preston-tower," with—it is supposed—the
stones of a neighbouring religious house he demolished.
Three of these stones, apparently of some particular note,
fell into the Ythan and were lost : and not until they
are all recovered (which, in the above words of Thomas
the Rhymer, will never be) will the family for the time
being owning the castle perpetuate itself beyond the next
generation.

This doom of sacrilege (which has not always come to
pass) befell Sir Henry Preston himself, for he left an only
daughter, who married a Meldrum, and thus conveyed
the property into another family. In the possession of
the Meldrums, however, it remained until 1596, when it
was purchased by Alexander Seton, who was thereupon
created Lord Fyvie and Earl of Dunfermline. This was
a distinguished nobleman, tutor to Charles the First,
Lord Chancellor, and an amateur architect. He added
the Seton tower to Fyvie Castle, and left a son who
suffered as a partisan of the King, and so died, childless
and in poverty, an exile at St. Germains. In 1726
Fyvie was purchased by the Earl of Aberdeen, head of
the Gordon family, and in 1746 was bequeathed by the

Earl to his son, whose descendants died out in 1884. Since that date Fyvie has belonged to Mr. A. J. Forbes-Leith, created Baron Leith of Fyvie in 1905. He died November 14th, 1925, aged 79. There is no heir to the title.

Like Glamis, Fyvie has its walled-up chamber. This is situated beneath the charter-room in the south-west tower, and remains closed owing to a legend which holds that disasters will befall the owners of Fyvie whenever it is opened and explored.

The ruins of the great seventeenth-century mansion of Moreton Corbet, in Shropshire, are associated with a not very convincing legend. Sufficient remains of the shattered walls to show that this residence was designed in a very restrained and chaste variety of Jacobean Renaissance. It was an era when almost every wealthy squire rebuilt his house and began to live with a romantic prodigality. Some, however, failing to count the cost of their rebuilding, were obliged to leave their magnificent new houses unfinished, as many a derelict pile, mouldering to decay, still exists to prove. The house of Moreton Corbet would seem to be a case in point.

The Corbets of Shropshire are an ancient family, bearing the raven, or *corbeau*, among their heraldic cognizances, in punning imitation of their name. Sir Robert Corbet, of Acton Reynald, it was who began to build this imposing new residence, in 1606, but he died in London of the plague before it had made much progress, and his brother and successor in the baronetcy, Sir Vincent, continued it. Sir Vincent Corbet seems to have been a kindly man. Not himself a Puritan, he nevertheless did not join his fellow-magistrates, or the country-side in general, in imprisoning or harrying them, even though their growing fanaticism began to assume a militant and aggressive character. One among their number, Paul Homeyard by name, he had indeed befriended in no uncertain manner when he was being sought after by the persecutors of sectaries; but becoming convinced that the increasing licence and political intriguing of these new religionists ought to be curbed, he warned Homeyard that no further encouragement could be expected. It was not long before Homeyard found it politic to fly from his house, to save himself from the pillory, and the ear- and nose-slitting that awaited him. He hid in the woods with the foxes and the owls, and in the crannies of old ruins with the rats and the jackdaws ; and, brooding there before he could safely shift to travel from the neighbourhood, he one day chanced to see Sir Vincent Corbet in solitude inspecting the progress of his mansion. To him the fanatic unreasonably ascribed his woes, and, assuming the manner of a prophet, he denounced the justly astonished baronet in the most melodramatic style ; ending with the prediction :

" Woe unto thee, man of the hardened heart : hardened even as the Lord hardened the heart of Pharaoh, to thine own destruction. Rejoice not in thy wealth, nor in the halls of thy pride ; for there shall never be a copestone set upon them, neither shalt thou, nor thy children, nor thy children's children, dwell therein ; but they shall be a ruin and a desolation, and the snake and the eft and the adder shall be found there, and thy house shall be full of doleful creatures."

It is wonderful what a course of short commons and skulking amid ruinous places can do in the production of prophets. On a generous diet, soft beds, and peace of mind, this sort of thing would be impossible. Our sympathies go out to Sir Vincent Corbet, who obviously did not deserve this abuse, and still less deserved that the prophecy should be fulfilled—as it was. The house appears never to have been completed, and was moreover battered by the Royalists in the Civil War, in which the Corbets garrisoned it for the Parliament.

Smithills Hall, near Bolton in Lancashire, is situated in a beautifully wooded park on a hill-side one mile to the north of that unlovely cotton-spinning town. In the park you may see myriads of black rabbits playing like kittens, and the scene is delightfully rural, but as you stand on the terraces in front of the house the countless factory chimneys of Bolton, trailing their smudgy wreaths of smoke across the sky, are all too evident.

Smithills owes its present form to Andrew Barton, who rebuilt it in the reign of Henry the Seventh. His

RUINS OF MORETON CORBET

rebus, a play upon the family name, is still found carved upon the ancient walls : a tun surmounted by a bar, and the initials A. B. are here and there displayed. The estate came into the Barton family in the reign of Henry the Sixth, by the marriage of a Barton to Joan, daughter and heiress of Sir Ralph Radcliffe. Bartons in their turn gave place to Byrons, from whom it passed by purchase to the present owners, the Ainsworth family.

It was in Bloody Queen Mary's day that the incident happened at Smithills Hall which has given the place its legendary fame. George Marsh, a Calvinist minister, was apprehended for his religious opinions, and brought before Sir Roger Barton at the Hall. He was examined here, and might have escaped by professing to conform, but he rejected all efforts made by his friends, and, stamping his foot upon the ground, exclaimed : " If my cause be just, let the prayer of Thine unworthy servant be heard."

Sir Roger Barton, as a magistrate, had no options but to remand him in custody, and Marsh was afterwards examined at greater length before the Earl of Derby, at Lathom, being at length burnt as a heretic at Chester, April 24th, 1555.

In the passage leading to the chapel in Smithills Hall, what appears to be a bloody footprint is shown upon the time-worn stone pavement. It is described on a wall-tablet as the " Footprint of the Reverend George Marsh, of Deane, Martyr."

Weird legends are told of the stone, particularly that which narrates the disturbances that followed upon its once being removed. The house, it is declared, knew no peace until it was replaced.

To the inquiring mind, not disposed to accept these fearful stories without examination, the stone is a fragment in which a large admixture of ferruginous sand produces a rust-coloured stain when moisture is applied. As the illustration shows, the stone is carefully preserved from rough usage by being encased in an ornamental iron covering with a hinged lid.

Inside the illustration, on the sign:

FOOTPRINT
of the
Reverend Martyr
MARTYR
Whence Quae
Queen Mary

THE MARTYR'S FOOTPRINT, SMITHILLS HALL

CHAPTER XII

OMENS AND WARNINGS

The " Radiant Boy " of Corby Castle—Lord Castlereagh—Lord
    Lyttelton's Warning—The Drummer of Cortachy—Roslin
    Castle—The Earls Ferrers and the Chartley Black Calves.

CORBY CASTLE, situated beautifully above the densely
wooded banks of the river Eden, in Cumberland, is the
" C—— Castle " referred to in Mrs. Crowe's often-quoted
but very out-of-date work, the *Night Side of Nature*.

This ancient seat has long been reputed the scene
of the wanderings, at intervals, of an alarming apparition
well known in Cumbrian lore as " the Radiant Boy."
Apparitions of this type are familiar in German spirit-
lore, and are traditionally said, in the fearful mysticism
that characterises ancient Teutonic legends, to be the
ghosts of children murdered by their mothers—the
kindermörderinn so frequently mentioned in the folk-lore
of Germany.

To the logical person it would seem that the
murderess should be condemned to perform the haunting, and that the murdered children should have peace ;
but we are dealing with a subject beyond the confines of
logic. Taking the general sense of apparitions of this
type, it would appear that they are sent to warn those
who see them of a violent end.

A possible explanation of a similar class of apparition
being found in Cumberland may be sought in the well-
ascertained fact of the district having been peopled in
the ninth and tenth centuries by settlers from Teutonic
and Scandinavian countries, who would naturally bring
their folk-lore with them.

The last authentic record of the appearance of the
Radiant Boy of Corby is referred to in the manuscript
volume dated from Corby Castle, December 22nd, 1824.

In this case, the vision does not seem to have had its usual significance, for the person who beheld it appears to have ended peacefully enough.

" In order to introduce my readers [says this account] to the haunted room, I will mention that it forms part of the old house, with windows looking into the court, which in early times was deemed a necessary security against an enemy. It adjoins a tower built by the Romans for defence ; for Corby was, probably, more a border tower than a castle of any consideration. There is a winding staircase in this tower, and the walls are from eight to ten feet thick.

" When the times became more peaceable, our ancestors enlarged the arrow-slit windows, and added to that part of the building which looks towards the river Eden. But many alterations and additions have been made since then.

" To return to the room in question. I must observe that it is by no means remote or solitary, being surrounded on all sides by chambers that are constantly inhabited. It is accessible by a passage cut through a wall eight feet in thickness, and its dimensions are twenty one feet by eighteen. One side of the wainscoting is covered with tapestry, the remainder is decorated with old family pictures and some ancient pieces of embroidery, probably the handiwork of nuns. Over a press which has doors of Venetian glass is an ancient oaken figure, with a battle-axe in his hand, which was formerly one of those placed on the walls of the city of Carlisle, to represent sentinels. There used to be also an old-fashioned bed and some dark furniture in this room ; but so many were the complaints of those who slept there that I was induced to replace some of these articles of furniture by more modern ones, in the hope of removing a certain air of gloom which I thought might have given rise to the unaccountable reports of apparitions and extraordinary noises which were constantly reaching us. But I regret to say I did not succeed in banishing the nocturnal visitor, which still continues to disturb our friends.

" I shall pass over numerous instances, and select one as being especially remarkable, from the circumstance of the apparition having been seen by a clergyman well known and highly respected in this county, who, not six weeks ago, repeated the circumstance to a company of twenty persons, amongst whom were some who had previously been entire disbelievers in such appearances. The best way, however, of giving you these particulars will be by subjoining an extract from my journal, entered at the time the event occurred.

"'Sept. 8, 1803.—Amongst other guests invited to Corby Castle, came the Rev. Henry A—— of Redheugh, and rector of Greystoke, near Penrith, with Mrs. A——, his wife. According to previous arrangements, they were to have remained with us some days, but their visit was cut short in a very unexpected manner. On the morning after their arrival we were all assembled at breakfast, when a chaise-and-four dashed up to the door in such haste that it knocked down part of the fence of my flower garden. Our curiosity was, of course, awakened to know who could be arriving at so early an hour, when, happening to turn my eyes towards Mr. A——, I observed that he appeared extremely agitated. "It is our carriage," said he. "I am very sorry, but we must absolutely leave you this morning."

"'We naturally felt, and expressed, considerable surprise, as well as regret, at this unexpected departure, representing that we had invited Colonel and Mrs. S——, some friends whom Mr. A—— particularly desired to meet, to dine with us on that day. Our expostulations, however, were in vain ; the breakfast was no sooner over than they departed, leaving us in consternation to conjecture what could possibly have occasioned so sudden an alteration in their arrangements. I really felt quite uneasy lest anything should have given them offence ; and we reviewed all the occurrences of the preceding evening, in order to discover, if offence there was, whence it had arisen. But our pains were in vain ; and after talking a great deal about it for some days, other circumstances banished the matter from our minds.

"'It was not till we some time afterwards visited the part of the country in which Mr. A—— resides that we learnt the real cause of his sudden departure from

CORBY CASTLE

Corby. The relation of the fact, as it here follows, is in his own words :

" ' " Soon after we went to bed we fell asleep. It might be between one and two in the morning when I awoke. I observed that the fire was totally extinguished ; but although that was the case, and we had no light, I saw a glimmer in the middle of the room, which suddenly increased to a bright flame. I looked out, apprehending that something had caught fire ; when, to my amazement, I beheld a beautiful boy clothed in white, with bright locks resembling gold, standing by my bedside, in which position he remained some minutes, fixing his eyes upon me with a mild and benevolent expression. He then glided gently towards the side of the chimney ; where it is obvious there is no possible egress, and entirely disappeared. I found myself again in total darkness, and all remained quiet until the usual hour of rising. I declare this to be a true account of what I saw at Corby Castle, upon my word as a clergyman." ' "

For many years afterwards, this seer of the Radiant Boy spoke of the occurrence, always with the greatest seriousness ; but the visitors to Corby in these opening years of the twentieth century will not find any belief in the supernatural lingering at Corby Castle, which, as the illustration shows, is a typical eighteenth-century mansion, and not at all ghostly in general features. The Howards have long been, and still are, owners of Corby.

The room associated with this legend, and commonly styled " the Ghost Room," is in the older part of the house. It is now a study. The ancient tapestry and the dark panelling still remain, and the material circumstances are such that no ghost should despise ; but candour compels the admission that the Radiant Boy of Corby no longer alarms the household.

Mrs. Crowe is also responsible for the story of the vision of a Radiant Boy appearing to Captain Robert Stewart, afterwards Lord Castlereagh and second Marquis of Londonderry, very many years before he committed suicide by cutting his throat at North Cray Place, in 1822. Unfortunately, the place where this spectre appeared is but vaguely referred to as in " the north of

VISCOUNT CASTLEREAGH

Ireland," at some country house when the then Captain
Stewart was staying as a guest. The narrative is stated
to have been derived from a relative of the ill-fated
Marquis :

" Captain Stewart, when he was a young man, happened to be quartered in Ireland. He was fond of
sport, and one day the pursuit of game carried him so
far that he lost his way. The weather, too, had become
very rough, and in this strait he presented himself at
the door of a gentleman's house, and, sending in his card,
requested shelter for the night. The hospitality of the
Irish country gentry is proverbial ; the master of the
house received him warmly, said he feared he could not
make him so comfortable as he could have wished, his
house being already full of visitors—added to which,
some strangers, driven by the inclemency of the night,
had sought shelter before him ; but that such accom-
modation as he could give he was heartily welcome to ;
whereupon he called his butler, and, committing his
guest to his good offices, told him he must put him up
somewhere, and do the best he could for him.

" Captain Stewart found the house crammed, and a
very jolly party it was. His host invited him to stay,
and promised him good shooting if he would prolong
his visit a few days ; and, in fine, he thought himself
extremely fortunate to have fallen into such pleasant
quarters.

" At length, after an agreeable evening, they all
retired to bed, and the butler conducted him to a large
room almost divested of furniture, but with a blazing peat
fire in the grate and a shake-down on the floor, composed
of cloaks and other heterogeneous materials. Nevertheless, to the tired limbs of Captain Stewart, who had
had a hard day's shooting, it looked very inviting ; but,
before he lay down, he thought it advisable to take off
some of the fire, which was blazing up the chimney in
what he thought an alarming manner. Having done
this, he stretched himself upon the couch, and soon fell
asleep.

" He believed he had slept about a couple of hours,
when he awoke suddenly, and was startled by such a

vivid light in the room that he thought it was on fire ;
but, on turning to look at the grate, he saw the fire was
out, though it was from the chimney the light proceeded.
He sat up in bed, trying to discover what it was, when
he perceived, gradually disclosing itself, the form of a
beautiful naked boy, surrounded by a dazzling radiance.
The boy looked at him earnestly, and then the vision
faded, and all was dark. Captain Stewart, so far from
supposing what he had seen to be of a spiritual nature,
had no doubt that the host, or the visitors, had been
amusing themselves at his expense, and trying to frighten
him. Accordingly, he felt indignant at the liberty ; and
on the following morning, when he appeared at breakfast,
he took care to evince his displeasure by the reserve of
his demeanour, and by announcing his intention to
depart immediately. The host expostulated, reminding
hin of his promise to stay and shoot. Captain Stewart
coldly excused himself, and at length the gentleman,
seeing something was wrong, took him aside and pressed
for an explanation ; whereupon Captain Stewart, without
entering into particulars, said he had been made the
victim of practical joking that he thought quite un-
warrantable with a stranger.

" The gentleman considered this not impossible
amongst a number of thoughtless young men, and
appealed to them to make an apology ; but one and all,
on their honour, denied the impeachment. Suddenly a
thought seemed to strike him : he clapped his hand to
his forehead, uttered an exclamation, and rang the bell.

" ' Hamilton,' he said to the butler, ' where did
Captain Stewart sleep last night ? '

" ' Well, sir,' replied the man, in an apologetic tone,
' you know every place was full—the gentlemen were
lying on the floor, three or four in a room—so I gave
him the *Boy's Room* : but I lit a blazing fire to keep
him from coming out.'

" ' You were very wrong,' said the host ; ' you know
I have positively forbidden you to put anyone there,
and have taken the furniture out of the room, to ensure
its not being occupied.'

" Then, retiring with Captain Stewart, he informed

THOMAS, SECOND BARON LYTTELTON

him very gravely of the nature of the phenomenon he
had seen; and at length, being pressed for further
information, he confessed that there existed a tradition
in his family that to whomsoever the Radiant Boy
appeared would come at first the greatest prosperity.
He would rise to the summit of power; and then, when
he had reached the climax, would die a violent death.
' I must say,' he concluded impressively, ' the records
that have been kept of his appearance go to confirm
this persuasion.' "

As foretold, Captain Stewart rose to great eminence.
His father was first Marquis of Londonderry, but he was
himself only the second son, and had at the time of the
incident already related no very brilliant prospects. The
death of his brother in a boating accident, however,
produced a great change. He became Lord Castlereagh,
and occupied a prominent position in Irish affairs; being
one of the chief figures in the political manœuvres which
resulted in 1800 in the Act of Union between England
and Ireland. This was merely the opening of his career.
His abilities led him onward until he won a commanding
position in successive English administrations : as Secretary of War in 1805 and again in 1807, and as Foreign
Secretary from 1812 onwards. A man of cold and
undemonstrative nature, he was not merely unpopular
throughout his whole career, but was cordially hated,
even by members of his own party. Yet he was not
merely a strong man, such as the times demanded, but
also successful in most of his schemes as a Minister for
the welfare of the nation. He lacked, however, the
pleasing, if dissimulating, manners that make for popu-
larity. It was well said that he was " just and passion-
less " ; and that is a character which, however noble,
does not merely fail to attract friendships, but even,
by in some way implying superiority, creates active
dislike.

In 1821, by the death of his father, he became Marquis
of Londonderry, but he lives in history as Lord Castlereagh. In the following year he suffered greatly from
gout, and the continued anxieties of a long and trying
public career began noticeably to tell upon him. His

manner grew strange, and, on the suggestion of the Duke of Wellington, medical advice was sought, when it was seen that he was in imminent danger of losing his reason. So serious did his condition become that he was confined to his country house, North Cray Place, and his razors were removed as a precautionary measure. This care was, however, unavailing, for he committed suicide by cutting his throat with a penknife on August 12th.

The event was cruelly referred to by Byron, in the unfeeling couplet :

> " He's cut his throat." " He ? Who ? "
> " Why, he who cut his country's, long ago."

A house in the fashionable thoroughfare of Hill Street, Berkeley Square, and another in the old town of Epsom —once a village, and famous as a medicinal spa, but now almost to be reckoned a suburb of London—are associated with the remarkable story of " the Bad Lord Lyttelton." Pit (not Pitt) Place, a stately but somewhat gloomy old mansion near the parish church of Epsom, is the scene of this story's conclusion. The peculiar name of the mansion—which is generally mis- spelled, under the impression that it was connected with the Pitt family—is derived from the fact that it was built on the site of an old chalk-pit, some two hundred years ago.

The Lord Lyttelton referred to in this well-authenti- cated story, which is one of a death-warning rather than of promiscuous hauntings, was Thomas, the second Baron, who was born in 1744, and whose career might well form a study for any novelist wishful of drawing the character of a typical Wicked Lord.

The account given at the time of Lord Lyttelton's death by a friend who was then visiting him cannot be bettered, in spite of the nauseating repetition of " his lordship," which convicts the man of being some ineffable Tom Tufto. He said : " I was at Pit Place, Epsom, when Lord Lyttelton died. Lord Fortescue, Lady Flood, and the two Miss Amphletts, were also present. Lord Lyttelton had not long been returned from Ireland, and frequently had been seized with suffocating fits ; he was

LORD LYTTELTON'S WARNING

From a contemporary print

attacked by them in the course of the preceding month,
while he was at his house in Hill Street, Berkeley Square.
It happened that he dreamt, three days before his death,
that he saw a fluttering bird, and that afterwards a
Woman appeared to him in white apparel, and said to
him, ' Prepare to die ; you will not exist three days.'

"His lordship was much alarmed, and called to a
servant from a closet adjoining, who found him much
agitated and in a profuse perspiration. The circumstance
had a considerable effect all the next day on his lordship's
spirits. On the third day, which was a Saturday, his
lordship was at breakfast with the above personages,
and was observed to have grown very thoughtful, but
attempted to carry it off by the transparent ruse of
accusing the others at table of unusual gravity. ' Why
do you look so grave ? ' he asked. ' Are you thinking
of the ghost ?   I am as well as ever I was in my life.'

"Later on he remarked, ' If I live over to-night, I
shall have jockeyed the ghost, for this is the third day.'

"The whole party presently set off for Pit Place,
where they had not long arrived before his lordship was
visited by one of his accustomed fits. After a short
interval, he recovered, dined at five o'clock, and went
to bed at eleven. When his servant was about to give
him a dose of rhubarb and mint-water, his lordship,
perceiving him stirring it with a toothpick, called him a
slovenly dog, and bid him go and fetch a teaspoon.

"On the man's return, he found his master in a fit,
and, the pillow being placed high, his chin bore hard
upon his neck ; when the servant, instead of relieving
his lordship on the instant from his perilous situation,
ran, in his fright, and called out for help ; but on his
return he found his lordship dead."

Thus died " the Bad Lord Lyttelton " in 1779, in the
thirty-fifth year of his age.

So Lord Lyttelton did not, after all, " jockey the
ghost," which is represented in a neat little copper-plate
engraving of the period appearing to him, in a not un-
pleasing form, at the moment of his decease. The
ghost, in this artistic effort, is represented in a decorative
attitude and with a smile midway between the seraphic

and the merely amused, while Lord Lyttelton dies in the foreground, facing away from the spectre, on a sofa too short for him, and with an unconcerned air by no means in accordance with the conventional last moments of a libertine.

The original of the apparition is said to have been Mrs. Amphlett, mother of the two Miss Amphletts, one (or both) of whom, it was stated, the wicked peer had seduced after the manner of wicked peers. The mother, it was said, had recently died of a broken heart.

A weird incident was told, as an addition to this story. It appears that Lord Lyttelton had purposed visiting an intimate friend, one Miles Peter Andrews, Esq., at Dartford, on the day which proved to be that of his decease; but, feeling unequal to the occasion, chiefly on account of his vision, he did not join the party at Dartford, nor did he send any explanatory excuse. Andrews himself, not feeling well, retired early to bed that night, and had not long been seeking repose when the curtains of his four-poster were drawn and the figure of Lord Lyttelton appeared, wearing a dressing-gown of a distinctive pattern that was commonly used by him when staying as a guest. The somewhat surprised Andrews at once thought his friend had made a belated arrival, and was bent upon some practical joke; and so called out to the figure, "You are up to some of your tricks. Go to bed, or I'll throw something at you." But the figure merely gazed at him sadly, and said, "It's all over with me, Andrews."

The thoughts of Andrews, however, were not at that moment running upon the supernatural, and he simply reached out for a slipper and threw it at the apparition, which then glided into the dressing-room. Still under the impression that this was part of a practical joke, he followed, and searched both rooms, whose doors were closed and bolted. Mystified, but still suspecting nothing but a trick, he rang the bell and asked the servants the whereabouts of Lord Lyttelton; but none had seen him, and the dressing-gown he used was found undisturbed. Exasperated at being so puzzled, Mr. Andrews still convinced that this was a trick, forbade the servants

CORTACHY CASTLE

to give Lord Lyttelton a bed. Let him, he said, find
one at one of the inns in Dartford.

It was not until late the next day that he heard of
his friend's death. He fainted when the news was
brought, and " was not his own man again for three
years."

The Drummer of Cortachy is a well-known legend
attached to Cortachy Castle and its owners, the Ogilvys,
Earls of Airlie, by which it would appear that when the
sound of the drummer is heard, a death in the Ogilvy
family may surely be expected. The legend is of a piece
with many another weird story long current in Scotland,
whose origin can only be vaguely guessed at, but whose
existence shadows forth a very terrible picture of Scotland
in mediæval times. The original drummer whose ghostly
playing is so unwelcome a sound to the Ogilvys appears
to have been the messenger of some hated chieftain,
bearing some unwelcome message. The most appropriate
act of defiance in England in those times would have been
to make the messenger eat his missive—and probably,
in the more extreme cases, his drum too ; but they
looked on life more sternly in Scotland in that era, and
the pleasantries of the savage chieftains took a more
tragic turn ; and, in short, the Ogilvy of that time—
history, or legend, is not particular to a century or so—
had the drummer stuffed into his own drum, and flung
from the topmost battlements of Cortachy. We will
not stop to inquire whether it were a very small drummer
and a very large drum ; but will dwell upon the threat
of the boy, or man, to haunt the family for ever after.

According to ancient legends, every now and again
brought up to date by the alleged reappearance of the
ghostly drumming, the unfortunate emissary kept his
word. The incidents chiefly dwelt upon are those that
took place at Christmas, 1844, when a Miss Dalrymple
was staying as a guest at Cortachy. When dressing for
dinner on the first evening of her arrival, she heard
music under her window, which presently resolved itself
into the sound of a drum ; and, having at that time
never before heard of the family legend, she asked her
maid, when she next came into the room, who was the

drummer who could be heard playing near the house. The maid knew nothing about it, and the subject ceased for a time to occupy Miss Dalrymple's mind. But it recurred to her at dinner, and she said, addressing Lord Airlie, " My Lord, who is your drummer ? " upon which his lordship turned pale, Lady Airlie looked distressed, and several of the company, who all heard the question, embarrassed ; whilst the lady, perceiving that she had made some unpleasant allusion, although she knew not to what their feelings referred, forbore further inquiry until she reached the drawing-room, when, having mentioned the circumstance again to a member of the family, she was answered, " What ! have you never heard of the drummer-boy ? "

" No," replied Miss Dalrymple. " Who in the world is he ? "

" Why," replied the other, " he is a person who goes about the house playing his drum whenever there is a death impending in the family. The last time he was heard was shortly before the death of the late Countess (the Earl's first wife), and that is why Lord Airlie became so pale when you mentioned it. The drummer is a very unpleasant subject in this family, I can tell you."

Miss Dalrymple was naturally much concerned, and indeed not a little frightened at this explanation, and her alarm became augmented by hearing the sounds on the following day, she took her departure from Cortachy Castle.

This affair was very generally known in the North, and events were waited with interest. The melancholy death of the Countess about five or six months after-wards, at Brighton, sadly verified the legend. A paper was said to have been found on her desk, after her death, declaring her conviction that the drum was for her ; and it has been suggested that probably the thing preyed upon her mind and caused the catastrophe. But in the first instance, from the mode of her death, that does not appear to have been the case ; and in the second, even if it were, the fact that the prognostic was verified remains unaffected—besides which, those who insist upon taking refuge in hypothesis are bound to admit that people like Lord and Lady Airlie, living in society not prone in modern times to believe unreservedly in old family legends, must, before they could attach such importance to the sound of the drum outside their walls, have already had very good reasons for believing in its ominous character.

A pendant to the story of 1844 is that of 1849, when it was said that, on the evening of August 19th, as a young Englishman, a guest of the then Lord Ogilvy, heir to the Earldom of Airlie, was making his way to a shooting-box belonging to his host, known as the Tulchan, accompanied by a Highlander for guide, he heard in the darkness that had fallen upon the brooding moors the sound as of a far-away band, in which a drum took a prominent part. At the same moment the lighted windows of the shooting-box came into view.

The Englishman asked his guide what such sounds of rejoicing could mean, but the Highlander, saying that such things were " no canny," declared that he had not heard anything.

Curious though he was to hear whence these sounds had proceeded, especially as he saw no musicians around the house, the Englishman forgot further to inquire ; for, on entering, he learned that Lord Ogilvy had been obliged to leave hurriedly for London, where, he had just been advised, his father was lying dangerously ill.

It was on the succeeding day that the ninth Earl of Airlie died.

But the Drummer of Cortachy, it would seem, has sounded his last note, for nothing was observed upon the death of the late Earl of Airlie, who was killed in 1900, in the Boer War ; and now the Reverend John Strachan, minister of the Established Church at Cortachy, informs me that the legend " is no longer believed in. Superstition dies very hard, and while there may be a lingering doubt in one or two minds, the Drummer has certainly passed away. No one, as far as I know—and I have every opportunity of knowing—professed to have heard him before the lamented death of the late Earl."

Roslin Castle, near Edinburgh, is the home of a good many legends of the picturesque mediæval type, and its

ROSLIN CASTLE

CHARTLEY PARK

beautiful chapel, on the hill-side, above the gloomy castle, is famous all the world over for the exquisite beauty of its interior, and especially for the supremely beautiful " 'Prentice Pillar," whose carved stone wreathed decoration was, according to the fearful old story, the work of an apprentice whose master, maddened with jealousy at being surpassed in his own craft, killed the lad.

The 'prentice does not (as he should do, by all the canons of the supernatural) haunt the chapel. The legend attached to it concerns much more important people : none others indeed than the St. Clair-Erskines themselves, the Earls of Rosslyn. These legends of supernatural manifestations belong really to the ancient line of St. Clairs, who ended in 1778 ; but the Erskines, who have taken their name and succeeded to the property, and enjoy the Earldom of Rosslyn, created in 1801 for their benefit, claim a continuance of the old portents. These are nothing less than that the chapel, on the approaching death of a descendant of its founders, seems to be on fire. Sir Walter Scott was well acquainted with the tradition, and explained it in his *Lay of the Last Minstrel :*

> O'er Roslin all that dreary night
>   A wondrous blaze was seen to gleam ;
> 'Twas broader than the watch-fire light,
>   And redder than the bright moonbeam.
>
> It glared on Roslin's castled rock,
>   It ruddied all the copse-wood glen ;
> 'Twas seen from Dryden's groves of oak,
>   And glimpsed from cavern'd Hawthornden.
>
> Seemed all on fire that chapel proud,
>   Where Roslin's chiefs uncoffin'd lie ;
> Each baron, for a sable shroud,
>   Sheathed in his iron panoply.
>
> Seemed all on fire, within around,
>   Deep sacristy and altars pale ;
> Shone every pillar, foliage-bound,
>   And glimmered all the dead men's mail.
>
> Blazed battlemen and pinnet high,
>   Blazed ev'ry rose-carved buttress fair.
> So still they blaze when fate is nigh
>   The lordly line of Hugh St. Clair.

The allusion to the old St. Clairs " sheathed in their iron panoply " refers to the old custom of burying the lords of Roslin in their armour.

The fortunes of the Shirley family, Earls Ferrers, are, or were, associated with the birth of a black calf among the herd of wild white cattle that is still a feature of the romantic park of Chartley, near Stafford. The tradition that the birth of a black or parti-coloured calf in this herd is a certain sign of a death in the family within the year is traced back to the remote times of Henry the Third, when the appearance of a black calf among the white cattle preceded by a few months the battle of Burton Bridge, in which the Ferrers of that day, a prominent figure among the turbulent Barons who were then in arms against the King, was defeated and slain. All the property of the family of the Ferrers thus slain in rebellion was confiscated, with the exception of Chartley Park, then in possession of the Earl's widow, under her marriage settlement. There is no chain of record to prove the correctness or otherwise of this legend ; and we do not find, in any account of the circumstances which led to the hanging of Earl Ferrers in 1760, for murder, any mention of a black calf among the white cattle of Chartley Park anywhere about that time.

It was noted, however, by the *Staffordshire Chronicle* in 1842 that calves of that description had been seen for some years past in the herd at Chartley, and that a death in the family had inevitably followed. Seven black calves, and seven subsequent deaths, were noted in that journal : the death of the seventh Earl Ferrers, in 1827, of his wife, of his son Viscount Tamworth, and of his daughter, together with those of the eighth Earl, in 1842, and of his daughter, Lady Frances Shirley. In 1835 the birth of a black calf was followed by the death of the Countess Ferrers, second wife of the eighth Earl.

The white cattle of Chartley Park are, like those of Chillingham Castle, Northumberland, supposed to be survivors of the original wild cattle, the *Bos primigenius*, of Europe. They are by no means so inoffensive as the usual cattle of our pastures, and it is considered dangerous

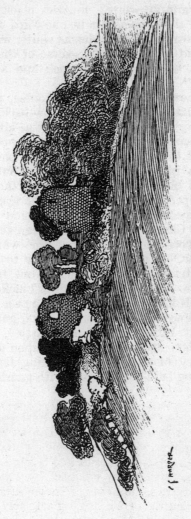

RUINS OF CHARTLEY CASTLE

for a stranger to approach them. They have been carefully described in the following terms : " Their colour is invariably white ; muzzles black, the whole of the inside of the ear and about one-third of the outside, from tips downwards, red ; horns white, with black tips, very fine, and bent upwards ; some of the bulls have a thin upright mane, about an inch and a half, or two inches, long."

The occasional black calf is, of course, well known to students of natural history as a throw-back to some early black ancestor ; and it would be not at all a remarkable thing in the course of centuries for the appearance of the ominous calf to be coincident with, or shortly followed by, a death in the Shirley family ; but the strange succession of black calves recorded by the *Staffordshire Chronicle* helped amazingly to keep the tradition alive.

After many centuries, the connection of the Earls Ferrers with Chartley has recently been severed, for the estate has been sold, and even the white cattle are becoming few. A mixed breed is now to be found in a remote quarter of the park, and no one troubles in the least as to the significance (if any) of black calves.

Chartley Hall is a building of picturesque outline, placed in a low situation beside a lake, and within sight of the great ruined castle of Chartley, crowning an adjacent ridge, and looking down upon the somewhat weird scenery of the park, consisting largely of wild, prairie-looking land interspersed with gnarled oaks.

CHAPTER XIII

Calverley Hall—Sykes Lumb Farm—Samlesbury Hall—Heath
Old Hall.

THE reader of these pages will have already gathered
that the twentieth century is inimical to ghosts. Few
believe in the supernatural, and the diligent inquirer
may quarter England and at the end find that almost
everywhere his inquiries have been met with the blank
look of ignorance, or with contempt for the foolishness
that impels an otherwise sane person to look for haunted
houses. But in the Yorkshire village of Calverley, four
miles from Bradford, if they do not now actually believe
in Calverley Hall being a haunted house, they do still
speak of the ghost of the wicked Walter Calverley with
a certain amount of respect. This is the more remarkable because Calverley is by no means a rustic village
steeped in bovine agricultural superstitions, but a grown,
and growing, place of woollen factories, living rather in
the forefront of affairs.

Everyone in Calverley knows the Old Hall, and
most are familiar with more or less authentic versions of
its story. It is a long, low building with traces of fourteenth, fifteenth, and sixteenth century work, but now
divided into a number of small residences. The exterior
is less pleasing than it might be if built of different stone ;
for the quarries of Calverley yield stone that with age
turns an ugly grey-black hue.

It was in this building that the bloody deeds were
perpetrated on April 23rd, 1604, that led to the execution
of Walter Calverley, the squire and descendant of a long
line of squires who were in possession of Calverley so far
back as the time of King Stephen.

Walter Calverley, although married to an estimable
and virtuous lady, was a wild and reckless man, whose
errors are said to have been due to a strain of insanity

inherited from his mother. He was at last driven completely off his tottering mental balance by the desperate financial position in which he found himself. Moneylenders were pressing him closely, and it seemed as if he must part with his ancestral home. The fear of impending ruin goaded him into an insane frenzy in which his hand was turned against those he loved best. Rushing on that fatal day into the house, he snatched up one and then another of his children, stabbed them to the heart, and then attempted to kill his wife, who was only preserved by the dagger striking her corset. Thinking, however, that he had slain her, among the others, Calverley took horse for Norton, near by, where he had an infant son out to nurse, thinking to kill him too. But the hue and cry was raised, and the entire village was in pursuit. The horse fell, or shied, and threw him, and thus he was secured and handed over to justice—as justice was understood at the opening of the seventeenth century. Brought to trial at York, he recovered his reason in so far that he refused to plead, incurring thereby the penalty of *peine forte et dure* awarded to the contumacious in that respect.

The reason for a criminal brought to trial refusing to plead is found in the fact that in the event of his pleading, and being eventually found guilty, his property was, by law, forfeited to the Crown. Refusing to plead and being found guilty, he incurred the fearful penalty already named, which, in plain English, was the prolonged agony of being slowly pressed to death under heavy weights. This terrible martyrdom was often incurred by criminals for the sake of their families, for by it they saved their property from being escheated to the Crown.

Walter Calverley, then, was duly pressed to death at York Castle. Tradition long told how an old and faithful servant was with him at the last, and how the wretched man begged him to end his sufferings the sooner by sitting on the weights that were crushing his chest. The old retainer did so ; but, according to the story, was hanged for his pains. Traditions proceed to tell how Calverley was buried at St. Mary's, in Castlegate, York,

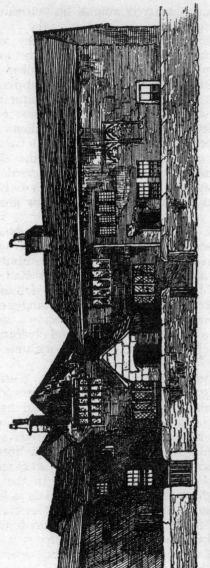

CALVERLEY HALL

but was afterwards reinterred among his ancestors in Calverley Church.

It is perhaps not remarkable that Calverley village and the roads around it became soon afterwards haunted by a fearful spectre of a horseman riding a headless horse and acting as captain to a number of other apparitions similarly mounted. These horrible nocturnal equestrians delighted to ride down any villagers who were foolish enough, or unlucky enough, to be out o' doors after nightfall. They then disappeared into a cave in Calverley Wood, and only ceased to trouble when the double indignity befell them of the cave being quarried away and the vicar " laying " the ghost of Walter Calverley until such time as the hollies ceased to grow green in the wood.

Then the village had peace, but somewhere about the close of the eighteenth century the Reverend Mr. Burdsall, a preacher in the Wesleyan connexion, invited to stay a Saturday night at the bloodstained Hall, over against his preaching on the morrow, had a most unpleasant experience. He has left a harrowing account of it, in which, after narrating how he was shown upstairs into a large oak-panelled bedroom, and bidding his friends good night, he performed his devotions and retired to rest.

" I had not been asleep long," he says, " before I thought something crept up to my breast, pressing me much. I was greatly agitated, and struggled hard to awake."

Up to this point we suspect that generous supper which the reverend gentleman's warm-hearted Yorkshire hosts had doubtless pressed upon him. It is astonishing what fearsome spooks are to be evolved in the silent watches of the night from such crude materials as lobster salad, or pork-pie, and certainly the Reverend Mr. Burdsall's initial feelings are symptomatic of nothing more other-worldly than nightmare.

But to resume the narrative : " The bed seemed to swing as if it had been slung in slings, and I was thrown on the floor. When I came to myself, I soon got on my knees and returned thanks to God that I was not hurt, and, committing myself to His care, I got into bed a second time. After lying for about fifteen minutes, reasoning with myself whether I had been thrown out of bed or whether I had got out in my sleep, to satisfy me fully on this point, I was clearly thrown out a second time, from between the bedclothes to the floor, by just such a motion as before described. I quickly got on my knees, to pray to the Almighty for my safety, and to thank Him that I was not hurt. After this, I crept under the bed, to feel if there was anything there, but I found nothing. I got into bed for the third time. Just as I laid myself down, I was led to ask, ' Am I in my right senses ? ' I answered, ' Yes, Lord, if ever I had any.' I had not lain a minute before I was thrown out of bed a third time. After this, I once more crept under the bed to ascertain whether all the cords were fast, and examined until I touched all the bedposts, but I found all in order. This was about one o'clock. I now put on my clothes, not attempting to lie down any more." And there, with the adoption of that wise decision, the minister's uncanny experiences concluded.

It is to be noted that he did not until afterwards learn the history of the house. In his own words : " I was afterwards told that this very house had formerly been the residence of Calverley, who, in the reign of King James the First, was tried at York for the murder of his wife (?) and two children, and, standing neuter, was pressed to death in the Castle."

About 1872, according to an account published in a local paper, the village of Calverley was thrown into a state of consternation by the inexplicable tolling of the church bell one night, or rather, at one o'clock in the morning. The sound continued a long while and aroused the whole of the inhabitants, ceasing only when the keys were brought and the church unlocked. The combined intelligence of the village unanimously associated the occurrence with the unquiet spirit of Will Calverley ; but what it portended none knew.

Sykes Lumb Farm, situated near the village of Mellor Brook, between Preston and Blackburn, was, very many years ago, reputedly haunted by the ghost of a certain

Mrs. Sykes, who with her husband is said to have lived there in the far-off days of Edward the Sixth and Henry the Seventh. We need not, however, be particular, in this instance, to a hundred years or so, for the surviving house is certainly no older than the Elizabethan age ; and in any case the story is not affected by the difference in time.

Sykes and his wife owned the farm, and were wealthy with the hoardings of their forbears and their own savings. They were a lonely couple, with no children and only distant relatives, whom they discouraged. Troubled times of civil war and general social and religious unrest gave them—and more particularly Mrs. Sykes—anxious thoughts for their wealth ; and, after much consideration, they at length decided to fill a number of earthenware jars with their gold, and to bury them in the orchard. And there it remained. The farmer in the course of years died, and after him his wife. They never again looked upon their hoard. You see, the opportunities existing in those times for such as they using an accumulation of money were few. Had they lived in our own age they would probably have bought a motor-car and become a nuisance to other users of the road, travelling at an illegal speed and putting up at hotels for bounders, and bragging of their pace. Unhappily, they lived in the dark ages, and knew nothing of those joys.

Mrs. Sykes died suddenly, and was not able to disclose the spot where her wealth lay hid. Relatives distant in kinship and in place of abode flocked to the farm, and a general upheaval in search of the hidden treasure resulted ; but no success rewarded their efforts. Years passed, and the farm many times changed hands ; but the troubled spirit of Mrs. Sykes was constant to the place. Often, as dusk fell, the peasants would meet an old wrinkled woman, dressed in the fashion of a bygone age, but none dared speak to her. Alas, poor ghost ! In the etiquette pertaining to such, she only desired to be spoken to first, to be able to communicate her secret to the living, and be at rest ; but the fears of those she met kept her for generations patrolling the marches of the visible and the invisible worlds.

SYKES LUMB FARM

And so she might have continued for years to come—
might indeed even yet be haunting the spot, but for the
happy chance of the then farmer seeing her one evening
when, primed with generous liquor, he had courage
sufficient to hold parley with even more terrible shapes
than that of an ancient dame hobbling along and supporting herself with a stick.

He asked her why she haunted the place so persistently
but received no answer. Instead of speaking, she moved
slowly towards the stump of an old apple-tree and pointed,
with a great show of meaning, to a particular spot.

Search was afterwards made there, and in the course
of digging, the ghost of Mrs. Sykes was observed for the
last time. When the hoard was discovered and the
last jar lifted out, a radiant smile illuminated her face,
and her figure melted imperceptibly away, never more
to be seen.

At another, and later, time, Sykes Lumb Farm was
haunted by a mischievous, prankish spirit, or " boggart,"
as in Lancashire they style the *poltergeists*. Nowadays,
however, the stranger finds that it is only the older people
who know anything about these things, or of Sykes Lumb
Farm at all. The modern young men who read the
weekly ragbag journals and buy picture-postcards of
actresses with greasy smiles and teeth like dentists'
advertisements know nothing of the old lore of the
country-side. In short, it is a difficult matter to be
directed to what was once Sykes Lumb Farm. It has
now taken a very humble position indeed, being a portion
of a gardener's cottage in the rear of a fine modern house
belonging to a local timber-merchant. The older portion
of the house, seen in the illustration, is the original of the
story. It is not now inhabited, and is given over to the
purposes of a wash-house, wood-store, etc. : less from
any surviving superstition than from the smallness, the
dampness, the darkness, and the general inconvenience
of the rooms. The wing in the foreground is quite
modern.

Not more than two miles from Sykes Lumb is Samlesbury Hall, standing beside the broad highway between
Preston and Blackburn. It is a fine specimen of the

ancient Lancashire type of manorial residence, being built almost wholly of timber framing, with sparing use of masonry and plaster. The present Hall dates from about 1370, when the site was very differently circumstanced from what it is now. Instead of giving upon a broad and much-travelled highway, it was then in midst of a dense forest of oaks.

The ancient family who took their name from the place had become merged into that of the Southworths, in the second half of the thirteenth century, by the marriages of Cicely de Samlesbury with John de Ewyas, and of her only daughter with Sir Gilbert de Southworth, long before the existing hall was built ; and the Southworths themselves were finally dissociated from it when John Southworth sold the property in 1677. It was during the Southworth period that the tragedy occurred which has given Samlesbury Hall a place in legends as a haunted house.

Sir John Southworth, who ruled the place in the time of Queen Elizabeth, was an important personage : had held high military command at Berwick and elsewhere, and was sometime Sheriff of the County Palatine of Lancaster. But he was a stubborn Roman Catholic : rigid in an age when only suppleness ensured safety, and exclusive in dealing, wherever possible, only with those of his own faith. Conceive the bitter opposition of such a convinced Papist when he learnt that one of his daughters had formed an attachment for the Protestant heir of a neighbouring knightly house ! He refused to sanction the engagement ; but, as ever, parental opposition merely served to increase their romantic attachment. The lovers met and agreed upon an elopement ; but the time and place agreed upon were overheard by an eavesdropping brother of the lady, and he determined to prevent their flight.

On the fateful evening the lovers met at the appointed place, and as the young knight moved away with his betrothed, her brother rushed out from his hiding-place and slew both him and two friends who accompanied him. The bodies were secretly buried within the precincts of the domestic chapel of the Hall, and, according to Harland's *Lancashire Legends,* " Lady Dorothy was sent abroad, to a convent, where she was kept under strict surveillance. Her mind at last gave way—the name of her murdered lover was ever on her lips, and she died a raving lunatic. Some years ago three skeletons were found near the walls of the Hall, and popular opinion connected them with the tragedy. Still, according to the legend, on quiet, clear evenings, a lady in white may be seen passing along the gallery and the corridors, and then from the Hall into the grounds. There she meets a handsome knight, who receives her on his bended knees, and he then accompanies her along the walks. On arriving at a certain spot, most probably the lover's grave, both the phantoms stand still, and as they seem to utter soft wailings of despair, they embrace each other, and then their forms rise slowly from the earth and melt away into the clear blue of the surrounding sky."

I suspect Harland must have added a good deal of imaginative embroidery of his own to the original legend ; for, inquiring on the spot—not with any great expectations of these details being confirmed—the chauffeur overhauling a motor-car in the courtyard, in a halo of blue, stinking smoke and a morass of lubricating oil, had never seen the like : nor had the cook : while the cotton-spinning owner of the Hall at the present day, mildly indulgent, scouted the entire story.

However that may be, Samlesbury Hall is worth seeing, if for itself alone. Many years ago it fell upon evil times and was even let out in tenements, and then became a farmhouse ; but was afterwards restored. The building is closely hemmed in and overhung by trees. It gives the impression of being so slightly constructed that the very varnish, plentifully smeared over the external woodwork for the purpose of preserving it against the weather, seems to take a prominent part in holding it together. Modern greenhouses and the like out-buildings, constructed in imitative style, throw unwarranted doubts upon the genuineness of the original building. The carved devices under the windows and on diamond-shaped panels along the front are curious and interesting. One of them, representing a sportive

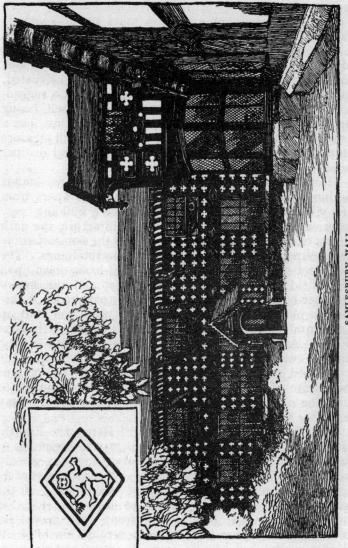

SAMLESBURY HALL

and grinning devil, with a toasting-fork, is shown in the margin of the accompanying illustration.

Heath Old Hall, not quite two miles to the south of Wakefield, is one of the grandest among houses owning a ghost-story. The colliery and manufacturing interests of Wakefield and the vicinity do not improve the surroundings of the village of Heath, which is still situated, just as its name would imply, at the summit of a rugged, wild expanse of heath-land ; but the village itself, facing upon a picturesque green bordered with tall elms, has a remarkably striking appearance, due in no small measure to two of the no fewer than three separate and distinct noble Halls that dignify the place.

Heath Old Hall, the subject of the legends, stands within its own wooded grounds, somewhat apart from the village green. It is a tall, upstanding building, very impressive by reason of its ornate architecture, the dark hue of the stone of which it is built, and the semi-defensive arrangement of its courtyard and outbuildings. The park (for such it may almost be styled) looks down upon Wakefield and the valley of the Aire, and the smoky smother of the commercial operations that render Wakefield a place very different from the place conjured up in mental pictures of the scene of Goldsmith's famous *Vicar*. Among the trees you notice a defensible-looking tower ; while another of the same character flanks the courtyard entrance to the Hall at the side. The curious hesitation of the builders of the Old Hall between defence and the display of assured safety is shown by the easy entrance in front.

The Hall was built in the reign of Henry the Eighth, when the early Renaissance movement was beginning to influence architecture. The new style has not greatly affected the exterior of this building, but may be distinctly traced in the decorative detail of the cresting of the parapets. The arms of John Kaye of Dalton, together with the initials I. K. over the front door, reveal for whom the house was built, but the heraldic shield of the Kayes, sculptured here in stone, is immeasurably more enduring than the Kayes themselves, for in less than thirty years they were succeeded by a certain William

HEATH OLD HALL

Witham, who himself died in 1593, supposedly from the effects of the sorceries and " devilish arts " practised upon him by one Mary Pannal, who was duly executed at York, as a witch.

Henry Witham, son of this victim of infernal agencies, died childless, and was succeeded at Heath by his sister, who had married one Jobson, of Cudworth. Becoming a widow, she married again, Thomas Bolles of Osberton, and was widowed for the second time. In 1635, for services to the King's cause, Mrs. Mary Bolles was the recipient of a very unusual honour, being created a female baronet, or " baronetess "—if such a term is admissible—with special and plenary remainder to any heirs. The honour descended to her daughter by the second husband, who subsequently married Sir William Dalston.

Old Lady Bolles lived many years at the Hall, in considerable splendour, and died in 1662, in her eighty-third year. She left elaborate and most precise instructions respecting her funeral, upon which £1,220 was to be expended, including £700 for mourning, £400 for actual funeral expenses, and £120 for the hospitable purpose of freely entertaining all comers during the six weeks that were to elapse between her death and burial. Great stores of wine, beer, and general provisions were provided for the occasion ; and the whole country-side must have regretted that there were not more such liberal ladies to die more frequently. In addition, £200 was set aside for erecting a monument to her memory in Ledsham church. Her will, executed only the day before her decease, most earnestly and emphatically conjured her executors to scrupulously fulfil all the provisions contained in it (as though she had reason to anticipate opposition to her wishes) ; and, as a clinching clause, any person benefiting by her testamentary dispositions who should seek to oppose her executors should thenceforward be deemed to have forfeited all claims.

It is the ghost of Lady Bolles that is said to haunt the stately rooms of her old home, and to particularly affect the handsome apartment still known as the " Banqueting Room," which includes among its features a finely-sculptured chimney-piece displaying the Witham arms. Whether, as being herself a Witham by birth, and troubled in some manner by the tragical circumstances of her father's death, or whether the provisions of her will were not faithfully fulfilled after all, the authorities could never determine ; but her spirit was at last " laid " and confined to a hole in the neighbouring river, still sometimes pointed out as " Bolles' Pit." This appears to have been only for a term of years that has expired, for every now and then rumours of old Lady Bolles being again at large may be heard.

CHAPTER XIV

LUCKS

JEALOUSLY preserved and carefully guarded, there are hidden away in English country houses (or sometimes stored in the strong-rooms of banks, for greater security) certain weird objects called "Lucks." They are not weird in their appearance; but their origin is legendary and generally uncertain. Chief among these family talismans, whose safe keeping is supposed to ensure good fortune, and whose loss or breakage implies disaster, is the famous "Luck of Eden Hall."

The mansion of that name, on the river Eden in Cumberland, is not now an ancient house, it having been rebuilt in the eighteenth century. The story of this "Luck" is that, at some time unspecified, the butler, sometimes called the "seneschal," of the establishment, going to draw water from the well of St. Cuthbert, found a group of fairies disporting themselves about the rim of it. Amid their frolicsome circle he observed standing a curiously painted glass cup which, in spite of the fairies' protests, he seized. Finding him more than a match for them, they vanished, leaving the glass in his possession. As they went, the leader of them delivered this parting warning:

> "If that glass either break or fall,
> Farewell the Luck of Eden Hall."

It is not necessary to believe this story of fairies. At any rate, no butler to-day, even if we were to go so far as to style him a "seneschal," would dare so much. Butlers who see fairies in these times get a month's notice, under suspicion, not of going to wells for the purpose of drawing water, but of resorting to the cellar for the stronger stuff there reposing.

EDEN HALL

The Musgrave family, in whose keeping was the famous Luck, held Eden Hall from the days of Henry the Sixth until 1927, when the thirteenth Baronet (mark it, the " thirteenth " !) sold the estate. He gave the Luck into the keeping of the Victoria and Albert Museum at South Kensington in the autumn of 1926. The Eden Hall estate was sold by auction in May, 1927 : 3,250 acres, with seven miles of salmon and trout fishing in the river Eden. Most of the farms were acquired by the tenants.

The Luck is yet unbroken, has often been written about and illustrated, and was lent for display at the Exhibition of 1862. It is a beautiful example of enamelled and engraved glassware, of a yellowish green in hue. Fairyland, you will think, who see this illustration of it, was more strongly influenced by the Moorish style of ornament than Queen Mab's domains might be supposed capable of. The design is traced on the glass in blue and white enamel, heightened with red and gold. Those provocating people who do not believe in fairies, or in butlers who are alleged to have seen them, declare the glass to have come from the south of Spain ; and say that its use was that of a chalice, probably in Holy Communion. They point, in confirmation of this, to the leathern case, of *cuir bouilli*, which goes with the glass cup ; for it is of mediæval character and bears the I H S monogram.

A hundred and seventy years ago, the Luck of Eden Hall had a narrow escape from destruction, when the Duke of Wharton, a guest of Sir Christopher Musgrave, accidentally let it fall, during a drinking bout. The butler dexterously caught it in a napkin. The Duke subsequently celebrated the occasion and his own clumsiness in verses beginning :

> " God prosper long from being broke
> The Luck of Eden Hall."

There is a " Luck of Workington Hall," in Cumberland, one not very well known ; traditionally said to have been presented by Mary Queen of Scots to Sir Henry Curwen, on the occasion of his aiding her in 1568, when she crossed the Border after the fatal Battle of Langside. It is an agate cup, still in possession of the Curwen family.

According to received legend, the " Luck of Muncaster," preserved at Muncaster Castle, Cumberland, was given by Henry the Sixth, that most unlucky of monarchs, to Sir John Pennington at some time after the Battle of Hexham in 1463, when that unfortunate King was in flight and in sore distress.   Pennington gave him shelter and comfort ; and on leaving Muncaster Castle, Henry gave its castellan this curious and beautiful fragile glass bowl.   The ancient legend (if it be no more) certainly was believed in the time of Sir John Pennington himself ; for the gift is recorded at length on his tomb, in Muncaster Church :

" Kinge Harry gave Syr John a brauve workyd glasse

MUNCASTER CASTLE

cuppe with his word before yat whyllys the famylie shold keep it unbrecken thei shold gretely thrif, and never lack a male heir."

And so the Penningtons for centuries thrived, and became ennobled, with the title of Baron Muncaster, in 1783.   But the luck ran out at last ; and in 1917 the last and fifth Baron died without an heir.   Sir Josslyn Pennington, fifth Baron Muncaster, had succeeded his elder brother, the fourth Baron, who was childless. Another brother had died in infancy, and a younger brother also died without issue.   The last Lord Muncaster

held the title from 1862, when it was merely an Irish one.
He was created Baron Muncaster in the peerage of the
United Kingdom in 1898.

So lapses an interesting honour ; and thus passed
away a family of great antiquity : having, it is said,
been settled in the Furness region of Lancashire before
the Conquest.

The " Muncaster Luck," still, however, at Muncaster
Castle, now the property of Sir John F. Ramsden, Baronet
—the late Sir John Ramsden, Baronet, was a cousin of
Lord Muncaster—is a glass bowl of, apparently, Venetian
workmanship and of fifteenth-century date. It is of a
pale violet hue, and is decorated with a gold band and
with white spots of enamel in groups of three, and having

THE " LUCK OF MUNCASTER "

a row of gold billets below. Beneath these billets is a
band of purple spots, in three's, reversed.

The romantic history of the Penningtons was not
without a modern chapter. The late Lord Muncaster
had, in 1863, married Miss Constance L'Estrange, a niece
of the seventh Earl of Scarbrough (the title so spelled,
not like the original place-name, Scarborough in Yorkshire). They travelled largely in the East, and at length
reached Athens and arranged a trip to the historic Plain
of Marathon. With Lord and Lady Muncaster were a
Mr. and Mrs. Edward Lloyd and their child, Mr. Frederick
Grantham Vyner, a brother of the Marchioness of Ripon,
Mr. Edward Herbert and Count Herbert de Boyl, Secretary of the Italian Legation. Returning from Marathon

they were surprised and captured by a band of brigands ; all of them being at first roughly used. But before nightfall the ladies and children were released, the men being taken to the brigands' secret lair in the mountains.

That was on April 11th. The next day the brigands decided to allow one of their captives to proceed to Athens, for the purpose of negotiating a ransom. Their impudent terms were : £30,000 in gold, a free pardon for past and present offences and the liberation of several of their gang then in prison. Lots were drawn to determine who thus should go to Athens, and the lucky straw was drawn by Mr. Vyner, but as he was unmarried, he heroically offered Lord Muncaster his chance—which he took.

Lord Muncaster on April 13th accordingly left, the brigands finally assuring him that if any expedition were sent out to rescue his friends all their captives would be murdered. The Greek Government, while making a promise that at all costs they would see the captives freed, secretly prepared an expedition. The news of these preparations was conveyed to the bandits by means of spies in Athens, and as a result their prisoners were conveyed further into the mountains ; and on April 21st, Mr. Herbert and Count de Boyl were shot, and on the next day Mr. Vyner and Mr. Lloyd met the same fate.

Intense and very natural indignation was felt in England at this extraordinary outrage, and it was by no means allayed by the news that, some ten days later, the band of brigands had been routed out, and most of them brought to Athens and executed.

It was said that Lord Muncaster never quite threw off the gloom of this terrible experience. A stained-glass window was erected by him in Muncaster Church in memory of his unfortunate fellow-travellers.

In the Castle is the " King's Room," occupied by Henry the Sixth on the occasion when he gave the " Luck " to Sir John Pennington. In it is a massive oak bedstead, shown as that on which he slept. A feature of the park is the extensive heronry, which, together with the great colony of black-headed gulls, was one of Lord Muncaster's hobbies, being as he was a lover of birds.

The " Luck of Burrell Green," in the same county of Cumberland, near Great Salkeld, in the region between Penrith and Carlisle, is preserved at a house formerly occupied by the Lamb family. It is a very curious example of these strange talismans ; but, technically, it

THE " LUCK OF BURRELL GREEN "

cannot be, in the more intimate sense, a " luck," for it is not a fragile article : the essential quality of a " luck " being this very fragility, rendering due care of it a matter of pains and anxiety.

The " Luck of Burrell Green " is, on the contrary, a brass dish, not easily to be injured. The luck here consists in the keeping of it ; as the inscription on the dish hints, not obscurely. The brass dish is 16¼ inches in diameter, with a depth of only 1½ inches. In the centre, in " Old English "—that is to say Gothic—lettering, is

the inscription: "Mary, Mother of Jesus, Saviour of Men";
and in an outer circle, in more modern characters appears:—

> "If this dish be sold or gi'en,
> Farewell the luck of Burrell Green."

Evidently, from the general character of this dish and
from the original inscription, this was in the first instance
one of the items in a service of church plate. To what
church, or to what religious house, it belonged does not
appear; nor in what way it came to Burrell Green.
The Lambs, or those into whose secular possession it
first came, added the "luck" inscription, greatly daring;
for it has generally been supposed, alike by Spelman,
author of the *History of Sacrilege*, and by others, that

THE "LUCK OF WOODSOME HALL"

the holders of despoiled Church property have "luck"
only of an evil sort.

A "Luck" which obtained the name in some
unknown way, and cannot really be a "Luck" in the
true sense, is the trumpet called the "Luck of Woodsome
Hall." The Hall, near Huddersfield, is a seat of the Earl
of Dartmouth, into whose family the estate came by the
marriage of the son of the first Earl, Lord Lewisham, to
the daughter and heiress of Sir Arthur Kaye, two centuries ago. The "Luck of Woodsome Hall" was sold
at auction by order of Lord Dartmouth at the rooms of
Messrs. Puttick and Simpson in March, 1922, and was
purchased for seventy-five guineas by Mr. Percival
Griffiths, of Sandridgebury, near St. Albans. It is
correctly to be described as a herald's trumpet, made of
an amalgam of tin and brass, with silver mountings. It
is a handsome object, and well-preserved. The bell is
delicately ornamented with cherubs, and bears the
inscription: "Simon Beale, Londini, Fecit 1667."

It does not appear how this trumpet came into possession of the Legge family, who have held Woodsome Hall since about 1730. It is to be presumed that it was already there. The generally-received legend is that failure to blow it on certain specified occasions was provocative of ill-fortune. Simon Beale, the maker, twice finds mention in Pepys' Diary, where he is styled " the Trumpeter." The first entry is on December 16th,

" THE LUCK OF EDEN HALL," WITH ITS LEATHERN CASE

1660 ; the second, September 26th, 1668. On the second occasion he is described as " a very civil man " and as formerly " one of Oliver's and now of the King's Guards." By this it would seem that Beale doubled the parts of maker and performer on trumpets.

The family of Dundas, of Arniston, have also a " Luck," an ancient Venetian glass, or goblet, once belonging to a sixteenth-century ancestress, Katharine Oliphant. Like most of the other glass lucks it is carefully cherished, in view of a legend that dire misfortunes will follow upon it being broken.

INDEX